OUT OF NIGERIA

A log raft on the Cross River, Nigeria

OUT OF NIGERIA

Witness to a Giant's Toils

J. L. BRANDLER

The Radcliffe Press
London · New York

First Published in 1993 by
The Radcliffe Press
45 Bloomsbury Square
London WC1A 2HY

175 Fifth Avenue
New York
NY 10010

Reprinted 1995

In the United States of America
and Canada distributed by
St Martin's Press
175 Fifth Avenue
New York
NY 10010

A full CIP record for this book is available from the
British Library

A full CIP record for this book is available from the
Library of Congress

ISBN 1 85043 732 7

Library of Congress catalog card number: 93-60680

Typeset by Spectrum City
Printed and bound in Great Britain by
WBC Ltd, Bridgend, Mid Glamorgan

Contents

Part II

General Foreword
to the Series

A. H. M. KIRK-GREENE

Lecturer in the Modern History of Africa, University of Oxford, and
formerly of the Colonial Administrative Service, Nigeria.

A whole generation has passed, nearer two in the case of the Asian sub-continent, since Britain's colonial territories in South-East Asia, Africa and the Caribbean achieved independence. In the Pacific the transfer of power came about a decade later. There was little interest in recording the official or the personal experience of empire either in the inter-war years – viewed by some, often among those personally involved, as the apogee of the British empire – or in the immediate aftermath of empire. And in this latter period attitudes were largely critical, largely condemnatory and even positively hostile. This is not surprising: such a reaction is usual at the end of a remarkable period of history.

With the passing of time and with longer historical perspective it was possible to see events in a better and more objective light and the trend was gradually reversed. In due course there came about a more sympathetic interest in the colonial period, both in Britain and in the countries of the former empire, among those who were intrigued to know how colonial government operated – in local, everyday practice, as well as at the policy level of the Colonial Office and Government House. Furthermore, those who had themselves been an integral part of the process wanted to record the experience before, in the nature of things, it was too late. Here was a potentially rich vein of knowledge and personal experience for specialist academic historians as well as the general reader.

Leaving aside the extensive academic analysis of the end of empire, the revival of interest in the colonial period in this country may be said to have been stimulated by creative literature. In the late 1960s there were novels, films and radio and TV programmes, now and again tinged with a touch of nineteenth-century romance and with just a whiff of nostalgia to soften the sharp realism of the colonial encounter. The focus was primarily on India and the post-1947 imagery of the 'Raj': there were outstanding novels by Paul Scott – surely destined to be one of the greatest twentieth-century novelists – J. G. Farrell and John Masters; epic films like *A Passage to India* and *Gandhi*, the charming and moving vignette of *Staying On*, and, for Africa, *Out of Africa* and *Mister Johnson*.

In the second half of the 1970s there emerged a highly successful genre of collective 'colonial' memoirs in the *Tales of... format: Charles Allen's splendid trilogy Plain Tales from the Raj* (1975), *Tales from the Dark Continent* (1979) and *Tales from the South China Seas* (1983), followed by others like *Tales of Paradise*: *Memories of the British in the South Pacific* (1986) and *Tales of Empire: the British in the Middle East* (1989), all good history and good reading.

Throughout the period from India's independence until that of the last crown colony there had, of course, been those splendid works which combined both academic history and creative literature: for example, Philip Woodruff's *Men who Ruled India: The Founders* (1953) and *The Guardians* (1954); and *Jan Morris's Heaven's Command, Pax Britannica* and *Farewell the Trumpets* (1973–8).

Finally, as the 1970s gave way to the 1980s, those voices which had remained largely silent since the end of empire now wanted to be heard. The one-time colonial officials, be they district officers, agriculturalists, veterinary, medical or forestry officers, policemen or magistrates, and just as often their wives, began to write about their experiences. They wrote with relish and enthusiasm, with a touch of adventure and few personal regrets. There was a common feeling of a practical and useful task well done, although some thought that more could have been achieved had independence come about more slowly.

These memoirs often began as little more than a private record for the family, children and grandchildren, some of who had never seen a colonial governor in full fig, shaken hand with an emir or paramount chief, discussed plans with a peasant or local politician, or known at first hand the difference between an *askari* and an *alkali*, an *amah* and an *ayah*. By 1990, the colonial memoir had begun to establish itself as a literary genre in its own right.

The initiative of the Radcliffe Press in harnessing and promoting this talent, primarily autobiographical but also biographical, promises to be a positive addition to both the historical and the literary scenes. Here is a voice from the last Colonial Service generation, relating from personal experience the lives and careers involved in the exercise of latter-day empire. They were part of what was arguably the most influential and far-reaching international event of the second half of the twentieth century, namely the end of empire and the consequent emergence of the independent nations of the Third World. It could also perhaps be argued that this is part of an even greater process – decolonization 'writ large', a sea-change in world affairs affecting greater and lesser powers into the late twentieth century.

It may well be that by 2066, the centenary of the closing down of the Colonial Office, great-great-grandchildren will find the most telling image of Britain's third and final empire in these authentic memoirs and biographical studies, rather than in the weightier imperial archives at the Public Record Office at Kew or in Rhodes House Library, Oxford.

Acknowledgements

I am much obliged to many friends and acquaintances for giving me advice. Some of these read selected sketches, and some of them all of the sketches in draft form, offering suggestions and corrections even if they did not always agree with my interpretation of events. I can name but a few in alphabetical order: Professors O. O. Akinkugbe and L. Ayo Banjo of Ibadan University; Chief Joop Berkhout of Spectrum Books, Ibadan; Professor Alex Boyo of Warri, one-time Fellow of King's College, Cambridge; Mr. Fred Egbe of Lagos and Warri; Alhaji Kamilu Ila of Kano; Mr. Anthony Kirk-Greene, M.B.E. of St Antony's College, Oxford; Mr. Louis Nnamdi Mbanefo, S. A. N. of Lagos and Onitsha; H. E. Brian Michael Fraser Neele, Ambassador of Brazil to Nigeria; Mr. Abimbola Oladapo of Lagos and Ondo; Miss Jaiye Sowemimo, of Lagos and Ogun State; Mr. George A. Trail III, Minister-Counselor of the US Embassy in Lagos.

Dr. Lester Crook of the Radcliffe Press in London guided my inexperienced hands through the pitfalls of duplication and irrelevancies.

My wife Pamela showed much patience and understanding, putting up with my typing at all hours of the day and night when at Tilbrook.

I was encouraged to write these sketches by Dele Fatayi-Williams, who used to visit me and listen to my tales; by Freddie Scott of the West Africa Committee, who felt they might be of interest to younger generations; and by Bob Fleming, one-time head of the Rockefeller Brothers Fund in West Africa, with whom I have kept up a lively correspondence over the years. Lastly, I must put on record that I could not have completed this work without the effective and sympathetic co-operation of my secretary, Susan Finch Noyes.

Lagos – Banyoles – Tilbrook 1990 – 1992

Author's Note

I changed the names of individuals in only two of these sketches.

I had to omit about twenty sketches to keep the length of these memoirs within reasonable bounds. There was the strange career of Freddie Mann, the Manager of Barclays Bank in Lagos when I arrived in 1947; the story of Ani, my army batman in Egypt, who later joined me in Lagos and stayed for twenty years as messenger, ill-fated in his marriages; the adventures of Dan Daura, my horseboy, and the first member of staff of the Lagos Polo Club to go on a pilgrimage to Mecca – with my encouragement; and my meeting with Chief Akintola, at the time Premier of the Western Region, in Sir Mobolaji's office.

I have not had time to describe the arrest of our receptionist's brother for alleged murder, and her attempts to get him out of gaol. And I have been forced to leave out the extraordinary saga of the compulsory acquisition by Lagos State of our prestigious office block, Kajola House, the jewel in our crown, and the long, drawn-out and vexatious negotiations with many Ministries over compensation – often leading to bizarre complications.

Also omitted are long descriptions of a visit to Germany in 1949, my first journeys to the USA in 1951 and 1952, and a trip to Brazil and Peru in the 1970s – interesting experiences not directly pertinent to Nigeria. In a lighter vein, the tales of how the Jujumen righted the wrongs of aggrieved parties, and how they assisted a barren wife to conceive have also, sadly, become victims of the demands of space.

Late in my career I established close relations in northern towns like Kano, Kaduna and Gusau, and wrote about them. All this and more I hope to offer the reader some time in the future.

List of Maps

Maps drawn by Russell Townsend

Foreword

I have known Mr. Brandler since my school days in the late 1950s as a man highly regarded by my late father, Sir Louis Mbanefo. He regards me as representative of the new generation of Nigerians brought up to reason in the Western way, whose formative years of intellectual development post-dated Independence; a generation which has learned to regard the world objectively and which is prepared to criticize and be criticized; a generation which is impatient to see a Nigeria which operates by reason and not by emotion or naked materialism. I believe that it is to my generation and to my children's generation that Mr. Brandler addresses this work.

Yet it is a book which will appeal to a wide readership – from expatriates eager to learn more about Nigeria and Nigerians to sociologists and historians. For the older generation of Nigerians, it will provide fond reminiscences of life in the 'good old days'. For the generality of readers it provides a fascinating account of commercial and social life, as well as a highly perceptive commentary on life in Nigeria.

Many expatriates who have lived and worked in Nigeria derived their knowledge of Nigerian society largely from conversations with their cooks and stewards and drivers – many of whom made much capital out of fanciful exaggerations and distortions. Unlike them, Mr. Brandler mingled freely with Nigerians at all levels and was accepted by them as a friend and confidant. It is not surprising that he loves Nigerians and feels at home in Nigeria. He enjoyed the sense of adventure, the patience in adversity, and the entrepreneurial spirit that is the hallmark of the Nigerian.

In the past two decades there has been a spate of biographies and autobiographies of Nigerians. With some notable exceptions, these works have dealt almost exclusively with the individual and his role in society. Not so with this work. Apart from a few comments in the early chapters, Mr. Brandler says remarkably little about himself and his family. Whilst this is in keeping with the admirably modest nature of the man, it deprives us of some insight into the makings of a remarkable gentleman – soldier turned businessman turned diplomat turned raconteur. His early tutelage under T.S. Eliot clearly manifests itself in his lucid and effective style. Perhaps because of his multi-faceted nature, he has been able to appreciate and paint vivid and fascinating pictures of life in the forests, of interactions with Nigerians from chiefs to labourers, of the timber trade and other spheres of business, and of the political and social life in Nigeria as well as the Cameroons and Liberia.

I do not flatter Mr. Brandler when I say that this book is a valuable historical document. The reality of Nigeria is fraught with enormous complexities. Yet he has unravelled and laid bare the atoms that coalesced to form Nigeria as it is today. He has criticized where criticism was called for and praised where praise was due. Yet at all times he emerges as a friend and well-wisher of Nigeria. Some of the episodes he describes, notably in 'Black Gold', 'The Rice Deal' and 'How Many Beans Make Five', must have caused him much discomfiture. But he recounts all with a sense of humour – an attribute without which he would have found Nigeria unbearable. He describes with scrupulous fairness and shrewdness some of the personalities with whom he interacted; some noble, others not so noble.

We live in exciting times. A new political order is about to emerge. The problems facing Nigeria have never seemed so acute. Cynics are asking whether Nigeria can still hold together. In these times of stress and confusion, Mr. Brandler brings us words of comfort:

> One must admire the patience, sense of humour and drive that keep most of the inhabitants going, where other peoples would long since have given up or rioted and revolted. That is their strength, and out of this they will in

the end build a better Nigeria, time permitting. Such is the verve and potential of Nigeria that she can afford to lose one quarter of her efforts through waste, and another quarter through dishonesty, and still make spectacular advances.

From a man who has devoted forty-five years of his working life to our country, such a prognosis should not be dismissed lightly. He deserves our warm thanks for telling us so much about ourselves.

Louis Nnamdi Mbanefo
Lagos
December 1992

1

Introduction

The sentiments mirrored in these sketches, approving and critical, are subjective reflections of forty-five years' residence in Nigeria. Born in 1912, and by good grace writing in 1992, I have lived in a century of extraordinary dimensions, embracing all parts of the globe and many aspects of human endeavour.

The Nigeria of 1947 and the Nigeria of 1992 are very different. Much has changed and been achieved, and although these changes and achievements are uneven and do not always benefit a majority of the people, they are remarkable and must be recorded.

If today most men and women walk in shoes, forty-five years ago they walked barefoot. If today vast numbers can read and write, forty-five years ago many more were illiterate. If today we see large cities and their skyscrapers, cement-block houses with electricity and running water, forty-five years ago there were no skyscrapers and few cement-block houses with electricity and running water. If today we observe roads full of motorcars owned and driven by Nigerian men and women, forty-five years ago but a handful of Nigerians owned cars and I doubt if a dozen women held driving licences. If today thousands of young boys and girls go to universities and polytechnics, forty-five years ago the first of such establishments was only in the making. One can go on citing such comparisons. Last but not least, forty-five years ago Nigeria was a British colony and protectorate ruled from London by the Colonial Office; today she is governed by her own citizens.

Nigeria is undergoing a state of rapid transition: evolution from colonialism to independence; from tribalism to nationalism; from native rule and custom to administrative systems modelled on Western styles; from cottage production to mass industry; from predominantly rural living to dwelling in towns; from illiteracy to university teaching; and so on. That cannot be a smooth process. Some of the romantic fascination with Old Africa is waning as she turns ever more into a likeness of Europe and America.

Coming fresh from the war of 1939–45 and the upheavals which followed in its wake, and at the same time from a Britain with new social aspirations, one had visions of a very different path of African development from that which one actually witnessed. This perception may have been at fault but had its justification in the context of post-war expectations coupled with old African traditions as a base for the new. That was the liberal view of many of my generation, which had just passed through one of the darkest periods of modern history.

I ask myself whether these changes could have come about by a more even distribution of the wealth created, by a greater sense of social justice, by a more responsible approach towards their fellow citizens by the new and mainly self-made elite. It is a hypothetical question I cannot answer. It does seem to me, however, that the acquisition of wealth and power by the individual, however effected, has become in itself the justification for its success, and that those who have achieved it feel entitled to underpin their power by whatever means may be at their disposal. Right or wrong, I could not ignore that.

I would not have remained in Nigeria for forty-five years had I not been attracted to her and her people. That attraction was not a mercenary one – bread is baked in many ovens. It was exciting and stimulating to live in an atmosphere of change, endeavour and hope, where everything seemed possible. The conformity of West and East, tied to ever increasing mechanization and computerization, had not yet penetrated many facets of daily existence.

I met much kindness and consideration and retain great admiration for a spirit which, all obstacles notwithstanding, has propelled the people to sustain and improve their lives. I would at the same time be a poor friend had I remained silent over the shortcomings I perceived.

In writing these sketches I searched my notes and memory conscientiously and pray they served me well. The reader must bear with me for any errors and contradictions he or she may be able to point at: life is full of them.

2

The Royal West African
Frontier Force

In the third quarter of 1945 I was posted to Egypt, and after embarkation leave ordered to report to an Army depot in North Wales. Here I joined a batch of junior officers like myself with low demobilization numbers who were sent abroad to relieve those with longer service and due to be demobbed before us.

From Wales we set off by train, ferry and train again to Toulon where we were to embark for Egypt. It was a long journey through war-torn France all the way from Calais south to the Mediterranean. In Toulon we went on board a passenger liner converted into a troop ship, the *Champollion*, well appointed and most pleasant to sail in. At night we passed the Straits of Messina and saw the active volcano Mount Etna puffing away – a remarkable sight. After a smooth passage of a few days we landed at Alexandria.

Wherever we passed on land or by sea there had been scenes of war and fighting only a short while ago and in a way we felt a sensation of anti-climax, rather like the cleaners coming in the morning after the party. All the same it was something new for most of us who had never been to the Middle East; we looked forward to it and were ready to take it as it came.

After disembarking at Alexandria, we were transported by train to Abassia Barracks near Cairo to be detailed for further duties. Brief interviews with the officer in charge of postings had been laid on. Rumour had it that the thing to do was to get a posting to second echelon where there would soon be many vacancies and rapid promotion could be expected. When I was

4

called into the office, I was given the choice of being attached to second echelon or serving with African troops. To the mild surprise of the colonel who presided I opted for the African units. 'What made you pick them?' he asked.

I told him that one of the officers who had trained me had been with African troops and had found the appointment interesting.

'Have you ever served yourself with colonial troops?' asked the colonel.

'No, sir,' I answered correctly, 'I have not.'

'Very well,' he replied, 'we shall send you to the Royal West African Frontier Force. Good luck.'

The reader of these sketches should bear in mind that up to the late 1940s the average Briton (and European) may have gone through life without ever having set eyes on a black man or woman. If a child came across a black man or woman in the street it would turn its head to have another look (much as the African child did in Nigeria when it spotted a white). There were practically no immigrants: a handful of students, a few sailors in the ports, the occasional visitor. One heard of an artist now and then – Paul Robeson or Josephine Baker – or stories from a colonial stationed in Africa. Blacks represented the jungles of dark and mysterious Africa as seen in the cinema and read about in study books or adventure stories. And there were the negroes of the USA: *Uncle Tom's Cabin*, the Civil War, the Ku Klux Klan and the Hollywood bit-player, usually taking the part of a servant. They did not travel abroad. It was not until the 1950s and 1960s that blacks began to settle in numbers in the UK. They first came from the Caribbean and then from Africa south of the Sahara, spreading from Britain and France into other West European countries.

All I knew about Africa was what I had learnt in geography lessons at school. I had never come into contact with a black person. There had been a colonial exhibition of some importance in Paris in or around 1935 where little African villages had been reconstructed; one saw half-naked men and women in native fashion, the men brandishing spears and other weapons, the women pounding yams and attending to their small children.

During that visit to Paris, I went one evening to a night-club with friends who dared me to ask one of the black girls present for a dance. I accepted the challenge. The young woman I chose was a very good dancer and I was surprised how easy it was to be on the floor with her. She spoke some French (in which I was not very proficient) and after a few minutes on the dance floor that was the end of it. She was a Senegalese, that much I gathered. The Senegalese had been part of the French Army occupying the Rhineland in the 1920s and had there acquired a reputation for ferocity: for the Germans to be knocked about by black troops added insult to injury.

I recollected these incidents as I made my way to report to 2421 Company of the Royal West African Frontier Force doing guard duties around Cairo, employed mainly in manning the airport. It had its headquarters in a suburb of Heliopolis which was part of greater Cairo.

The officer in charge of the company, Major Powell, again asked me, 'Have you ever served with African troops?'

And once more I replied, 'No, sir.'

'You will have a lot to learn. Take it easy and start off by getting to know the names and faces of the sergeants.'

On parade the next morning I gazed at around 300 bodies, all of which looked alike to me; I could not tell one from the other be they thin or fat, tall or short. After a few days I con-fessed this to the company commander. 'I have the greatest difficulty, sir, in recognizing the faces, let alone remembering the names.'

'It will come,' he replied, and indeed after about a month or so I began to get the hang of it.

These troops were not a crack regiment. The three officers, the sergeant-major and a couple of colour sergeants were white. All the other NCOs and the men were black, hailing from Nigeria and the Western Cameroon – mostly from the south with a sprinkling of men from the Middle Belt of Nigeria. All this, however, meant nothing to me. Neither the company commander nor the officer I was to relieve had ever been to West Africa; they were relatively new to the unit but the second in command, Captain Ingram, had been employed commercially in Nigeria and had served with the RWAFF for some years. It was to him, a 'hail-fellow-well-met' type, that I turned to learn a little more about my charges. 'One has to get to know their ways,' he warned me; 'you are in for a few surprises.'

These were not slow in coming. The person I was to relieve was made orderly officer of the day for the last time and I was attached to him. We went off at night to check the guard posts and he always blew the horn of the car when he got to within about 100 yards of the location where we were to find them. 'Why do you do that?' I asked.

'To wake them up,' he replied.

'Well,' I retorted, 'I thought the whole idea was to make certain they are on the job.'

He laughed. 'That's the idea all right, but in fact it is rather cool here this time of the year and these fellows invariably put on every stitch of clothing they have got, sit down and fall asleep. If we were to surprise them all every time we inspect them half the company would be under arrest.'

I was horrified. Old Tringle, I thought, has been here too long. When it was my turn to be orderly officer, I did not blow the horn and I did find many asleep and put them on a charge, after which whenever they knew that it was my turn to be Orderly Officer they did not sleep.

In a way these men had been brought to Egypt under false pretences. On being recruited they had been assured that they, in contrast to other Nigerian Regiments, would never leave Africa – which to them meant they would never leave the West Coast. So when they were shipped to Egypt it caused some resentment; they had been promised that they would be sent back as soon as the fighting was over and here they were at the end of 1945, still hanging around North Africa.

I had arranged to get the London *Times* as regularly as possible. Copies arrived sporadically and when the Major spotted this he said sarcastically, 'Ah, a highbrow, you can take up the additional duties of education officer.' Much emphasis was laid at this time on education, partly to keep the men busy. I protested that I was no teacher but he waved this aside. 'There are plenty of guide books to show you how to go about it. Concentrate on the NCOs and appoint selected men to teach the rank and file how to read and write.' Many of the men were illiterate or semi-illiterate.

Orders are orders and I set about this unexpected task. After a few sessions with the sergeants, it became clear to me that these seemingly simple men were not as simple as they were made out to be. They even talked of self-government. Confronted with these sentiments my theme always was: forget about politics. You will never be independent until you learn how to repair a lorry, handle a radio set, and in general be on a par with the white man technically. I taught them according to the textbooks issued to me and in the process learnt quite a lot myself about Nigeria and the Nigerians.

After a few weeks we were transferred to guard a camp at Helwan, some distance south of Cairo at the approaches to the desert. It was then a transit station for a South African Division preparing to return home: a vast compound with a perimeter of some 15 km. The South Africans, who had not exactly distinguished themselves during the fighting in North Africa, were a very arrogant lot. They looked down on our black troops whom they considered to be very lowly.

Large convoys of 200 lorries would leave the camp in the morning bound for Suez where their equipment was to be loaded onto the ships, and would return in the evening for further loads the next day. We monitored these movements and found that invariably a few lorries less came back than had set out. We reported this to the major who took up the matter with the South African staff who were outraged and told us to 'mind our own bloody business'. Friction ensued. The next incident took place when their armoury was broken into and sizeable quantities of rifles and other small arms were stolen. In high dudgeon the South Africans accused us of failing in our duties and a court of inquiry was instituted.

We were not of course in charge of their armoury; all we could report was that we had seen some of their lorries load arms at night. The event was never clarified. Rumour had it that they had themselves organized the break-in and had sold the arms to political interests in the Middle East. Relations between us became more and more formal and frigid.

They were, however, quite smart and discovered that our men brought women into the camp. We could not believe it. But true enough, on searching our quarters we discovered that some of the platoon sergeants had set up brothels for their men and kept these girls under the floor boards of the tents whenever it became necessary to hide them. Who negotiated for them we did not know – some local pimps no doubt. They brought them in lorries carrying supplies in and rubbish out. The men had to pay a small sum to the sergeant each time they visited these girls and the girls saw very little of the money. We fished out these unfortunate women, most of whom were in their early teens. The sergeants so caught were prosecuted. It was one up for the South Africans.

Newly attached officers like myself were considered rather tough and unreasonable. The war was over and all the men could think about was going home. However, they realized that I sympathized with their position, for the weekly education sessions had brought us into closer contact. Thus it fell upon me to act as defending officer in a court martial of a soldier accused of stealing six pairs of socks whilst on guard duty. He had stolen them all right, but the Military Police had lost the evidence: namely the socks. Being a conscientious bloke I went by the MML (Manual of Military Law) and set off to the scene of the crime, an ordinance depot. Whilst there, I saw a corporal of the Military Police securing six pairs of socks which, he loudly proclaimed, he required as evidence in a case coming up in a few days' time.

When the case was called and the prosecution presented the evidence I challenged it by suggesting that the evidence had been procured recently from the depot and did not represent the facts. A minor sensation! The case could have been stopped, but since the soldier had confessed to me I felt I had to put him in the witness box and I regret to say that he had to spend three months in a military gaol. The corporal in turn had to face charges of misconduct. It was a small affair which had strange consequences for me.

There had been undercurrents of discontent for some time, even in our company, which we had managed to contain. This discontent blew up in a sister company, 2422, where the men rioted, refused to obey orders, made for the armoury, and had to be subdued by white troops. Eighteen soldiers were charged with mutiny whilst on active service: a very serious offence. On the strength of my case of the six pairs of socks, I was detailed to defend them. The offence in theory carried the death penalty and I felt totally inadequate to undertake the mission. The major understood my reluctance but said, 'Look, Joe, if it is not you it will be another chap like you. Have a go at it. At least you have done it once which is more than can be said of most of us. Interview them and see what they have to say for themselves.'

The men had been locked up in a Cairo prison. I had them called in front of me and addressed them. 'I have been appointed to be your defending officer; I am not a trained lawyer and you may accept me or refuse me; it is up to you.' The idea of refusing me never entered their heads – to them my appointment was part of army routine. 'Yes , sir, you defend us,'they said. I told them that I would be returning to take their evidence and left.

The task had me worried. There were to be three separate trials and to prepare for them would tax me beyond anything I had ever attempted. Before committing myself I went to see a friend, a half colonel in the Judge Advocate-General's Department, the army's legal body. I showed him the papers, told him what I knew, and asked, 'How am I to go about all this?'

He said he would look into it and asked me to come back after a few days. He then recommended more or less what the major had done – have a go – and promised to help if I needed advice. He pointed at some weaknesses in the charge and suggested a course of action.

So I plunged into the MML, studied all the documents on hand, and began to interview the accused one by one, having been excused routine duties for the time being. It soon became clear that the accused looked on me not as their guardian angel or Defending Officer, but as part of the army machine and the prosecution. They told me many contradictory tales and it was obvious that there was little truth in what they said. The lies were clumsy. I had them in front of me and gave them a little lecture: 'Look, you are telling me tales; I can see that and the prosecution will see that. You will end up before a firing squad if you are not careful. I will interview each one of you once again and you must speak the truth. If I find you do not I will resign.'

I began once more to take down the evidence of each man, cross-examined him on points which did not make sense, and went on to the next one. This took several weeks. I condensed my papers, prepared the case, and showed it all to my friend, who suggested that not only must I plead 'not guilty' but that I must also first of all plead 'In Bar of Condonation' under some obscure paragraph in the MML referring to something that had happened under Wellington in the Peninsular War.

The great day came. The court assembled, presided over by a Canadian brigadier with two majors as assessors. The prosecution was led by a captain of the JAG's office. The charge was read out and I was to reply.

Feeling nervous, I got up and read out my prepared response to the charge: 'Sir, we plead not guilty to the charge. If, however, we are found guilty we must plead "In Bar of Condonation" in that the men, after committing the alleged offence, were given duties of honour, to wit sent on guard duty in full possession of their arms.'

There was silence in court. The brigadier looked at me and muttered under his breath, but quite audibly, 'Where the hell did he dig that up? Well, we will have to deal with it first. I hope it will not take all day.'

It took more than that. At the end of the third day, the court threw out our plea of 'In Bar of Condonation' because, they argued, at the time the men went on guard duty they had not yet been charged. The trial on the charge was to begin the next morning.

We again pleaded 'not guilty'. My point was that whilst we admitted offering violence to our superior officers, we were not charged with that but with mutiny. This involved men combining with each other in collective action, and we would prove that such had not been the case.

I put the men in the witness box and my inexperience soon showed. Several times the president interrupted to say that my line of argument was irrelevant and would I please get on with the job and not waste everybody's time. He was quite kind about it and I apologized. However, I had to carry on in much the same vein, following my prepared course, since, if I dared to diverge from this, I would be lost completely.

The JAG captain then cross-examined and the accused answered, as they had to my own questioning, through an interpreter. This gave me a little time to collect my thoughts. I had warned the men not to tell lies but to answer truthfully, and that if they did they had a chance of being acquitted. If only one of them were found to be lying, the whole defence would crumble. Even so, the cross-examination had some peculiarities. An accused would be asked, 'Do you know Corporal X?' All he should answer was 'yes' or 'no'. The interpreter would pose the question and a lengthy discussion in the accused's own language would ensue. Eventually the accused would reply, 'No, sir.'

I later asked the interpreter why a simple question took so long to be answered, and he said that he had to make absolutely sure that the soldier understood the point. I must admit that I wondered whether they were discussing if it were better to say 'yes' or 'no'.

We won the case: the men were acquitted of the charge of mutiny, and rightly so. One of the sergeants exclaimed, 'That is British justice.' We also won the second case, in which some of the same men stood trial. I then went to the officer commanding and suggested that in the third case some of the accused had already been through two trials and it would not perhaps be in the best interests of the army to prosecute them for a third time. The charges in each trial concerned different incidents, and were quite properly laid, but it did look too

much like persecution. I asked, therefore, whether he
exercise his powers and cancel the last trial. After considering
the matter he gave orders to cancel.

This legal adventure lasted for several weeks. By the time
it was concluded, all West African companies had been
repatriated and I had lost my chance of being one of those
taking them home. I was ordered to locate the stragglers – such
as the accused, and others in gaol and hospital – and make the
necessary arrangements for their return. I was then posted to a
unit commanded by a colonel of the Royal Tank Regiment at
Tel el Kebir. I was really sorry not to have gone along with the
company to Lagos. I had looked forward to seeing the men in
their habitat and to experiencing something new.

The Egypt to which we came late in 1945 was in a state of
flux. Its heady days of the last few years were fading fast. Cairo
had been the headquarters of the British Middle East Forces
and British Troops in Egypt right through the war. The fighting in the desert had come as close as Alamein. The town had
teemed with officers and men of many nations; there was great
activity which spilled over to the social life, the shops and
everything else. Not much of that remained when we turned up
and it drained away daily.

The bar in the famous Shepheard's Hotel was not full
any longer. Groppi, the charming tea place, was still well
patronized but mainly by the large foreign community which
made up so much of Cairo. The same applied to the restaurants
at the Pyramids, the Opera, and the night-clubs like Madame
Badia.

One was struck by the stark contrasts in living conditions.
Much money had been made during the war and along the Nile
there were luxurious villas owned by Egyptians, Greeks, Jews
and Armenians. Heliopolis was a middle class suburb of tidy
appearance with its own racecourse, and in its stables beautiful
white Arab horses could be glimpsed as we passed. But the
great mass of the population lived in overcrowded slums of vast
proportions and there was clearly much poverty. Transport
was limited; the trams always over-full with passengers hanging on as best they could and sometimes being brushed off as a

tram passed in the opposite direction.

There was much to arouse one's curiosity: the magnificent museum, the grand mosques, the City of the Dead, the falukhas sailing along the Nile. There was social life organized by the army bodies and the hotels and various organizations, attended by good-looking and well-mannered young women of many different origins, but never by the Egyptians who had little time for the soldiery and were kept well away from it. I met many people but socially no Egyptians. We had two officers' clubs to go to and there was the famous Gezira Sporting Club, of which we would become temporary members.

One could have a good time in Cairo if one had the inclination and the money. I spent some months there on my case but could not take much advantage of the opportunities which offered themselves because I was so hard pressed with the courts martial. Once they were over I remained alone awaiting a new posting; they had forgotten about me and my office in Kasr-el-Nil, my kitcar and my driver. I was roped in by the garrison commander for jobs like courts of enquiry, until eventually I drew attention to the fact and was posted, as already mentioned, to Tel el Kebir.

I had a few adventures. I stayed at the West African Leave Camp. Coming out late one night from the Junior Officers' Club, I was shocked to see several little children aged four or less walking the streets alone picking up scraps of food from the gutter. I called a policeman to take them in and alert the parents. I really had no authority to give orders to the police but that never occurred to me. The policeman said, 'Sir, if you insist I will do as you ask but what can we do with them? There are thousands like that all over the town. To be frank, once you are gone all we can do is drive them out again.'

I visited the Pyramids and marvelled, and took a week-end off to visit Alexandria. Several times I went to Ismailia and the Suez Canal. I saw dead bodies floating in the Sweet Water Canal, and a drowned donkey. I took local leave to travel to Luxor and Aswan by train and saw the remarkable sights of old Egypt: Thebes and the graves of the Pharaohs; the Nilometer,

14

which told their administrators how good the floods were going to be, allowing them to budget the state's income for the year; an old synagogue where the Jews dispersed by the first destruction of the Temple had settled at Aswan; and the first Nile barrage, which was of a more modern construction.

During the trials I used to spend Sunday mornings in a small office run by the West African command to cater for its logistical needs. On one occasion an agitated Egyptian police officer drove up on his Harley Davidson motorbike; he had to see an officer immediately. Only a sergeant was on duty so he begged me to follow him on the back of his bike. 'What's the trouble?'

'You will see, sir,' was all he would say.

We set off at speed and ended up in a large girls' boarding school; it had an open space surrounded by its buildings and as we came in he pointed at a tree from which a near-naked black man was hanging, swaying gently in the breeze. 'He is one of yours,' the policeman explained.

As we were contemplating the scene, with the girls on the first floor looking down over the railings, the rope broke and the body came crashing down. The girls shrieked and I asked the matron to get her charges back indoors. We carried the body away. The poor young soldier had left a note to say that he was going to kill himself as he thought he would never see his people again.

One last tale worth relating. During my stay at Helwan with 2421 Company, serious political riots had broken out in Cairo. There were some casualties, the town was declared out of bounds, and troops were confined to barracks. Our company commander had urgent despatches for HQ and felt they had to be delivered. He consulted me and I volunteered to make the trip but asked for an order in writing.

I picked one of the drivers in whom I had confidence, checked the small truck we had for personal transport, and set off. We had to travel about 50 km. The driver, Edu Eze, drove at speed through almost empty roads. En route we had to pass the university which had been a hotbed of the troubles in Cairo. We were just about getting away from it when I smelled

15

some burning and in less than a minute the car came to a stop. That was not funny! I told Eze to open the bonnet and when we looked inside I thought I saw a wire smouldering. 'Get some insulation tape,' I said to Eze, 'and wind it round the wire. Perhaps it will get the vehicle going again.' We had stopped in a wide residential street with large apartment buildings on either side.

In no time a small crowd had gathered, getting larger by the second. They jeered at us and a hostile atmosphere prevailed. I urged Eze to make haste and as a precaution drew my revolver, and whilst he was working on the car patrolled around it to keep the onlookers at bay. I said that if the car would not start he was to walk some distance in front of me and make his way to the barracks in Kasr el Nil, our destination. I would follow behind. 'Whatever you do, don't run, walk briskly. If they dare to attack us they will go for me first and I am armed; with luck we will make it.'

He beavered away and the crowd, a hundred or so by now, kept on jeering but at a discreet distance. Then things – orange peel and suchlike – were thrown at us. They landed on top of the car's canvas and I could not make out where they came from as they seemed to fall vertically. This throwing gave the crowd new courage and they came closer and shouted. More rubbish landed on the roof of the vehicle. I looked up and saw on the second or third floor of one of the houses two young women throwing stuff at us. My first reaction was to shoot at them but at the same time I changed my mind and saluted them smartly. They hastily withdrew inside and the crowd laughed; we gained a respite. Just then Eze said, 'I have finished, sir,' and we went back into the car and started up. Would the engine fire? If not we would have to abandon it and proceed on foot through the mob. We were lucky and drove away.

In mid-December 1946, I was ordered to report to Port Said for embarkation to the UK. My time in the army was to come to an end. The ship taking us back was HMS *Battleaxe,* a regular troop carrier filled with several thousand men. Each officer was put in charge of a number of other ranks. It was a crowded vessel and the sea was rather rough. On the way we were diverted to Piraeus, the port of Athens, and we were lying off it for several days. Heavy fighting was going on in Greece's civil war and it seemed that we would be called upon to disembark and act as reinforcements. That, however, did not come to pass and we made for Toulon where I spent a week before getting onto Medlock, a special train arrangement for troops from Toulon to Calais and on to Aldershot for demobilization and paid leave. At Aldershot we were kitted out with a civilian suit, a couple of shirts, and other clothes. It was efficiently done, as were most such things in the army.

Before I left Egypt, my colonel asked me if I wanted to sign on for some years and they would send me to the Control Commission in Germany. He had endorsed my naturalization papers and was genuinely interested in me. He also felt that I would do a good job. I thought about it; army life suited me and I was unmarried, but I was already over thirty and a bit of an outsider and could not see myself getting very far. I would have to face an uncertain future sooner or later and decided sooner was better. The colonel said he was sorry but quite understood and wished me luck. So Aldershot it was, and demobilization in time for Christmas 1946.

The soldiers enlisted in the Royal West African Frontier Force under our command were mainly young men whose ages ranged between seventeen and twenty-two, with a sprinkling of older categories; some of the sergeants and others may have been in their late twenties, and were literate. Most of them had never been in regular employment: they had worked on family farms or done casual jobs in villages and small towns and often just hung around family compounds.

When the Force needed more men and recruiting started in earnest, the administration would call on the village chief and ask for bodies and by force of his authority he would persuade men to join. The companies I am talking about recruited mainly in the south of the country in contrast to the Nigeria Regiment which was predominantly composed of Northerners. (I say this generally speaking because there were many exceptions either way.)

Two divisions of West African troops were sent to Burma

17

and acquitted themselves well but we had nothing to do with them. Our lot were of the Pioneer Corps and similar service units. They did not join up to fight for king and country, or to save Nigeria from Japan and the Nazis, nor were they conscripted in the real sense of the word. They joined under pressure and because they had nothing better to do; they would earn some money and see something new, and perhaps find work when it was all over.

Before the war, men signed on for a number of years and were officered by British professional soldiers; they were regulars. This time they signed on for the duration of the War. They received their pay, most of which they saved and sent home to their parents or other members of the family. They saw new places and met different people and however poorly educated (something we improved as described) their minds were broadened and they took note. A few were trained as drivers and other trades and did their work well enough. They all spoke some English which was the *lingua franca* and understood the words of command. For all that, very few of them rose to prominence after the war, be it in trade or politics, because their background was too lowly and their education too limited. By the time Nigeria became independent fifteen years on, a new generation had come to the fore.

The white officers and NCOs in charge fell into several categories: the regulars who mostly became attached to the fighting divisions and had by 1945 all risen to high rank in the fast expanding numbers; the war-time officers who were split between men who had had commercial or administrative experience in West Africa; and fellows like myself who were attached without previous experience of Africa.

The Coasters, as one would call them, had very fixed ideas about the men. They knew them from past experience and looked at them paternalistically, whilst at the same time having a poor opinion of their abilities, reliability and honesty. We, the newcomers, were influenced by the Coasters but could not accept their views at face value. We tried to take the men as we found them. This disparity of approach did not always work out well. We could treat the men neither as children whose faults must be excused and at times overlooked, nor as fools who required only an iron discipline. It seemed to me that there was an ambiguity in this philosophy which must be detrimental to good order and discipline.

Working as education officer, and later being defending officer, brought me into closer touch. I realized that we officers were part of the government, of the alien rulers who must be obeyed and had all the power. To get by, West Africans had to be cunning and to stick together. The Nigerian sergeants were their real masters whom they addressed as 'sir' and to whom they would turn in case of need or trouble. (One was not supposed to address an NCO as 'sir' but the habit persisted amongst them.) There was much happening in the ranks that one could only guess at. 'Lending' money to their NCOs was an evil we could not eradicate. The medical staff would pinch pills, bandages and so on, and sell these to the soldiers. The socks which were stolen by the man on guard duty whom I defended were taken at the behest of and for the benefit of a sergeant.

It was the culture of their village which they followed, and the veneer of Western civilization which the army superimposed was thin. Even within the ranks of one company there would be tribal suspicions and rivalries, so that if the sergeant came from a different tribe or sub-tribe he would have less authority than one from another platoon who came from 'home' and literally spoke the same language. But they were not by nature a rebellious body and gave little trouble until they became restless, wanting to get back.

After a while, I came to understand the men and got to like them. I did not talk down to them or treat them as children and established a reasonable rapport. A few would come to me with their worries: they had sent money home but it had fallen into the wrong hands – what could they do about it? They had received news that their father had died – could they send an urgent message? Sometimes, off their guard, they would hint at misdemeanours in the platoon or company. When trouble broke out in the neighbouring company, one man came to me and warned about potential troublemakers in ours, on whom we could keep an eye. Such allegations had to be taken with a pinch of salt, of course - was the informer trying to get his own back for something or other? There was always this gulf between officers and men common in all armies, but accentuated here by the question of colour and the colonial mentality.

It was the courts martial which established me as the friend of the black soldier, although by the time they were over the men had gone back home. It was a mistaken judgement: I did not defend them because they were black, but because I had been detailed to do so and, having accepted the assignment, felt it my duty to do my best for the accused. That much I will concede - I would not treat the matter lightly because the defendants were black. This was commented on in the mess, *en passant.*

A few of the old soldiers re-enlisted during the Civil War in 1967, already middle-aged by then. Crossing the Niger Bridge near Onitsha I was stopped routinely at a military post guarding the approaches when suddenly a sergeant ran up to the car and said, 'Master, don't you recognise me?' He had been one of my soldiers in Egypt over twenty years ago. It was a sentimental reunion in melancholy circumstances.

I never felt that my time with the RWAFF had been wasted; the service was interesting and challenging, and it certainly helped me greatly when I went to Nigeria a year later. More than that: it made me want to see the country and when I had the chance to do so I took it, hazardous as it seemed and indeed was.

3

From London to Lagos

I had made no plans for the future whilst in the army. I did not even know where to stay on demobilization and before leaving Egypt had sent a message to the wife of an artist friend, Jan Kurzke, to ask if I could camp with her in Hampstead to give me time to sort myself out.

Jan and his wife, Kate, did not live together any longer. She had been an art teacher and was in her youth a beautiful woman, the toast of the town. Her father had been a solicitor in the Midlands, and her looks, wit and connections had landed her in high society. She met Jan in Spain and threw everything up to marry him. Relations became strained and they had parted. Kate had bought a house in Steeles Road, Hampstead, from where she worked again as an art teacher. She had one daughter, who lived with her, and she let out any rooms she did not require for herself.

Kate was very kind and responded to my appeal, sending a message that I was welcome to turn up any time. I phoned her from Aldershot to expect me and arrived with my loads one afternoon. Kate, in her early forties but still very attractive, and her daughter, Charlotte, about thirteen and schooling in London, made me welcome. 'You can stay as long as you like, Joe,' she said as she greeted me, 'and don't worry about paying rent.'

I was restless and my finances were in poor shape. My pay-off from the Army, plus a few hundred pounds I had saved, would see me through the next few months, but sooner rather than later I would have to earn some money. The BBC had told

21

me when I resigned to join the forces that I could re-apply for employment and consideration would be given me, and there was always old Lister, now in his eighties, who had promised to look after me. I did not fancy either alternative.

The winter of 1946/47 was one of the coldest on record. Going to the cellar to shovel coal into a bucket to keep the house warm was a major task. I felt honour bound to do so twice a day, a duty much appreciated by my hostess.

The festive season over, I was offered a temporary job by an old acquaintance, a corporal, who had been discharged from the RAF in 1943. He had done well working with a Northern Ireland yarn spinner and needed assistance. His number two who had worked with him before the war had been a major in the army and won the MC. I accepted his offer – it would give me time to make decisions and to meet my bills.

One day Kate said that there would be a private viewing of paintings by a young Nigerian artist studying at the Slade School. She thought I would be interested and suggested that I accompany her.

'Isn't it too damned cold to go out, Kate?'

'Come on,' she replied, 'you served with these people and can make the effort. I don't fancy going by myself.' So we went.

The show was held in a house within walking distance which some kind soul had made available to the artist, who had won a scholarship to the Slade. His name was Ben Enwonwu. About two dozen people had turned up; we were introduced to the painter and walked around the room looking at his work. A few of the visitors were Nigerians and I got talking to one lady who said that she came from Lagos and thought the paintings were wonderful. I agreed politely, feeling cold in the room which could have done with more heating.

'You must meet my husband,' she said, and took me by the hand to introduce me to him. He was a large, well-spoken, middle-aged chap, who pricked up his ears when I mentioned that I had served with Nigerian troops.

'But we must meet again, sir,' he insisted, 'and you must tell me what you think of my people.' I was glad to make contact again with Nigeria and readily agreed. An appointment was arranged. He said his name was Bank.

'I hope you enjoyed the evening,' Kate said, on our way home. 'I saw you talking to some people. Were they West Africans?'

'Yes, they were friends of the artist and came from Lagos. Do you know, Kate, this is the first time I have spoken to an African on assumed terms of equality?'

'I hope it didn't bother you, Joe?'

'It didn't trouble me at all, Kate, but subconsciously I was very much aware of it. It broke a barrier, so to speak. At least I hope it did.'

I had been given a small office in the West End of London to operate from, and Bank called on me there a few days later. 'I was interested to hear that you served in the army with our men so you must know my country. When were you there?'

'Our men', 'my country' – perfectly correct, of course, but it struck me as incongruous. I had looked on them as *our* men being in the Army for *our* country. 'No, Mr. Bank, I have not been to Nigeria. I met the RWAFF in Egypt, was attached to them for some months and in fact only left them fairly recently.' I expanded a little and mentioned the courts martial affair which had precluded my going to Nigeria. 'What are you doing in England?' I asked.

'I have come here with my wife in the interests of my business,' he replied, and went into detail. He had been to Europe once before the war, as a young man spending a few weeks in Hamburg at his father's request. His father was the largest undertaker in Lagos and interested in trade in general. The war had interrupted that and now that it was over he was in business for himself trading in alarm clocks, fountain pens and anything else that was going; he was also a specialist in marble gravestones. He was trying to make connections. His father-in-law had at one time been sole agent for Singer sewing machines but the business had been taken away from him and given to one of the large British companies. He was particularly interested in Smith alarm clocks.

'If there is anything you can suggest, Mr. Brandler, I shall be glad to hear of it. We Nigerian businessmen are up against the large foreign companies who monoplize our trade; we have to twist and turn to make a decent living.'

I liked him. He was self-possessed without being aggressive, polite and to the point. If there was an undercurrent of disbelief in me it did not surface; the scene was so different from what I had experienced before that it felt almost unreal. How to translate the men I had dealt with into this accomplished individual? Was there a catch in it? I had no colour prejudice at all but the colonial approach of the army had left its mark on me. Nor could I see how I might be of any assistance to Bank in his present task. I invited him and his wife to join me for lunch the following week to pursue the acquaintance.

The contact grew in intimacy. After I had shown him photos of myself with some of my men and told him about my activities as defending officer he felt I had more than usual sympathy for his country; he felt at ease with me.

I took Bank and his wife Lande to my father's flat near Regent's Park. They got on well. He brought several Nigerians to my office and to my father – 'just calling to say hello,' as he termed it. There was at the time an unofficial Nigerian delegation in London to talk to the Colonial Office about granting more political rights to the Nigerians (the Colonial Office refused to receive them) and Bank knew them all. Amongst them were Dr. Azikiwe, Prince Adedoyin and Bode Thomas. Bank's affairs made only slow progress. It was quite exceptional in those days for a Nigerian to turn up in the UK seeking to promote business.

One day Bank suggested that I should visit Lagos. 'There will be many possibilities in my country. You are young and have some experience and you are white. There is room in Nigeria for energetic men like you. Look around and you will find that I am right. There are opportunities. Anyway, come and see.'

That had not been my information in the army. We were told that the colony was run by a handful of large, mainly British, companies and that they guarded their position jealously. I told him so. He agreed it was so, but added, 'There is always a chance for something new. It's a big country and much will change. Anyway, come and look. I am there and perhaps we can do something together.'

It seemed a little odd to me for an African to make such a suggestion. How could he, whatever his local standing, promote the interests of a man like me? The idea seemed unrealistic. Besides, nothing concrete had been proposed. 'I will think about it, Bank, and keep in touch with you in Lagos.' He was to return there shortly.

Nevertheless, his comments had lit a flame and I did indeed think about it. There was little to keep me in London. The job I did might become permanent but did not attract me. I again discarded the idea of returning to the Monitoring Service of the BBC or of asking old Lister to take me back – six years was too long a break to take up a career with him successfully. The war and its aftermath had disillusioned me and perhaps I was not very sure of myself in the conditions then prevailing. Nor did I have great commercial ambitions: in truth, I had no ambitions at all that I could fasten on to. The spell with the RWAFF had been a success from a personal point of view, a time when I had accomplished something that satisfied me.

Perhaps I *should* break away, associate with new people, take on new challenges, be of importance in a new environment, and use my talents (such as I perceived them to be) to good advantage. It need not be with Bank at all. I could apply to the Colonial Office to become a development officer and ask to be posted to Nigeria – or elsewhere in Africa for that matter; I had heard that active recruitment was going on. I could ask for a job with one of the companies in Nigeria. Or I could just go there and look around, as Bank had proposed, and come back after a few months should I find nothing to keep me there. Now, surely, was the time to make a decision.

(Seven months later I flew to Lagos. More on that and Bank who ended his days as Chief Sir Mobolaji Bank-Anthony, KBE, etc. as the story unfolds.)

Shortly before they left, Bank and Lande introduced me to two young Nigerian girls recently arrived in England to study law. One was Funke Ransome-Kuti from Abeokuta, Lande's

25

home town, the other Grace Duke from Calabar. 'Both are from prominent families,' Bank assured me. 'Do help them to get acclimatized.'

They were in their early twenties, well padded against the cold, and seemed very shy. When they did open their mouths they spoke in such low voices that I could hardly hear them. I asked them for their addresses and phone numbers and promised to get in touch. Looking at their address, I was amused to discover that they lived in a boarding house in Bayswater which had been my home for a short period way back in 1932. When I rang them, only Funke was in and I arranged to pick her up and show her something of London. 'Do bring Grace along if she is free,' I added.

I borrowed my father's car and went to Bayswater. Funke appeared dressed in a gorgeous native gown in spite of the cold; she looked a different person. Grace, she said, had work to do. I drove her out to Hampton Court and we had tea.

'Are you on a scholarship?' I enquired. No, neither of them had a scholarship: they had been sent to England at their fathers' bidding. We talked about this and that, and I took her back. She then suggested that I come to visit them and they would cook me a Nigerian dish. I offered to bring along one of my brothers and we duly turned up for this culinary adventure.

The meal was served, well cooked but very spicy, and the crockery cleared away. We sat in a small overheated room and made hesitant conversation. Funke did most of the talking in reply to our questions. Grace sat quietly on a bed tossing her keys up in the air and catching them again and again. It so irritated me that I snatched them in mid-air and held on to them. She said nothing, but just looked at me.

On closer view, they were two attractive young women. To get the conversation into better flow, I recounted my army experiences with their countrymen and the ice slowly melted. When I mentioned that I had for a time been education officer, Grace sat up. 'Do you know Latin?' she asked.

'I took Latin at school,' I replied, 'Why do you ask?'

'I have to pass an examination in Latin before they will

26

accept me to read law. It's new to me and I am struggling to make progress. Will you help me?'

I had to confess that my Latin was rusty. 'Have you got any textbooks?'

'Yes, I have, and please, sir, do help me.'

'Do you need assistance as well, Funke?'

'No, thank you. I am all right.'

My brother was amused. 'It's good to know that our years of Latin are now of some use.'

'Very well, Grace,' I said, 'If you can come to my place with all your books and exercise papers some evening or at the weekend we will talk it over.'

'I will come tomorrow.'

As we said goodbye she reminded me that I still retained her keys, which I handed back in some embarrassment.

She turned up in Hampstead with a bag full of books and papers. I introduced her to Kate and we retired to my room.

'Your wife?' Grace asked.

'No, not my wife, Kate owns this house. Please show me your books.' It was *Latin For Beginners,* not hard for me to cope with, and I told her so. 'You will have to find a better qualified teacher before you can pass your exams, but for the time being I can help if you will co-operate and work at it.'

'My allowance is small,' said Grace, 'and I don't know...'

I interrupted her. 'Forget it. I cannot charge you any fee. ' We agreed to meet two or three times a week. 'Let's see how we get along.'

The first few periods went well. Grace was attentive and did her homework – as did I. I began to enjoy the experience. All was kept strictly on a teacher-pupil basis and I never looked at it as anything else. We generally finished with a coffee in a small café near the bus stop. After four or five lessons her concentration began to wander and her homework was unsatisfactory. I remonstrated and received a sullen response. I wondered what had got into her.

On her next visit this quiet girl exploded when I told her off. She accused me of treating her badly because she was black. 'If I were a white girl coming here you would not be so rude or treat me as a child.'

Her outburst took me completely by surprise. 'What non-sense is this? You come here to learn Latin. Black or white, boy or girl, has nothing to do with it. I am the one to complain, not you. I don't know what you're talking about.'

The row got worse and worse. She was in a fury, and threw her books at me and kicked me. I retaliated, whereupon she began to cry hysterically and threw herself on the bed in the corner of the room, sobbing uncontrollably. A fine kettle of fish, I thought. It took us ages to make peace.

'You snatched my keys,' she kept on saying, as she sat in front of the mirror repairing the damage to her appearance. 'You snatched my keys.'

Catching her keys had clearly been some signal to her, and she was baffled and offended by what she felt to be my subsequent coldness and indifference, so she came to the conclusion that racial prejudice had kept me from getting closer to her. She resented it as an African and a woman. I could not convince her that I saw myself only as her Latin teacher, and that sexual or racial instincts played no part in my relations with her. Nor did they. Not, that is, until she forced the issue.

We became good friends. I was not used to female company and could not at first interpret her affectionate and uninhibited approach to our reformed relationship. There was little I had to offer except my company and limited knowledge of a classic language; but I soon realised that she was lonely and frightened in a strange country, and in need of a friend in whom she could confide and whom she could ask for guidance. In her turn, she could offer comfort and feminine charm, and teach me something about Nigeria. A getting-together of two people who complemented each other at the time and in the circumstances in which they found themselves.

Grace did not become a lawyer; she took on office work instead. Funke Ransome-Kuti married a Swiss and went to live in Switzerland. Ben Enwonwu became an internationally acclaimed sculptor and painter, a professor of arts at various national universities, and his work today is highly prized. He is an acknowledged doyen of the arts world of Nigeria and beyond. He made a statue of the Queen which was installed in a prominent place in Lagos. He also made a bronze head of our eldest son and we have several of his works in our house now. We still meet frequently.

~ ~ ~

'I have decided to go to Nigeria,' I announced.

'What are you going to do there?' my father asked.

'I don't know yet, I'm thinking about it. I want to see it.'

As a trader, Bank had suggested I procure suitable goods to sell on the Nigerian market. 'What is suitable?' I had asked.

'Anything that makes money.'

I toyed again with the idea of applying as a development officer. I felt my qualifications were right and the work would suit me. Friends advised me against the move. 'Go out first and have a look at what is going on. You may hate the idea of being tied down to the country.'

I put an advertisement in the London *Times* to say that I would accept commissions from any firm interested in furthering business with Nigeria. I received replies from a trading house in Liverpool, two textile dealers in Manchester, and a bicycle manufacturer in London. I travelled to Liverpool and saw Mason, Ellis & Jones, a smallish trading concern who had shipped some goods to Lagos for which they had not been paid. Would I look into it? I went to Manchester and met a couple of cloth manufacturers who gave me their samples to test the market. And I called on the bicycle company, which I had never heard of, and they gave me specifications and brochures: they hoped to begin exporting there. None of these companies offered any financial assistance. If I were to sell any of these goods they had to be paid for before loading on board. My expenses were on my own account.

I went to see my father – fairly comfortably off but by no means rich – and asked for support. He would lend me a few thousand pounds if I needed it to establish myself, but not just to go sight-seeing in Africa because I was fed up with London. I assured him that I had enough money for the sight-seeing part of the trip.

Before I flew off, an old Leicester friend also gave me some cotton print samples from a producer he represented in the Midlands which he thought might be of interest.

It was all new to me. I had had a little experience of textiles under Lister but I knew nothing about bikes except that I had ridden them. However, if there was something I had learned in the army it was to study new situations, adjust myself, and get on with things as best I could. The idea that I might require some official sanction or permission to enter the country never occurred to me. It was a British colony, after all.

It was difficult to get a passage to Lagos, and Cook's Travel Agency in Mayfair could not book me until some five weeks ahead, 28 November 1947. The planes flying to West Africa were converted Halifax bombers called Haltons which flew with much noise and little comfort. The airline was the old Imperial Airways (by then I think already renamed). There were about twelve seats in each aircraft. All the passengers were British expatriates going out on duty. One of them was Professor Mellanby, proceeding to Ibadan to take up an appointment as first Vice-Chancellor of Ibadan University, which was in fact to become the first fully-fledged Nigerian University. We took off around mid-day. The adventure was under way.

Our first stop was Tripoli in Libya, whose airport was still showing many marks of the fighting during the war. Second stop was Kano, and we reached Lagos after about eighteen hours. I was met by my good friend Bank who was very happy to see me and hired a taxi to take us into town. (Most of my 'loads' I had sent on by ship and these were not due to reach me for another month.) We reached the Grand Hotel in the centre of Lagos, at that time one of the top two hotels in town (the other was called the Bristol Hotel). After hanging about the reception desk for a few minutes, we were greeted by a portly gentleman who looked at me, said nothing, and then looked at Bank and said, 'Yes, what can we do for you?' His name was Joe Harold.

'I have booked a room for my friend, Mr. Brandler,' Bank said.

'You have?' asked Harold.

'Yes, don't you remember?'

'Well, I do not remember that, but I'll check the bookings.' After doing so perfunctorily he said, 'There is no booking here for Mr. Brandler or anybody else you may have reserved a room for.' He turned to me and said, 'I am sorry, sir, there is no booking for you and we are quite full.'

Bank was very upset, querying the booking once more, but the proprietor would not budge: he had no room!

'Look,' I said, 'I have come a long way. Please see what you can do to accommodate me for one night at least, as I am quite exhausted and would not know where to go.'

'We will put you up in the corridor on the first floor.'

I thanked him, and thanked my friend Bank and said, 'Let me sort this out by myself and we will meet tomorrow.' I had my luggage taken up to the first floor where a camp bed was made ready for me. The hotel was not very large; it had about thirty rooms. Downstairs was the bar frequented by all and sundry, but as far as I could see only by whites. I met Mrs. Harold and we talked.

I said how disappointed I was that I had not got a room, since it had apparently been booked weeks ago. She laughed and said, 'My dear sir, we never take the bookings of the Nigerians seriously, as most of the time nobody turns up. You should have known better than that.' The remark irked me and I must have shown it. She said, 'You don't seem to know anything about West Africa.'

'Well', I said, 'I served in the Royal West African Frontier Force.' She was a good-tempered lady, and nothing more was said about it. Quite clearly there were two worlds, the white and the black, with the Syrians occupying the twilight zone. I settled down in the hotel and started to look around.

After one night in the corridor they gave me a room. The Harolds were kind to me. Joe had worked pre-war with the United Africa Company. When Italy had entered the fighting, the Custodian of Enemy Property had asked him to run the Grand Hotel, which had formerly belonged to an Italian.

Joe explained that most imports were handled by the large

companies, which had banded together during the war as the Association of West African Merchants (AWAM), and practically monopolized all imports which were under licence. Major exports were government-controlled by marketing boards which channelled their business through the same AWAM. 'I don't suppose you want to break into that.'

The companies distributed their imports to merchants, relying on some influential local traders and the Syrians (who specialized in textiles but also traded in other goods). The import licences were easing off for British goods. The principal marketing boards had taken charge of groundnuts, palm products, cocoa and cotton. The government fixed buying prices for the produce and sold at world market prices which were higher; the difference was put into an equilization fund to keep producer prices as stable as possible so as not to expose the farmers to wild market fluctuations. Joe gave me a few addresses to call on with my samples when I was ready to do so.

Bee, his wife, also gave me good advice and warned me to be careful of the women. She was an addicted poker player; her partners were mainly Syrians who liked to gamble. One evening she roped me in. I lost £20 after drinking many whiskies and was barely able to crawl up to my room. The following morning I decided to look for quarters. I had by then spent about ten days in the Grand Hotel. I had met a few birds of passage propping up the bar and dining room: some from abroad, others from up country. I had asked many questions and played cards with an American, Joe Costa, who, like me, had come to Lagos after army service to see what he could find. Solo was then very much in vogue and our stakes were modest. I also met Bank a couple of times.

I asked Joe Harold about accommodation, pointing out that I could not afford to live in the hotel for long. He replied that it was very tight. 'Rooms are at a premium in this town,' he emphasized, 'but I will make some enquiries and let you know.'

I went to Bank and asked him if he knew of any suitable place. He came back a couple of days later with the good news that a Syrian friend of his had a flat available and that he had arranged for me to meet him.

We set off to meet this man, Arif Barakat. Barakat owned cinemas in Lagos and traded; he had an employee by the name of Grizi who was to be moved and he would be happy to offer me his quarters. They had rented the house from the Nigerian owner, Issa Williams, and the lease had another year to run – it had been paid for in advance. 'You reimburse me the money I have laid out and buy the furniture and you can move in by Christmas,' he said. This was about two weeks ahead.

'Let's go and see it,' I said, and we drove to a house at 49 Docemo Street. It was a two-storey building: downstairs were stores with large wooden shutters used by the landlord; an open staircase on the outside of the house led to the flat upstairs. There was a corridor running one length of the flat which led into four rooms one after the other. The front room was wider because it took in the whole width of the house and had a small balcony. Then there were another three rooms, and at the end the shower and the kitchen. The furniture was limited but adequate. I asked Barakat how much money was involved and he mentioned a figure which relieved me after all I had heard about rents in Lagos. Nor did he ask much for the furniture. We shook hands on the deal there and then and I took a cheque to him the next day. 'There was no hurry about that,' he said, and thanked me.

I thanked Bank and mentioned that I thought the price reasonable. 'Yes,' he agreed, 'It was cheap. But then our Syrian friends are very clever. He liked you and thinks that in time the connection may be useful.'

Docemo Street lay in the heart of the town. It had houses like No. 49 on either side, all looking much the same, built about twelve feet apart with a low fence dividing the properties. It ran parallel to Balogun Street, a major road leading to Carter Bridge, at that time the only connection between Lagos Island and the mainland. The occupants of Docemo Street were better-off Yorubas or Syrians who had their shops in Balogun Street. The Oba's palace was close by.

No other white, i.e. European, man, lived there and Joe

Harold raised an eyebrow when I gave him the news, but that did not worry me. I had made up my mind to leave the past behind me and make a new start. Considerations of prestige could not enter my calculations. I was too conscious of the weakness of my position.

I was happy to find a base. I had never had a place of my own; all the years I had worked for Lister I had stayed in a boarding house in Oakley Street, Chelsea, where I had two rooms and was well looked after by my diminutive landladies, the Misses Jolly. Lister had often said to me, 'Surely, Joe, you can afford to take your own flat,' but I had never done so.

The flat had electricity and water. Not all houses in the neighbourhood offered such amenities. A few yards away was a stand pump in the street where, from the early hours of the morning, women would line up with their buckets to draw water. It was noisy as they kept up their conversations and sometimes quarrelled in loud voices. My neighbours were Yorubas and we soon got to know each other. All the houses seemed overcrowded. One could see the young girls walking bare to the waist sporting their firm breasts, and the older ones too – less enticing. There were children everywhere. A cockerel used to crow lustily next door. I bought it on condition that they did not replace it, which caused much amusement.

I would invite the men to come up for a beer. Some were minor civil servants, some worked for the mercantile houses as clerks, others were in the pay of the Oba's administration. A few of the women were petty traders showing their wares by the front doors: cigarettes, sugar, salt and such like. They were a friendly lot. I bought a car after a while and parked it outside. There were not many cars in the street, and no-one ever interfered with it. Telephones could not be connected in Docemo Street. I had called for my ex-batman from the army and he duly turned up; I gave him the last room of the flat.

I moved into Docemo Street just before Christmas 1947 and remained there for two years until I moved to Campbell Street in 1949.

~   ~   ~

Established in Docemo Street, I was soon visited by some of Bank's friends. Among them were T.A. Doherty, who later became a chief and an important banker, and S.O. Gbadamosi, who opened the first ceramic factory near Lagos and became a prominent figure after independence. I also called on the addresses that Harold had given me.

I could see that Nigeria was very much a semi-closed market, still in the hands of the war-time coalition of the Association of West Africa Merchants (AWAM). Only the crumbs were left, but it seemed that there were many of these around if one knew where to find them.

I set about trying to trace the trader who had not yet paid for the combs he had bought from the Liverpool merchants. I found their man, an ex-policeman named Sodipo. He called on me, and complained that the combs were not what he had ordered – they were unsaleable since they were quite unsuitable for African hair.

We talked and I discussed with him the various lines I had to offer and he became very enthusiastic about the bicycles. 'There is a great shortage here and we can sell them easily – but you must first import them and then the Ibo traders will buy them.'

Bringing them to Lagos meant buying and paying for them before they were shipped, and then offering them out. It would take between eight and ten weeks before they arrived. It was a risky business to go into cold, but I thought I had better try it and ordered something like 200 cycles. When they eventually arrived I sold them at a fair profit but did not repeat the order. The timber business beckoned and would not allow other activities.

Meanwhile I had got an order for some textiles from Chellarams, one of the few Indian traders then active in Nigeria, and an order from Bank-Anthony for some soap via my new Liverpool friends. It was all very small beer.

Before long, however, Liverpool asked me to get them some raffia mats to be shipped to the UK and I asked Sodipo to assist. We went to the market where such mats were sold in twos and threes and bought all the mats available, about 300 at 2/-

each. This caused quite a commotion, especially when we said we could buy more. Next day hundreds of mats were offered to us but the price had gone up to 2/9 each! We declined to buy and Sodipo suggested I keep away from the sellers. 'If they see a white man the price will go up too much.' We kept on buying at 2/3, later rising to 2/6, until we had about 1,000 mats. As our target was three times that figure, Sodipo set off north to Zaria and returned with another 1,000 mats bought at the same price. We stored them in my quarters.

Before the shipping date, Sodipo had asked me to visit Ibadan with him where a local company was anxious to buy buses. We set off and arrived at the house of one of his friends' father, a Chief Agbaje, who put me up for the night. The Chief proudly told me that he was nearly eighty and had learnt to read and write only after he had reached the age of fifty-five. He was a most interesting and caring host who kept me up half the night talking about old times, going back before the colonial days. 'The white man is teaching us new ways; we must learn, even we old men.'

Nothing came of the bus business.

Returning to Lagos after three days, I was told by Eugen, the clerk I had engaged, that Elder Dempster's ship to carry the mats had arrived early and he had arranged to load them.

'Where are the mats now?' I asked.

'On board ship, sir.' I was staggered but all went well. It was another lesson well learned: don't underestimate the Nigerian staff – if motivated they will perform well. We made a shilling profit per mat.

Eugen stayed with us until the Civil War forced him to leave; when the war was over he felt too old and too ill to resume his duties. He had brought up five well-educated children, some of whom went to University.

~   ~   ~

What would you like to see in a man you want to marry?

It was the early 1940s and I was in a bus travelling from Richmond to Darlington. I had come down from Catterick Camp, having been given a day pass to take up a lunch invitation from the mother of a young landgirl I had met a couple of times. She told me that her younger sister aged nineteen had got married and that perhaps she had been in too much of a hurry. The boy was young too and in the army. So I posed the question, 'What would you like to see in a man you want to marry?'

She replied, 'He must have a good job; he must notice what I am wearing, and he must be strong at night.' I thought that was a splendid answer, to the point, and dealing with the essentials.

This was war-time Britain with backs to the wall. The hypocrisy of the Chamberlain years had been blown away. War was a great equalizer: the bombs fell on the East End and on the exclusive Café de Paris night-club alike. There was a great sense of belonging to each other. There was little showing off by the men in uniform – Dunkirk had sobered them up, as had the fall of Poland and France.

What did you look for in a man? That he could earn his keep and take care of his family; that he had some social graces and took note of what those around him were doing; that he had natural instincts. The basic requirements of a sound society.

I mention this because such, by and large, was the life and attitude of the average Nigerian when first I met them. There was no war in the country, but there was the colonial master to act as the equalizer. There was a lack of industrial wealth and ready access to the luxuries associated with it, a lower standard of living, and a creaming off by the foreign power. There was, for all the country's ills, a community spirit, however localized, which vanished quickly as modern conditions were imposed and accepted.

At the time of my arrival in 1947, the atmosphere in Lagos was still very colonial. The administration was totally in the hands of the Colonial Office and so were the various bodies answerable to government: customs, health, police, army, ports, inland waterways, law, education, etc. All had white officers at their head and in key positions.

Within the service, rank was important; one rose slowly up the ladder and did not necessarily remain in the same country for long. The administrative officers, starting as assistant district officers and rising to governor, were all men educated at university, mainly Oxbridge graduates, carefully selected and highly motivated. They were firm, fair, efficient, intelligent and incorruptible. They could also be very arrogant. Their task was to rule on behalf of the British government and to make sure that the interests of that government were paramount. To retain that paramountcy they had to ensure that the country was run smoothly and its inhabitants were happy. One must admire the fact that a few hundred of these men could run a country of thirty million people, and run it well.

I never could see the point of the argument by my Nigerian friends complaining about colonial exploitation. How did it come about, I would enquire, that so few Britons could take over these vast areas? Surely you must blame yourselves? Nor could one expect the colonial power not to look to its own advantage; nobody conquers a country for the benefit of its population, although sometimes interests may coincide. I knew many of these government officers, and had a great respect for most of them.

Commerce and industry were also in the hands of white companies: mainly, but not exclusively, British. They too were run by whites, with Nigerians working in the lower echelons: to a ratio, perhaps, of 1:100, or even more. These whites were of a different calibre. They were rarely university men, but had started their careers after leaving school when recruited for service overseas. Some spent all their working lives in the same country. The government officers kept themselves distant from these 'commercials'. There were, of course, many contacts and the heads of companies had ready access to the relevant officers in government.

Colonial government is a dictatorship. There may have been fruitful contacts between rulers and ruled, but in the end decisions were made by the colonial civil servants and there was no constitutional appeal against them. Several generations of Nigerians grew up in this system, which was to be significant later. When I came to Lagos, having just spent several years under Army discipline, I was not put out by these proceedings and never gave them much thought.

I signed the governor's book, I met people in the ministries, and I called on the only English connection I had been given, one Williams, who was at the time financial secretary. His house was on the racecourse around which several senior officers had their quarters. I joined the Ikoyi Club, which was a social and sporting club for whites; later I also joined the Polo Club.

In the Ministry of Commerce and Industry sat a retired ex-Indian army Lieutenant-Colonel who, *inter alia*, dished out permits to send locally cured hams back to the UK, which many did. We got quite friendly. He was opposed to the slightest concessions to the 'natives'. 'This place will go the same way as India,' he moaned, 'mark my words.'

'Surely not?'

'You will see, friend. This Labour government in London has no idea how to run an empire. Well, I am only here on contract so I will not see it. What did you come for, a ham permit?'

'No, we want a permit to buy a kitcar.'

'That can be arranged if you have the money to pay for it.'

The economy was still more or less on a war footing two years after the war had ended. There was food rationing – which included whisky – and one needed a permit not only to buy a car and petrol, but also to journey outside colony limits. Going to Ibadan, for instance, meant showing one's papers at checkpoints at Otta, near Lagos, and at Ilugun, near Ibadan. All that, however, did not last very much longer.

There were still white locomotive drivers working on the railways, a rough lot who let their hair down in these foreign parts, and the Railway Club in Ebute Metta was renowned for its wild scenes. They too had gone by the end of the decade, to be replaced by the Nigerians they had trained. A Nigerian engine driver who had taken over from a white expert had a high standing in Nigerian society.

Further up the road from the Railway Club stood the white sergeants' mess near the ordnance depot. Opposite it was a nightclub where many of the sergeants gathered with their girlfriends or went to find girls; loud music played, blaring out the latest popular tunes. No decent Nigerian would be seen dead in such places, at least no Lagosian. They had their own entertainment.

We all walked about in shorts and open-necked shirts during the daytime; in the evening one wore long trousers, long-sleeved shirts, and tie. A tie was also worn with shorts if one had to call on a government officer. On independence, suits became *de rigueur.*

Every expat slept under a mosquito net. Many boiled and then filtered their water, although it must be said that Lagos tap water was perfectly safe: I drank it and suffered no ill effects. (Once the town expanded rapidly in the mid-1950s it was a different story.) Most drains in the town were open and regularly sprayed with anti-mosquito chemicals, health inspectors would walk around the domestic quarters to ensure that no water was lying around in little puddles in the compounds. In Ikoyi, a suburb reserved for whites, for instance, it was forbidden to grow bananas because their leaves collect water. Some of these precautions may have been exaggerated, and some may have been wasted, but they all disappeared once the town grew and its administration could no longer cope.

It was rare for whites and blacks to mix socially. The Freemasons made no distinctions, and there were also clubs which tried to ensure that the races mixed, but it was a forced show of unity and rarely a spontaneous getting together based on socially or culturally shared interests. The native and the colonial were two parallel societies with their own traditions, rules, priorities and ranks which met only on official occasions. The British had to ensure that they were feared and respected, and undue intimacy would mitigate against that.

Moreover, it must be remembered that nearly all whites were birds of passage whose stake in the country was transitory: this applied to both government officers and to many company employees. Everyone lived in an official residence belonging to either government or company, and did not necessarily return to the same one after coming back from leave. Tours of duty ran generally to eighteen months, with three months' leave in between: houses were not left empty during this period and occupants changed. Promotion would in any case entitle one to a larger house.

Most people still travelled by sea until the early 1950s. Elder Dempster provided a good service with their mailboats which took thirteen days from Lagos to Liverpool, stopping on the way in Takoradi on the Gold Coast, and either Freetown in Sierra Leone or Bathurst in the Gambia. These trips were great fun and very relaxing. There was also a French line which ended in Marseille and was equally enjoyable. Nigerian students returning home after completing their studies invariably used these mailboats, bringing many goods like refrigerators, record players, and sometimes the tools of their trade. Once on board in Lagos, Nigeria was forgotten; once on board in Liverpol, it loomed large. All this has long since gone; mail boats were scrapped as hardly anybody travelled on them, and only a few people, mainly Nigerians, used them to return home.

Cigarettes were bought in tins of fifty. Beer was imported, usually from Holland and Germany: Amstel and Beck. Few Nigerians drank beer – they could not afford it. One could buy a box of twenty-five local cigars, made (I think) in Abeokuta, for four shillings. Tailors would call; many were very efficient and would make one's shorts and servants' uniforms and even long trousers. They did not, however, make jackets very well. Material was bought in one of the many stores. It was customary to give the tailor an advance and very few ran away with it.

Air-conditioning did not come in until the 1950s and caused havoc, architecturally speaking, because the houses had been built for maximum through-draught, which of course did not suit the air-conditioning.

Government officers, if I recollect rightly, bought their own cars but had Land-Rovers, etc. at their disposal when they went 'on tour'. Company employees were given transport and drivers.

The many Nigerians employed by government or company would never cross swords with a white man, but they did have considerable powers when dealing with their compatriots and were treated by them with caution, respect, and even fear. It depended, of course; they would not dare offend a chief from their own background – on the contrary they would do their best to help him. Staff, such as customs or police, were often posted to areas where they were comparative strangers and could not know whom to trust if asked for favours. White man's business was white man's business. One did not owe any loyalty, but one pretended to do so.

From time to time a bold character would venture into the unknown. I had bought a second-hand car soon after my arrival; one evening I went back to the Grand Hotel for a meeting and parked my car alongside a dozen others. None had their lights on. As I came out a policeman stood waiting for me. 'You parked your car without lights, sir.'

'Nobody else has lights, constable.'

'They are all committing an offence, sir.'

'Too bad, constable.' I got annoyed; what the hell does this fellow think he is doing, talking to me like that!

'Well, sir, I am only doing my duty and you have committed an offence. May I see your driving licence please.'

I was dumbfounded; the cheek of it! 'My driving licence is in my home – why don't you come and have a look at it? I'll give you my address.'

Next day he turned up in Docemo Street. 'You are new here, sir?'

'Yes, I am new here but I served with your men in the RWAFF. You're not a Lagos man, are you?'

He said that he came from the east, that his name was Henry, that he did not want to offend me, and that if ever I needed any help he could be found at such and such a place. 'We will forget about the parking offence, sir.'

When I told Sodipo about it he said, 'Don't worry, this man wanted a "dash" but was afraid to ask you for it and felt he had made a connection he may be able to use in future. These men are poorly paid and look for their advantage.'

'What if I report him?'

'Don't do that, there will be endless palaver and he may lose his job. He may help us some time.' Sodipo, of course, had been a policeman himself and knew the game. Henry called every now and then to see how I was getting on, but we never needed each other. He got the occasional beer out of it.

I wondered if the white police officers knew that their men were on the scrounge. If a white man like me could be so handled, how might a black man be treated? Not many had cars but there were other ways of holding people to ransom. Street trading, for example, was one of them. I am sure that these petty traders were molested by policemen for some extra income even if they were not of their tribe. Who wants to be arrested? And, after all, one had heard similar stories about New York and Chicago, though not about London or Liverpool.

Perhaps the officers knew but did not want to make too much of a fuss. If they caught a fellow red-handed they would take action but otherwise their main preoccupation was political. Any hint of agitation would be severely stamped out. It worked, and the ordinary policeman would take care not to overstep the mark. It was rather like my fellow officer in Cairo blowing his horn when making the rounds of the guard posts to wake up the men before he reached them.

Social life was active: there were the sporting clubs; private dinner parties within fairly narrow circles; official functions crowned by the garden parties in Government House, invitations to which were highly prized: and receptions for visiting VIPs. In all of this rank played its part. On official occasions privileged Nigerians were invited. There were charitable and educational organizations run by the wives.

On Saturday nights people went to the open-air cinema on the marina which featured fairly recent international films; if it rained the show was off. This was attended mainly by the expats. There were a number of other open-air cinemas in the town patronized by the Nigerians; their entrance fee was not only cheaper, but their films, often Indian, were more to the taste of the viewers. As the action unfolded they would hiss the villain and applaud the hero.

On a higher plane was Ogunde's Theatre Party. This was a

Yoruba troupe performing in a large hall near our logging beach office, whose theatre I visited a couple of times. I understood very little Yoruba and much of the play – folk stories turned into colourful action – went over my head. The stagecraft was rather primitive – a raised podium with little extra lighting – but the actors played with enthusiasm and conviction. Ogunde carried on for a long time and became a doyen of the Nigerian stage. Nearly all of the spectators were local Lagosians and the troupe also went on tour throughout Yorubaland. (In Calabar, too, one could see amateurs perform in the Efik language, similarly depicting local folklore turned into drama. Once the number of universities increased, a lively, mainly amateur, theatre developed, performing modern Nigerian authors who wrote plays on topical, sometimes political, subjects.)

Last, but not least, there was the twilight zone of the less reputable night-clubs, with their heavy drinking sessions and black girls.

There was an efficient public transport service run by a Greek entrepreneur, Zarpas, whose buses plied the streets regularly; they were British Guy models with Gardner diesel engines. Zarpas had allowed soldiers to travel free during the war, for which he was decorated with the OBE. He and his wife, an accomplished pianist, lived in a luxury flat over his bus depot by the waterside where they entertained royally, often bringing over renowned artists for an evening's soiree; the Governor and his wife would be present when their duties allowed it. Following independence in 1960, Zarpas sold out to Lagos Town Council and took a suite in the Waldorf Astoria Hotel in New York.

Some of the smaller transporters also ran bus services, among them the Benson family from Ikorodu and Elias, a Muslim, who was to rise to commercial prominence after independence. He looked after the education of his younger brothers, one of whom, Taslim, became a lawyer academician of note, a lecturer at Manchester University, Chief Justice of the Federation, and a Judge at the International Court of Justice in the Hague. Once Zarpas was out of the way these two, Elias and Benson, became the new lords of the Lagos bus world only to fade in their turn as other entrepreneurs pushed their way forward. Whites rarely made use of these facilities.

Quite a curiosity were the launches run by the Ricketts which connected Lagos with the Ikorodu end of the lagoon, a run of about thirty minutes. Travellers trying to reach Ijebu Ode would patronize these waterways to cut short the long journey east via Abeokuta; the fare was one penny. Once a road was cut through the swamps to Ikorodu these launches lost their *raison d'etre*.

Even in those days the colonial administration became concerned at the ever-increasing numbers of men streaming into Lagos to find work. To stem the tide special permits, little red cards, were issued to legitimize this flow and employers were urged to hire only these permit holders. It was a forlorn attempt, leading to minor corruption and exploitation.

One of the highlights near the end of the colonial regime was the Queen's visit in 1956. It started off in Lagos where the streets had been gaily decorated and schoolchildren lined the roads waving little Union Jacks. Her Majesty declared the Apapa wharf extension open – a function with limited seating capacity which left many expats disappointed. The Governor-General held a garden party in the grounds of his residence and there were other official gatherings, an invitation to which was considered to be a rare honour. The local press gave extensive coverage of all the details with full reports and photographs. From Lagos the royal party went up-country. It was impossible then to imagine that within a few years Nigeria would declare herself an independent republic, albeit within the Commonwealth. There was not a single hostile demonstration during the whole of the visit.

The Syrian/Lebanese colony (at first they were all Syrian but later divided themselves into Syrian and Lebanese, the latter in the majority) lived its own existence mixing little with either the Nigerians or the Europeans. They specialized in trade and were strong in textiles and in transport. In the North they were also prominent produce agents.

In 1950 total imports were valued at £62 million, more than

45

50 per cent of which came from Britain. Exports for that year reached £90 million, mainly represented by marketing board sales through its London offices. The 1952 census showed a total population of 31.55 million, which included a non-African figure of 15,400, of which 4,000 resided in Lagos. Two-thirds were British, the balance being made up of Lebanese/Syrians, Americans, Irish, French, Dutch, Indians and others, in that order. It was a small foreign community where most people knew each other or of each other – gossip was rife, yet not too vindictive.

For white bachelors, sex was a major problem. Most had African girlfriends but few would admit it. The girls in turn often thought little of their secret white lovers, who were mainly a means of economic advancement.

I am not referring here to the prostitutes picked up at one of the nightclubs. These girls knew little of hygiene and VD was rife. The sailors off the ships were very prone to this disaster. The girls in these clubs came from well outside Lagos: many from the Delta areas, others from the eastern provinces. Occasionally one would find a very young Hausa or Fulani. They had been sent to Lagos because their parents could not feed them, or they had run away and stayed with some countrymen who sent them out to make money. This is a phenomenon known to all large cities and Lagos was no exception.

One of the more famous nightspots among the whites was the Yaba Rex Club, commonly known as the Yaba Sex Club, owned by a man who later rose to prominence in politics. The resident at the time, the colonial officer in charge of Lagos, took it upon himself to control the morals of his white subjects. He posted policemen in the vicinity of the club who would stop a car carrying a mixed couple. The girls picked up in the club would crouch on the bottom to keep out of sight. If caught it might cost a pound. Above all, the girls dreaded being taken away to the police station where the men on duty would use them sexually before letting them go.

There were many young unmarried whites in Lagos who had taken up posts with the banks, shipping companies, trading houses, and so on. They had been warned against associating with prostitutes, although not a few had been made to learn the hard way. 'Get your contacts at work to find you a nice girl' was the motto. Or the servants would do so, but that was not to be recommended – it was too close to home. To the average Nigerian matron, the sight of an unattached white man was like a red rag to a bull. Surely this man needs a woman, and if we can find him one it will be to our advantage!

Liaisons were formed but rarely openly acknowledged. Some senior employees would have their wives out and these wives would look askance at these attachments. Single senior men in the same position were even more discreet about their African girls than the younger men.

However, once these couples got to know each other better, and especially among the unattached men, matters progressed down an established path. To the men these women were a revelation, sexually speaking. The girls took it as a challenge and gave themselves to the pleasures of sex with an abandon which astounded and highly flattered their partners. They had never known anything like it. There were no inhibitions or false shame. The girls, alas, did not think so highly of their white lovers: they were too quick – like chickens, they would complain – and too self-conscious. But they would obtain useful presents like bicycles and sewing machines and if the liaison lasted they would 'educate' their men to give them more pleasure. The French boys had the best reputation in this respect.

Although there were many exceptions it was often as Fanny Hill said: 'But though, amongst the kept mistresses (and I was now acquainted with a good many, besides some useful matrons, who live by their connexions with them) I hardly knew one that did not perfectly detest their keepers, and, of course, made little or no scruple of any infidelity they could safely accomplish.' The girls knew very well that sooner or later their lovers would return home. The Lebanese and Syrians were in a different category as they felt no need to hide their girlfriends and took a more natural approach.

Few of these women conceived, and mixed children were not common. It happened occasionally, of course, and then the men would make suitable arrangements to maintain their offspring. How the majority escaped getting pregnant was not clear to me. There must have been abortions. A few white men lived openly with their women, had children and seemed happy enough, but they were outsiders even if they did well financially. The whites were seen as the master-race and it would not do to acknowledge that the people who had been conquered could aspire to equal status. This sexual hypocrisy oppressed and tainted life.

Homosexuality was unknown in the south. If it did exist, it was kept so secret that nobody knew about it. To the Africans sex was a natural thing and meant the fusion of male and female, although this changed with independence and the influx of foreigners from many parts of the world.

It was absolutely unheard of for any of the unattached white women working in government as confidential secretaries to strike up a friendship with a black man. If a whisper reached official ears she would be packed off at once, but I must admit I only ever heard of one such occasion. In any case, these white girls were much sought after by white boys and had no shortage of suitors. Nor did one hear of white women being raped by their servants, for instance, who would have had opportunities to do so. The gulf was too deep, the fear too great, and perhaps the inclination too suppressed. Whether a frustrated woman would bestow her favours on a black boy in her household is not known. I doubt it, although it may have happened.

Affairs, however, between white wives and their husband's white friends were not infrequent, sometimes ending in divorce. The men drank, played games, and would neglect their duties as husbands, and there was always someone ready to oblige. The lot of the white married woman who had no children to look after was a dull one. Rounds of morning coffee, playing bridge, charitable duties, and giving orders to gardener and servant made up the day until husband appeared, only to go off again to play polo, golf, tennis or squash, and thereafter drink with his pals. It was much better in the outstations where husband and wife were more of a team and the woman could take an active interest in the man's work.

In time this changed. Young Africans would go overseas to study and sometimes would return with a white wife, perhaps a fellow student. It was hard for these people, too, because they were not fully integrated in either society and some of these marriages did not last.

All that came later. I would add that, temporary as the liaisons between white men and African girls were, they benefited both parties. They began with the physical need and attraction, but slowly the relationship would grow. The girl would learn something of the white man's society and customs; this might fire her ambitions, and it would teach her how to handle the European if she later traded or went abroad to study. Those who were still at school would find not only financial security, but also assistance with their lessons. In her turn, she could warn her lover of pitfalls over dealings with her countrymen: this chap will cheat you; this chap is lying; don't give money to so and so; he is going to use it for something else and not what you are giving it to him for. The man would also learn much of her society: the close family ties and obligations; the intrigues and in-fighting; the rumblings of discontent in one sphere or another.

It was amazing how neat and tidy these women kept themselves. They would live in cramped quarters, many to a room, and yet come out as though they had spent hours getting ready. It was a pleasure to see them and a minor miracle how they managed it. The African woman was never the chattel she was made out to be in European folklore, but she did have a hard time. It was a man's world.

Into this man's world the women brought their femininity, in the end as equal partners: I need you and you need me. The way they dressed, the way they walked and danced, clothed from head to foot with *buba* and *lappa* (blouse and wrap-around), carrying themselves straight, moving slowly and deliberately, hips swaying sensuously and naturally, they revealed and offered as much as the London girl in her miniskirt, black stockings, and off-the-shoulder blouse. Seemingly demure and obedient, nothing would escape her and woe betide any man who failed to deliver financially or physically.

At functions it was (and still is) customary for all members of a wider family to be dressed alike: an expression of solidarity and belonging. Those who could afford it would show off their gold jewellery, blending it into their overall appearance with elegance and little obvious ostentation. They knew how to carry it off. They still do. And if today millions are educated and tens of thousands have university degrees, few have lost their instincts of old. They do not repress their sex – not yet at any rate.

They still do much of the hard work and bear children. Taking employment in the cities, they are faced with the problem of how to look after their young when married. Sometimes grandmother is at hand to help out or a young relative joins the household to act as nanny. Some can afford to employ paid staff. Few will settle down to become housewives until the second or third child comes along, and even then many prefer to keep on working.

At first a women seeking independence met many obstacles. Getting a job even once she had some education, was difficult – nursing and teaching excepted. With education came some hope but also new dangers. A young working woman was exposed to much harassment by her colleagues. Even schoolgirls had to submit to unwanted attentions by the male teachers, especially if the girl did not come from a prominent family. She might be threatened with failing her exams if she did not submit, an obnoxious practice never eradicated. Yet to fail such exams would be a disaster and incur the wrath of parents or guardians.

Today these hazards are probably no greater than in Western society: sheer numbers have reduced the risks. Liaisons between blacks and whites of equal status cause little comment, although these are still not very common. The practical adjustments of everyday life mitigate against them.

4

The Brandler & Rylke Timber Company

I had met Bill Reeks in the Grand Hotel where Joe Harold introduced us, and saw him from time to time after leaving for my new quarters. He had been sent out to West Africa by one of the big British hardwood companies, Glikstens, to find areas where his company could expand: the choice had been narrowed down to either Nigeria or the Gold Coast.

Bill had chanced on the Ondo Native Administration Forest Area No. 4 (ONA 4), a local reserve let out to one Chief Fawehinmi. He had taken a verbal option on the forest.

'Head Office haven't decided yet where to go,' he told me, 'but it looks like the die is cast in favour of the Gold Coast. I have been instructed to stall. Look, Joe, maybe meantime you'd like to dabble in the timber business?'

'How?' I asked.

'Contractors bring rafts of mahogany logs to Lagos on the lagoon for sale. You make a connection in the USA, get a contract, and on the strength of that we buy the logs and ship.'

'But Bill, I wouldn't know a good log from a bad one. I wouldn't even know a mahogany log from a sow's ear.'

'Ron and I will help you; we will go partners.' 'Ron' was Captain Pedlingham, who had also been sent out to look at the timber scene by Finch & Co of London, and was now kicking his heels while they studied his reports. Bill had been an officer in the RAF at the tail-end of the war, Ron was ex-Army.

'All right, let's give it a shot,' I said. I went to the Department of Commerce and Industry to obtain names of US importers, wrote to several, and in the upshot had a contract for 100 tonnes to be shipped to New York for the Pierson Lumber Company. We bought the logs, rolled them up for inspection behind the police barracks at Iddo (courtesy of the officer in charge who was a friend of Bill's) and loaded them on the Barber West Africa Line.

In spite of the help of my two expert friends, the result was disappointing. The buyer wrote that the measurements were incorrect and that a few of the logs had toredo worm damage. He paid only 90 per cent of the invoice value and there was not much left for us.

But I had smelled blood, or rather timber, and insisted we try again. Ron's company had by then decided to go ahead in Nigeria and he had to bow out. Bill's bosses had advised that they thought the Gold Coast offered them better prospects; he was to wind up in Nigeria and proceed to Accra within the next two months.

'I will have to inform the Chief that we are not going ahead. He will be very disappointed. It's a good concession, about 200 square miles, plenty of mahogany. Why don't you take it, Joe?'

'I don't know the first thing about logging in West Africa, Bill. And what about the finance?'

'I think you may have enough to kick off with and I would join you. First we'll make some money buying logs in the lagoon and then we'll travel to Ondo to see the Chief. We've got a few weeks.'

It sounded simple enough and was made simpler still when an Ondo man by the name of Roberts whom I had never met came into the office to say that he understood that I was in the timber business and that he had several contracts with an English firm which he would like to pass on to me for a consideration.

I said, 'Well, Mr. Roberts, I am not really in the timber business but am interested to hear what you have to say.' He showed me three contracts, each for 15 tons of Abura species, from a London company called Cobbett & Co. 'Why don't you want to handle it yourself? The contracts are made out in your name.'

'You see, Mr. Brandler, I thought I would be able to do it but it requires money and I'm short of cash. These people won't open a letter of credit. They say I should ship the goods and they will pay me on arrival and after inspection. How do I know they will pay me? In any case, that means my money will be tied up for several weeks, maybe three months.'

'How did you contact Cobbett & Co?' I asked, 'Where did you find out about them?' He replied that a relative of his was a clerk in the Ministry of Commerce and Industry and he had found the name in the files and passed them on to him.

'Mr. Roberts, before I can even look at this seriously you must write to the London agents telling them that you wish to pass the contracts on to me, and asking if they'll re-issue them in my name. We'll take it from there.'

Roberts did write to Cobbett & Co, the agents he had contacted, and by return of post he received corrected papers in my name which he brought to me. I had done nothing about them, and when Bill Reeks came up with the idea I showed him these papers and he said, 'OK, it's a start. Let's deal with them.'

'How do we know we're going to get paid?'

'Well, I should think we'll be paid. After all, it's a small amount. I don't think they'll cheat us out of it.'

'All right, let's go ahead.'

We drew £100 to buy logs. The money was in shillings – 2,400 of them – in a heavy bag which Bill carried back to his hotel. He was staying in the annex of the Grand Hotel some distance away the main block. That very night the annex caught fire, Bill had to jump out of the window, and hurt his back in the fall. The money melted in the heat. Bill was taken to hospital and the doctors decided he had best be evacuated to England for observation and treatment.

'Sorry, Joe, I can't go on, but I think you should. I know a very good man who could perhaps join you. He is been working in Ijebu Ode for a timber concern for one tour and knows something about bush work. I'll send a note to the Chief to say that you'll be coming to look at his bush, but first you must meet Sandy Rylke. He's the chap I think you could team up with.'

A meeting was arranged.

Sandy Rylke was a Pole, about forty years of age. He had been a regular officer in the Polish Cavalry, and a member of their Olympic equestrian team at the Berlin games of 1936, where they had won a medal. When war broke out, his division had been pushed south towards Romania, from where he had made his way via France to Britain and had ended up in No. 3 Regiment in Nigeria.

His wife and only child had been left behind in Poland and they had only recently been reunited. On demobilization he had taken a job with a timber company and although he knew nothing about the work or commerce he was a good organizer and had done well, except that he could not get on with his resident director, Annesley, who terminated the appointment when the contract for the first tour of duty was at an end. They were in Lagos looking for a passage to the UK and in effect at a loose end.

Bill Reeks explained the circumstances and my experiments in timber. I pointed out that I was uncertain what to do in Nigeria; I had several options. Timber looked interesting: what was his position and what did he feel about the timber business?

'Don't answer now. Think about it, talk to your wife, and let's meet again in a couple of days.'

We went to the cinema, after which he introduced me to his wife at their temporary abode provided by the company he was to leave. Two days later we met again in Docemo Street.

'I have got little to lose, Mr. Brandler.'

'Call me Joe.'

'Joe, Reeks thinks the bush is good. Perhaps we should go and have a look at it.'

'Well, Mr. Rylke...'

'Call me Sandy.'

'Sandy, it will mean little to me looking at the bush. How about finance? I can put up some money – how much could you bring in?'

'£600,' he replied.

'That's not very much, Sandy. I would put up double that

amount and could lend the venture an additional £3,000. Would that get us anywhere? If we proceed, we form a partnership and split it two to one.'

'I have to see the bush first.'

We sent a messenger to the Chief in Ondo to tell him that we would be coming, gave him the date, and made preparations for the trip.

Bill Reeks recovered but never returned to Nigeria. He bought a London taxi and kept himself busy with that until he decided to emigrate to Australia and to fly there in a small plane with a friend. They had to make an emergency landing on a small island in the Pacific from where they were rescued after having been posted as missing. That was the last I heard of him.

Ron Pedlingham's company did well. His main claim to fame was that he managed to insure his rafts with Lloyd's of London and then had them towed bigger and faster than anyone else dared do. Inevitably some of them came a cropper, especially during the rainy season. It took Lloyd's some time to realize that they could not win. He later became the managing director of an important timber concern in London. I last met him by chance walking in the City with bowler hat and umbrella.

5

Chief Seriki Fawehinmi

B ill Reeks had walked Fawehinmi's concession area
several times and told us all that he knew about it.
However, if we were to take over, we needed to look not
only at the bush but also at the licencee, his work force, and the
conditions in which he operated. Then we would have to
confirm terms of co-operation, and budget for what would be
involved financially.

The camp was in a village, Kajola, which fell under the
domain of the Oba ('King') of Ondo, although it was quite
some distance away from the town (a day's march, I would
guess, taking the shortest route through paths and local roads).
To reach it we had to drive from Lagos to Ibadan, on to Ife,
where we branched off onto the Ondo Road and crossed the
Oni River on a wooden bridge. We would pass Ondo town and
reach Okitipupa Road where we left the public highway to join
a road constructed by UAC (United Africa Company). We
were to skirt UAC's concession and HQ offices at Bulawayo
to reach their boundary with the chief's concession. From
there a rough, single-track road would take us to Kajola, some
fifteen miles away. It was a journey not far short of 300
miles.

About ten miles from Kajola camp we got stuck. One of the
wooden bridges had had its decking and one of the runners
removed and the car could not pass. It was late in the afternoon
and we had no choice but to leave the driver and one boy
behind to guard the car and loads and set off on foot.

The road was a very rough and ready path enlarged to take a

motor vehicle, with plenty of potholes and temporary bridges similar to the one that had forced us to leave our car. It took us about three hours to get to Kajola and it was quite dark by the time we arrived.

Chief Seriki Fawehinmi had given us up and retired to his quarters. Not a soul stirred but the occasional dog began to bark. We sent a man forward to announce our arrival to the chief who came out of his hut and greeted us with some surprise. We explained our difficulties. Then Sandy insisted that the chief got people together to collect our loads from the car which was unlikely to reach us for at least a day.

So the chief got his clerk to drum up some fifteen hands to set off to collect our belongings. To my great surprise they were all women. 'Why does he pick women?' I asked Sandy.

'Carrying loads is a woman's job,' he replied, 'They are used to it.'

These poor women were none too pleased at the prospect of having to walk over twenty miles in the middle of the night and took some persuading; Sandy promised them a big 'dash' and off they went. They returned many hours later carrying our loads on their heads, obviously tired and glad to be back. Sandy gave the senior £2 to be divided between them and they seemed happy with that. To put this into perspective, at this time (1948) one penny would buy ten bananas. For all that, I was still surprised that fifteen women could be mobilized at a moment's notice to go off for twenty miles, in the dark, to collect our loads.

We were quartered in a mud building with palm leaf thatch and wooden shutters. The goats had to be driven out and someone came and brushed out their droppings while we waited for our camp-beds and other belongings.

Next morning the chief sent his clerk to guide us to his camp a short distance away. The chief greeted us formally, a fine upstanding figure belying his age – he was said to be in his late seventies – and made a little speech in Yoruba which the clerk translated. He was glad to see us and happy that we had reached Kajola. He would make sure that the bridge was repaired and that such hold-ups would not recur. He would show us anything we wanted to see. We could then discuss terms.

Chief Seriki Fawehinmi was not a local chief but a senior chief in Ondo town. The title 'Seriki' meant he was head of the Muslims in Ondo. The family was large and highly respected. His junior brother had become Chief Lisa, second only to the Oba in rank, when Fawehinmi had declined the honour because he preferred the Muslim title. The Chief had a large house in Ondo town, several wives, and many children of all ages. He understood English but would not speak much, and although he wrote Arabic and read the Koran he did not read or write English.

Kajola was a small Ondo settlement of no more than three dozen mud houses. Farmers lived there and the farms belonged mainly to Ondo people who kept relatives in the village. Then there were Seriki's people, and a blacksmith, Dare. The village was right in the middle of the bush and the farms were all very small. It looked as if the Chief's timber activities dominated the village. The village had a *bale* (a headman), known to us as 'Daniel'.

To our knowledge no car had ever reached Kajola, although I cannot be sure of this: certainly no lorry had ever done so. The chief's labour camp was a few hundred yards outside his headquarters, which themselves were on the edge of the village and its largest compound by far. There was also a tiny school and a teacher.

Goats, hairsheep and chickens ran about freely. Men and women were dressed in native Yoruba garb. During the season in daytime, such villages would be almost deserted except for the small children and the very old; everybody was out working. In the compounds there were flowery shrubs and sometimes orange trees, as well as the inevitable banana and plantain plants.

Each morning under the watchful eye of the headman, the houses and paths would be swept out and the rubbish dumped, to be burnt later or left to rot in the bush. It was a well organized community run on traditional lines isolated from the nearest public highway by many miles. People walked to Ondo or they walked to the highway from where they would, with luck, pick up transport: a mammy waggon which catered for passengers and freight but did not follow any scheduled timetable.

There were many streams which during heavy rains would become impassable torrents for hours or days. They provided water, although in the dry season this would be reduced to a trickle and not very clean. Some of the farmers had daneguns with which they hunted. There were also professional hunters living in Kajola.

We spent three days in Kajola. Sandy was satisfied with what he saw and after several hours of talking we drew up a provisional agreement of co-operation. Chief Seriki then informed us that the agreement would have to be approved by the Oba, the Oshemawe of Ondo, and that he would ask for an interview to introduce us and get the Oba's approval. He took along his English speaking clerk and when we reached the town (Ode Ondo) we put up in the Government resthouse high up on a hill for the night. He would send for us next morning.

Ondo was a smallish provincial town, not even the administrative capital of Ondo province. Why this was so we did not understand, but believed that at some time or other the town had fallen foul of the colonial power, which kept a district and assistant district officer there. We paid a courtesy visit on them but only the ADO was in – the DO was on leave. He was very correct but not too friendly and complained that we had gone to the bush without advising his office of it first. We explained our mission and apologized for our lapse.

'I thought a large British company was to work with the chief in ONA 4?'

'We have taken over their interests.'

'Really? I understood that UAC were next in line. Have you signed an agreement with the chief?'

'We are about to do so.'

'I see. Well, keep us in the picture.' We took our leave after briefly giving him the background to our affairs. The meeting disconcerted us. Had we blundered in some way? Did he think we were deliberately acting behind his back? What did he mean about UAC's interest in the area?

The chief called on us to say that the Oba would see us next morning. We mentioned that we had heard that UAC wanted the concession. He confirmed that they had approached him, but said that he had preferred Glikstens because they were new on the scene. Now that they had fallen out, he would rather deal with us. 'It is the Oshemawe who has the last word, not the DO. Don't worry.' (The expression 'Don't worry' has since been replaced by 'No problem': in both cases it means all is not well.)

The audience with the Oshemawe took place the following morning. We went to his palace, a large compound in the town surrounded by high mud walls and entered through a great iron gate. A uniformed servant led us into an antechamber where we waited to be called into the Oba's presence. Eventually we were ushered into a big room at the end of which sat the Oba on a chair – I suppose it could be termed his throne. The chief immediately prostrated himself before the Oba. Sandy and I looked at each other as we remained standing. The Oba signalled for the chief to rise, got up himself, held out his hand, and greeted us. 'You are welcome,' he repeated several times.

He asked us to sit down and resumed his seat. At a signal a steward came, brought glasses and filled a tumbler full of gin for the two of us and for the Oba. The chief, being a Muslim, took plain water. 'You are welcome,' he said again, as he raised his glass. We followed suit.

He was a middle-aged man, dignified and well-proportioned, with cunning eyes and a friendly demeanour. Round his waist he had a wide belt from which hung a key-ring with many keys dangling. He had taken one of the keys and given it to the servant to bring the gin.

A long conversation ensued between the chief and the Oba in Yoruba which we could not understand. We thought we heard the word UAC but could not be sure.

After a while the Oba turned to us. He congratulated us on finding such a worthy man as his good friend, Chief Seriki, to do timber work with, and he was sure all would work out well for both parties. He had heard from the chief that the local manager of UAC, Maclaren, had immobilized a bridge to keep us out and that was not acceptable. 'Please call on me any time you are driving through the town. As you can see, we need much development and are always happy to meet new faces who want to work with our people. We have no electricity yet nor running water. We have been neglected by the Government.'

He rose to bid us good-bye and we took our leave. The chief asked us to wait a few minutes. He stayed behind to talk to the Oba and soon joined us; he was in a good mood. 'The Oba is on our side and we will succeed.'

We drove to the chief's house where we were offered soft drinks and met his senior wife and some other members of the family. We then signed a short agreement setting out the salient points of our co-operation and fixed a date for Sandy to come back to discuss practical matters.

'Please, gentlemen,' he said through his interpreter, 'remember that the Oshemawe is with us. You will know how to show your appreciation in due course.'

We drove the long journey back to Lagos. En route we stopped for the night in Ibadan which had a good resthouse where we could take a bath rather than just a shower, a practice we followed for the next few months.

6

We Team up with the
City of London

Having come to an agreement with Chief Seriki Fawehinmi, we had to sort ourselves out. Our first and most urgent task was accommodation. The Rylkes could not remain where they had been quartered by his old company which was expecting their early departure to the UK. To find living space in Lagos was not only difficult, but also expensive. One could not rent a house or a flat in Ikoyi, the normal residence for expatriates, since all properties were owned either by government or by the big trading houses. There were the suburbs of Yaba and Apapa, but rents there were high and we could not afford them. The same applied to Lagos Island.

'I have four rooms in Docemo Street,' I pointed out. 'You can occupy two of them, one can be the office and one can be my bedroom. Let your wife Musia have a look. It's not ideal but it would do until we find our feet. We can put the steward downstairs.'

The Rylkes moved in. It was the best we could do in the circumstances. It was only then that I was told that Musia was expecting a child, after a lapse of over ten years. It complicated matters but could not be helped. The child was born a few months after they joined me; she grew into a delightful young woman. Their boy, aged eleven, had been sent to the American school in Jos, on the plateau, a long way from Lagos but still in Nigeria. I wondered why they had not sent him to a boarding school in Britain and was told that after the long separation they had wanted the child to be reasonably near them.

We lived together for eighteen months. It was a difficult and cramped existence, very unlike that of other Europeans and Musia felt it keenly. After a few months she began to complain.

'We've made some money. Why can't we rent a house or a flat?' she kept on crying, 'There is no room here and I can't entertain my friends.'

'Give us a little more time, Musia. We need all the money we make to run the business and establish ourselves.'

I don't think she ever forgave me for being so rigid, even when later she lived in one of the finest houses in Ikoyi. I think she thought, 'Here is this bachelor who has no idea what it is like for a woman like me to live in these conditions with a baby, and he is so mean he won't spend money on renting a decent place for us to stay.'

For my part I thought, 'Here is this woman who miraculously survived the war and Nazi atrocities [she had been forced to work in a factory by the Germans during the war] for over six years, at last re-united with her husband who has a chance to make good, and she will not put up with a few more months of discomfort. She's prepared to risk our progress just to entertain her friends in better style.'

There was no answer to the problem and I prevailed by force of having the deciding voice. Sandy saw my point but she did not. We never became close friends. The fact that it cramped my style as well as hers, that I was not used to living with a new-born baby, probably never entered her head.

Sandy had learnt what he knew of Nigeria through his attachment to the Nigeria Regiment and his work with the company in the western bush. He was a strict disciplinarian and his attitude to the Nigerians had been shaped by the prejudices of the white army officers and his English employers thereafter. The collapse of his world and the vicissitudes of war-time had, however, opened his mind and made him surprisingly flexible. He learnt quickly and accepted my philosophy that in order to succeed we needed to establish a good rapport with the Nigerians, to make them trust us and feel at ease. At first it went against the grain but he was an intelligent man and quite liberal at heart.

He used to tell me stories of his army life, of how, when he was posted to an eastern Poland mostly populated by Ukrainians, the army used to break up demonstrations by force, often having to shoot the demonstrators. Even so, they never subdued the inhabitants or got them to accept Polish rule.

'I can see now,' he said, 'that we would have been better off to be rid of them, but of course most of the land belonged to Polish grandees who would fight to retain their estates rather than concede. Now they've got Moscow to take care of them.'

He was nobody's fool and always on the look-out for people trying to cheat or get the better of us. His suspicions often paid off. I remember one occasion when we had timber lorries running on the Ondo – Agbabu road and we had gone there to inspect the work. We ran into one of our lorries on the way back, carrying passengers dangerously perched on the open truck. We stopped and made them get off. The lorry went on its way.

After a few minutes Sandy said, 'Let's turn round and follow the lorry to see if they obeyed our orders or took the passengers on again.'

We did this, and soon caught up with the lorry, once again carrying the passengers. Great consternation ensued: the passengers were told to get off, and there was a dispute between the driver and the clerk, each accusing the other of having taken back the passengers.

'Turn out your pockets,' Sandy shouted to both of them. The driver's pockets were empty but shillings rolled out of the clerk's. 'Aha! You have taken money for this, you rogue! What if the people fall off the lorry and get killed? You're sacked!' The clerk was in tears and begged for mercy. Sandy said he would deal with him later and sent them off to continue their journey.

'I know them,' he laughed. 'He couldn't resist making a few shillings extra, and having taken their money wouldn't return it to them when we ordered them off. He took a chance, bloody fool.'

We worked as a sort of double act. Sandy was the tough guy, I was the conciliatory one, and so we could play hot and cold as it suited us. Many years later the roles were reversed. He mellowed with success.

Sandy and Musia led an active social life. He had become the head of the Polish community in Lagos, a great entertainer in the fine houses which we had built for each of us. He also bought a house near Ascot where he spent his leaves. He had his mother and his wife's mother come to stay with them in both Lagos and Ascot, and even went to visit them in Poland.

We were friends to the end. There were, inevitably, differences of opinion, but they never led to rows. It was a good partnership because we complemented each other. Success never went to our heads; we were too conscious of the wheels of fortune which affected not only our families, but also those of so many of our circle since 1914.

Sandy turned into a good businessman. He was a quick learner. In his short career with the Ijebu Ode company he had learnt that mahogany was very good wood and abura was not so good. When we began buying logs to augment our production, at first he could not understand why I would increase the buying price for abura but not for mahogany. 'Abura is bad timber. Why pay more?' he asked.

I explained, 'If we buy mahogany for 2/- and sell it for 3/-, we gain 50 per cent. If we buy mahogany for 4/- and sell it for 5/-, we make 25 per cent. The price for abura at the moment is 1/6 and there's competition to get supplies. So let's raise our offer to 2/-. We'll steal a march on our competitors and still make more money out of it than out of mahogany. Remember – a good timber is one you make a profit from, a bad timber is one you lose on.' It sank in.

Nigeria was a hard school. I always maintained that two years in business in Lagos was equal in training to two years at Harvard Business School. The Englishman who ran the local newspaper, the *Daily Times*, ended up as editor of the London *Daily Mirror*, and there were many other similar success stories. Individuals either made it or fell completely by the wayside.

Sandy was always a stickler for detail. He had the offcuts

piled on one side and they were sold as firewood. He loved haggling with the market women who came to buy them, even though it was only a matter of pennies. When I suggested that we leave them as perks for the labourers as it was hardly worth our while to waste time selling them, he was surprised and disagreed: he feared the men would cut off more than they needed in order to have firewood for sale.

'You have a point, Sandy, but I think we can risk it. It will bring in goodwill in return.'

He saw the argument. 'All right, no more firewood transactions. But you know, Joe, you're depriving me of one of the little pleasures of life.'

~ ~ ~

'How are we going to sell these logs?' asked Sandy.

'How did your old boss, Annesley, get rid of them?'

'I have no idea.' Nor had Pedlingham or Reeks. They were in Africa to find timber, not to sell it.

'There are Roberts' people, Cobbett & Co, and there must be more like that in London. Let me go to see our colonel.' I called on our Indian Army friend.

'Yes, there is a list; Cobbett & Co. are on it. They seem to be of medium size. – Here are the names of a few others. Why not write to all of them?'

'Are they reliable?'

'We get these names from Whitehall; they must think they're all right. In the end it's your pigeon, Joe, we accept no responsibility.'

'Thanks. We'll contact Cobbett first.'

'Do you know them?'

'We had an enquiry from them by chance. Besides, I like the name, William Cobbett, and all that.'

'Who is he?'

'An English politician of the last century. I rather cared for his views when I read him.'

'First-class recommendation, first-class recommendation. You can give me as a reference if you need one,' he added, 'Let me know how you get on with your politician. How about a drink in the house this evening?'

We wrote to Messrs Cobbett & Co. Ltd, Cross Keys House, Moorgate, London EC4 – right in the City of London. We were impressed, almost standing to attention as we sealed the envelope. We kept the letter short. We were now Brandler & Rylke Timber Company, we were ready to process their abura contracts, we had taken a large concession, and would soon be producing different species in fair quantities. Would they be interested in working with us and, if so, on what terms?

They replied promptly (airmail in the 1940s took about four to six days each way). They were interested; they urged us to load the abura and to offer anything else we might have, especially obeche. Terms initially would be cash against documents, 90 per cent balance after arrival and inspection. This was a lot more favourable than what they had offered Roberts.

Sandy became concerned. 'How do we know they're going to pay? Why don't they open a letter of credit?'

I waved this aside. 'Let's look at it this way: these people are in the City and on a government list. Their first attempt to deal with Nigeria via Roberts came to nothing. We're talking about a small amount of money – maybe not small for us, but small all the same for a London City firm. We're wondering if they'll take up the documents when our bank presents them, they must be wondering if we'll ship rubbish. Letter of credit or not, they won't see the logs until after they've paid.'

'Unless,' intervened Sandy, 'they're rogues.'

'They'd be more like pickpockets, playing games with such a small amount. Let's take a chance, and not bring this matter up. We'll load and ask for cash against documents through the bank. It's a trial for both parties. We'll go ahead.'

And we loaded. We did not even send the document through the bank for collection as they had expected, but posted them by registered mail. First set one day, copy set two days later, as was customary. We were paid by return.

Cobbett then wrote that they were very interested in the obeche species, a large tree of white wood, relatively light in weight, and coming strongly in the market. We should try to send them some tonnage as soon as possible. They further mentioned that a good friend of theirs, a Mr. Poole, still employed by government in timber control and before the war a senior manager at Gliksten's, would soon be visiting Lagos; they had asked him to meet us and hoped we would show him our beaches and our logs.

We met this Mr. Poole. It was pouring with rain as we took him to our beach, which was under water. We drove as near to it as we could. Poole got out, the rain still coming down in buckets, saw some logs in the distance and said, 'All right, chaps, I see you have got logs. That's all my friends want to know. Quite a few obeche, eh? Very good, very good.' The obeche he saw, alas, were not on our beach, but we kept silent and took him back to his hotel. Oko Baba beach had had its first foreign visitor.

We shipped more abura; we bought obeche logs from contractor Egbegbe and sent them to Cobbett; we then loaded our first mahogany from Fawehinmi's bush. We never asked for a letter of credit and always got paid promptly against documents sent by mail. We wanted as little to do with the banks as possible. Mutual confidence grew.

We came up against a great problem in Fawehinmi's bush during that very first year, 1948. The little stream to which the logs were hauled was temperamental. The rains had been exceptionally poor and the waters did not rise enough to float them out. The logs were lying exposed to the sun and began to split at the end, to be attacked by pinworm making small holes, often more than an inch into the surface of the log. Most of our fortune was tied up. We were lucky that heavy rain came late in October and early November which enabled us to float the timber downstream to the Lagoon where the first raft of mahogany was picked up by Elder Dempster's tug and towed to Lagos. This was so dire an experience that we made up our minds to find a deeper channel to dump the logs all the year round, so as not to be dependent on seasonal fluctuations and to avoid our money being tied up in stock for longer than was economical.

We consulted the chief. 'Yes, if we make a road to Ayesan,

some twenty miles from Kajola, to the Ofara River we will have permanent water. We will need a lorry or two to carry the logs to the village and dump them in the river.'

'How much will it cost us to make such a road?'

The headman, Daniel, was called in as local contractor. 'Can you quote us?'

He quoted. 'All told £100 per mile. All to be done by labourers with shovels, axes and matchets. By hand.'

'How long will it take?' I asked.

'About four months and I can start in November after the rains. You pay as we go along.'

'Will the road be passable in the rainy season?'

'Absolutely,' he assured us. This it turned out, was an exaggeration *par excellence*.

'£2,000!' Sandy cried when we discussed the project. 'Where do we find that sort of money?'

'We'll approach Cobbett's,' I replied. We wrote to them and advised them that we needed funds for road construction and that I would shortly be in London. We implied that if they could or would not accommodate us, we would have to look elsewhere. We also wrote that they should not worry about a hotel as I would be staying with friends (it was essential to keep expenses to a minimum).

I called on Cobbett's the morning after my arrival. George Cobbett, the head of the firm, greeted me heartily. They had good offices, about four or five rooms. I was introduced to Mr. Dyer, the accountant, and to Mr. Branchflower, the salesman, whose name was shortened to 'Twig'. I was told that another Cobbett – a senior brother, Sydney – spent most of his time in America. They were a private concern founded by the father, Colonel Cobbett – now dead. They had specialized in American woods and their business had fallen flat because of the war. They were trying to build it up again and West Africa was one of the possibilities they were considering. They were glad to meet me.

George Cobbett was a tall, elegant gentleman, well spoken with suave manners. Dyer, a fussy chap, looked after the finances. Both were in their mid-forties. Twig was younger.

He had joined the company as an office boy aged fifteen and by dint of hard work, a likeable personality, and a sharp brain had risen to his present position. He was, as it turned out later, the heart and soul of the business.

I presented my case. 'How much do you need for this road?' Cobbett asked.

'£3,000,' I replied, allowing an extra thousand and feeling very cunning in doing so.

'We'll think about it,' came Cobbett's response. 'What are you doing for dinner?'

'I am free.'

'All right, let's have dinner together. Meet you at...' and he mentioned a posh restaurant in the West End (I think it was Scott's).

Cobbett brought his wife, Thelma, along to the meal. She was a very prim and proper, well-dressed lady, clearly concerned that this stranger from darkest Africa would get her husband to lose money in a wild venture (he had apparently done so once in his youth in South America).

'What security can you offer?' Cobbett asked, over a brandy.

'None,' I replied. 'Come out, or send your man out to have a look.'

'How will you repay?'

'You will deduct 10 per cent from each shipment until the loan is repaid. By the way, what interest would you charge?'

'If we give you the money, we will charge you the going bank rate plus one and a half per cent – no more.'

We had another brandy and even Thelma relaxed a little. I had the impression that they were keen to conclude a deal. They were looking for new fields. 'Mr. Cobbett, this is a risk for you, but it is a good risk. Don't keep us waiting with your answer because we must take advantage of the dry season. We need the funds now.'

'Are all the logs you want to ship coming over this proposed new road?'

'No, we also buy in from small contractors who bring their logs to Lagos.'

'Fine. Let's have one for the road and meet tomorrow morning. You go and have a good sleep.'

We met next morning. 'We have agreed to take a chance, Mr. Brandler, and give you the money,' Cobbett said. Dyer and Twig nodded approval. 'We'll draw up a short agreement. It must be understood that you will channel all your shipments through us. You can have a draft tomorrow. It won't take us long to put this on paper.'

Next day we signed, I received the draft, and in less than a week I was back in Lagos, mission accomplished. Neither side ever regretted the connection. The advance allowed us to expand and we were able to repay it long before the agreed terms. It revived Cobbett & Co., as I found out much later when they in their turn owed us £30,000. Twig told me then that they had feared I would ask for an advance of £15,000 while their bank had set a limit of only £10,000.

When I visited London a year and a half later, they booked me into the Savoy Hotel, one of the most expensive in town. I protested. 'We've made a few pennies, George, but we're not show offs.'

'We put you in there for our prestige, not yours! Our shipper must be seen to be a man of importance. You're getting known in the trade.'

On that visit they invited me for dinner in their house. Twig was one of the guests. He confessed that it was the first time he had received such an invitation. That, after having been with the firm for well over twenty years! 'For Thelma I am still the Cockney office boy.'

'Do you mind?'

'Not really; that's the way it is.' The class system accepted.

Good old Twig. He was as short as George was tall, popular, hard-working, astute. It was he who had thought of Africa and he who went around trying to sense the trends of the market and to place our supplies to best advantage. They sent him out shortly after the road was completed. He would not fly and travelled by mail boat. He was apprehensive of the 'jungle', and as so often happens came across some unusual adventures.

On his first day in the bush with Sandy, a snake fell on him

71

from a tree. I never heard of such a thing before or since. In Kajola one night there was a drunken altercation amongst some villagers brandishing matchets in which he somehow got mixed up. He hated jumping on the rafts in the water or sitting in a canoe to have a look at the logs. To cap it all, his boat on the return journey ran aground in the mud in Lagos Harbour for a few hours until the tide released it. He dined out on his Nigerian safari for months. He had a pleasant wife and three children. He was a good man and a loyal friend to the end.

Our association with Cobbett's lasted many years. Eventually, our ever-growing turnover stretched their finances, and when we called for funds to go into the Cameroon it was too much for them. We had made many friends in the trade ready to support us but were reluctant to drop Cobbett's and in the end we persuaded one of the big concerns, Price & Pierce, a quoted company, to form a joint venture with them – *de facto* to take them over under a separate flag. Twig became managing director of this new business and George remained on the board. His health was failing and he died soon afterwards of a stroke.

7

Sergeant Bragg and the Lorries

We would soon have our road to the waterside at Ayesan; now we needed to get lorries.

'I have just bought five ex-army Bedford lorries for £15 each,' crowed Annesley, Sandy's ex-boss. 'They have auctions every month at the ordinance depot in Yaba. All you have to do is to get to know one of the sergeants to tip you off which are in good shape and which are duds.'

We took his advice and went there to see what was going on.

'Can I help you?' asked a white sergeant. We told him why we had come. 'OK, let me give you a hand.' He recommended two Albion lorries. 'Buy them. They are almost new and one is a workshop lorry with all sorts of tools inside. The army doesn't do the auctioning, we get a local professional in to do that. Keep your eyes skinned.'

We both attended the auction. When it came to our Albions the bidding climbed to £45. 'Going, going...' shouted the man with the hammer.

'£50!' we shouted.

Down came the hammer. 'Gone,' said the auctioneer, 'for £45 to that gentleman over there.' He pointed to a portly African. It was Elias, a local transporter. He came over to us and said we could have them for £65. We bought, having learnt a few more lessons.

'Sorry,' said Sergeant Bragg, 'that's how it goes. The auctioneer didn't know you, did he?'

'Smart fellow, that,' we thought. 'Come and join us in the timber business.'

'You will have to buy me out of the army.' And we did.

Bragg got the lorries to Kajola. He drove over the UAC connecting road at night and when stopped by the night watchman gave him five shillings, which settled the matter. 'It is a one off affair,' he explained.

The excitement in the village was unbelievable. Men, women and children ran out of their houses to look at the lorries. There had never been any in Kajola nor in the villages on the way to Ayesan. Some of the children had never set eyes on one. They would run behind for miles shouting for joy. Everybody sensed that their world was changing, as indeed it was.

Daniel's road went in a straight line – no contours for him! Up and down, up and down, and the Albions groaned, carrying their loads. They broke down quite often. During that year, 1949, it rained and rained; the road became a quagmire; the villagers' help had to be begged to push the lorries out of potholes or from the verges inundated with water. The lorries had to be assisted up some of the hills. One such (which we called 'number five hill') was so steep that, whenever a lorry approached, one of the farmers (who was called 'the Bishop') – Oni Paraga was the location – came out of his hut dressed in his white robe and, positioning himself at the bottom of the hill, vigorously rang his large handbell to give the driver faith and courage and to make sure he did not muff his gears. This happened twice a day and rarely failed.

We cursed and swore at fate, at the rains, at the drivers, and at Bragg, but soon realized that there was little to be gained by forcing the trucks to do the impossible: we would have to lose many days or risk the lorries breaking down irretrievably. A large labour force was detached to maintain the road with shovels and matchets.

If we were disappointed, all the villagers along the road and some miles either side of it were enthusiastic. No longer did they have to trek for miles carrying their produce to market on their heads. They could make visits to friends and relatives, they could go to town, traders would call, a hospital could be reached. Farms were extended, new farms established, and one large village, Araromi, became a town. We tried to restrict traffic, particularly when it was very wet, but never enforced this rigidly except for rival timber lorries which we would not allow to pass. The chief saw to it that this restriction was strictly adhered to. To do so was in the villagers' interest, since they wanted to see their part of the country opened up. Without wishing to boast, we were the heroes of that part of Ondo Province for a long time: we had put it on the map.

In our time we built hundreds of miles of timber extraction roads. We used modern equipment when we could afford it and soon learnt that spending money on a road was essential to get the best out of the trucks, which became heavier and heavier. The locals always welcomed us in this effort. Kajola had been our school.

We made other roads in Ondo, we made roads by the Cross River, we made roads in the Cameroon and Liberia: always opening up new areas, up and down hills, and across rivers. There were rarely any disputes with the inhabitants or the administration. Asking for compensation for spoiled crops became the game. As soon as they heard a road was coming, the farmers would plant like mad along the proposed path up to the last day. Some of these roads were later taken over by the Public Works Department and extended. We did accomplish something and never felt we were exploiting people or devastating the environment.

8

The Tropical Forest

The tropical logger is not popular in today's society. The uncontrolled felling of trees, particularly in the Amazon Basin, has given him a bad name. The colonial administration and its successor states were (and are) aware of the importance of forest management and conservation of trees. At the same time they knew that logging had to be supported and were careful to co-operate with the timber companies to bring order into the tropical forest management. I owe some of what I am about to write to the work of the late D.R. Rosevear, for many years Inspector-General of Forests in Nigeria, and gladly acknowledge my debt to him.

The use of timber for firewood, house construction, tools, weapons, furniture and so on must be as old as civilization itself. The abundance of trees in the forest belt of West Africa, stretching from Sierra Leone right down to Angola and south thereof, lend themselves to these activities. When Britain took over the rule of what is now the Federation of Nigeria in the last century, the administrators soon realized that the forests constituted a major asset of the country, not only commercially but also environmentally, and took steps to control their exploitation. Briefly, the policy was laid down that the interests of the people were to be secured by setting aside a minimum area of permanent forest which would satisfy their needs, that this forest was to be planned and managed in accordance with the principles of rational forestry, and that such planned forests were to be as far as possible inviolate. The Forestry Department divided the forest areas into:

76

1 government reserves
2 native administration reserves
3 local free areas under the control of the villages where
   these areas were situated.

The term 'government forest' did not mean that the government claimed ownership but only the right to control the cutting of the wood in the areas for the common good. It did,
however, lead to many disputes. There can be a conflict between the farmer who wants to extend his land and the forester
who wishes to stop the farmer from encroaching into the forest
areas.

It is a matter of interest that at the turn of the century the
emphasis in tropical forestry was as much on rubber as on
timber, which then meant only a few select species of trees
being felled. The discovery of vulcanization, and the demand
for tyres for bicycles and then the automobile, gave rise to a
boom and a consequent combing of tropical forests for anything that would produce a coagulable latex. It was only later
than the Para rubber, *Hevea braziliensis*, the only species now
used, was found to be superior; in the meantime, balls of wild
and probably dirty rubber soon became one of the chief articles
of trade from the forests of Africa. Once the superiority of Para
rubber was recognized, that trade disappeared completely until
it was partly revived in the First World War.

In those early days trees for export, or trees to be shipped
to the big towns, were felled near rivers because they had to
be manhandled. Anything further than three miles from the
nearest waterway was left standing, unless the occasional pitsawyer felled a tree and cut it up on the spot, the planks then
being transported on the heads of carriers to a roadside from
where local traders would pick them up.

Although, generally speaking, felling took place near
waterways, there was one exception in Ondo Province where
we first worked. The United Africa Company, which had
licences for many Government Reserve areas, had constructed
a narrow gauge railway and used it to evacuate logs over twenty
miles, to a waterside at Okiti Pupa from where they rafted logs

to Sapele port. That was quite an exception in those days. Later, caterpillars and trucks were used for the extraction of timber and this extraction criss-crossed the forests far away from water. I would place the development of mechanical extraction in Nigeria to the mid-1950s, whereas the UAC's railway must have been built in the 1940s or even earlier. It was, of course, a great capital outlay which only a large company like the UAC could afford.

Felling was strictly controlled in the government reserves. The Forestry Department worked on the principle of a 100-year rotation, so that if a concessionaire got 100 square miles he was in theory to fell one square mile per annum. A further and important protection was that the regulations stipulated the felling of trees as to size – the trees had to be marked before felling and inspected by a forest guard who would then issue, or arrange to be issued, the necessary permits – so that young trees were allowed to grow. The tree permits had to be paid for and generally speaking the cost of a tree was measured by the volume of timber it yielded. All this was designed to perpetuate the government forest reserves. The native forestry reserves and local free areas had no working plan along the same lines. However, the restrictions on what trees could be felled were the same, and tree permits were issued accordingly.

The successful concessionaire would not necessarily be a logger or a logging company but could be an individual who would sublet his concession to a group or company interested in working it, for which the group would pay the concessionaire a commission per cubic metre.

Some illegal felling took place. Not all these vast areas could be successfully patrolled, nor were all forest guards a model of probity, but in our time illegal felling was limited to the odd pitsawyer. In the last twenty years the demand for timber increased very much and the firm control of forests became slack so that much timber was felled which should have been retained in the forest. The demand was not only for the export of wood but also to satisfy internal demand, and eventually the government had to put a ban on the export of all timber. Whether this policy was wise or not is difficult to say. In my opinion, a cubic metre of mahogany exported would generate enough foreign currency to import three cubic metres of softwood from abroad, but clearly the government was not of that opinion. One benefit of this enormous demand for timber was that many species which had been left behind in the old days, when about a dozen species were considered suitable for the trade, were now being felled. Inside Nigeria the most popular was the iroko tree, and a few other species like mahogany and abura were used. Much the same applied to the export business which was very selective, not only as to species, but also as to configuration of the log.

Our company worked in government reserves, native reserves and free areas in western Nigeria, in eastern Nigeria, in the Cameroon (both when it was part of the Nigerian administration, and later when it became part of the Republic of Cameroon), and it also had a large concession in Liberia. We worked under the rules and conditions described above.

A concession area might be gazetted inviting bids, it might be offered by private treaty, or it might be applied for by an interested party. In the west, in Ondo, we first worked as sub-lessees in area ONA 4, a native forest reserve. In the east, the concession area (which was very isolated) was suggested to us by the government which was anxious to have the area opened up. In the Cameroon, we worked as part of a consortium which had an agreement with the government. All of these are described elsewhere.

Before taking on a concession one would spend weeks and often months walking through it taking note of the composition of the forest, the terrain, its accessibility, and the cost of road–making and extraction, and, having come to the conclusion that the forest had commercial possibilities, one would sign an agreement. After that, one would send in teams of enumerators to get a good idea of the concession area in detail, dividing it into half square miles, sometimes less, sometimes more, and these enumerators would mark each commercial tree on a map. The company could then make its working plan, decide which part of the concession to work first, and plan its road-making, which had to be done one or two years ahead.

79

The proposed working plan would then have to be agreed with the Forestry Department. On the maps prepared by the enumerators, not only trees were marked, but also rivers, swamps, hills and other obstacles. It was an exact and costly procedure.

Walking through these forests to appraise them, generally early in the morning, was a great experience. One followed narrow paths, often hunters' paths, or paths between villages, and branched off to the left and right, with half a dozen boys assisting by cutting through the undergrowth. Next to the hunter, the logger was the man who opened up new areas and joined one village to another by his activities. It was always cool, the sun fully blocked by the crowns of trees. These forests were of lofty growth and included some of the giants of the tropical plant world. The canopy was irregular and covered several tiers of vegetation, each overtopping the other in turn. Liane, or epiphytes (which are like ropes hanging down from the trees), were all over the stems and branches of the larger trees. The soil was damp and covered by a deep layer of decaying leaves rich in fungi. The air was moist and remarkably still, even when storms raged overhead, and the whole formation irresistibly gave the impression that it represented the rich development of plant growth in the tropics.

One came across wildlife, an experience which vanished when the noise of the caterpillars, lorries, and mechanical saws drove all wild animals away from the working areas. One of the more common animals was the duiker, an antelope small enough to find its way through the undergrowth of the thick bush. One could trace their progress by the leaves they had nibbled for food as they made their way. They were lovely little deer and I once received a present of a young duiker which I took to Lagos and kept in the back yard. There were also tree bears, or bushbabies, so called because they made a noise like a little baby. Both were hunted for food.

There was a profusion of grey parrots which were caught by the villagers in two different ways. When they found a tree with a nest, they would either climb it carrying a stick on which they had put glue and thrust it into the nest removing the birds as they stuck to the stick, or they would cut down the tree and take the young parrots which survived out of the nest. Occasionally I came across bush cows, or water buffaloes, which were very dangerous. I only once saw an elephant from a distance and twice I came across leopards. I vividly remember one occasion at night on a narrow road in the Cameroon when a leopard, carrying something in his mouth, crossed the path in front of the car's headlights. He took no fright but looked up in annoyance as he disappeared into the thick of the forest on the other side. The elegance and power of the leopard as he made his way were memorable.

The most common animals we met were the monkeys, a great variety of them. I never saw a live chimpanzee but they were around and in the Oban Hills in the east, close to the Cameroon boundary, families of gorilla were known to exist. To witness the monkeys jump from tree to tree was amazing, their agility extraordinary. Driving uphill on a narrow road, I once saw a monkey jump right across the road high up in the crowns of the trees, clutching a tiny baby close to her breast with one arm whilst holding out the other to grasp the branch of the tree she was aiming for. She did so without fumbling and the branch bent under the impact to whip back into position with monkey and baby being carried upwards again to continue their journey. Unfortunately monkeys, too, were hunted for their meat; in the market the sellers would often leave the fur on the flesh to convince buyers that what they were offering was monkey meat, not human flesh. Monkeys still live in great numbers in the bush and seem in part at least able to adjust themselves to changed conditions and not to be too afraid of the noise of mechanized logging.

There were a great variety of snakes, some very poisonous, such as green mambas and gaboon vipers. These were very dangerous and we had cases where our workers were bitten and had to be treated on the spot by a native doctor who used herbs and leaves, his treatment generally proving successful. There were also pythons. None of these snakes attacked a human unless he happened to tread on them or they felt threatened. In our early treks through the bush we always carried a small bottle of permanganate of potash which could be used against snake bites. Fortunately we never had to test it.

The desirability of a concession varied, and inside information from local inhabitants of its composition before looking at it would be a great help. The government reserves before independence were generally allocated to foreign companies of substance and were initially hard to obtain for people like ourselves. The native authority reserves were very much a political issue, even in the days of colonial administration, because the ultimate say was at least officially with the native administration and its head, the Oba or king of a given locality. There was much intrigue and bartering going on. Sometimes one succeeded and sometimes one did not. In all cases money had to be spent.

Much the same applied to the small free areas. Bartering for them was quite a game. One would hear through an interested party that such and such a bush was available and one would hold unofficial discussions with the head of the village, the *bale*. One would promise to link up the village to a feeder or main road a few miles away. If a company had a good name and was known to keep its promises, to look after the people and employ them, it was an advantage.

An official meeting would be called in the local village hall, attended by as many bodies as were around, both men and women. The *bale* would preside, seated on a podium. The company's representative would state its case, having first put two or three money bags each containing £100 in shillings on a table on the podium. The villagers would ask questions, the *bale* would close the proceedings, and say that in a couple of weeks they would confirm or otherwise that they were prepared to give their bush to the company. These meetings were often a matter of form because much had been settled before, including a small gratuity to the *bale* which his subjects would not be aware of (they guessed it of course), but sometimes the decision went against the company – somebody else had been smarter – and the money which had been officially offered in the bags was returned.

If these local free areas adjoined government reserves and

native authority areas it would be an additional perk. Sometimes they would be a little distance away. One never took an isolated free area of five square miles or less unless it was in the close vicinity of forest already allocated to the company. When, however, more and more public roads were cut through the country these small areas became more interesting, the cost of reaching them being drastically reduced. I remember one such occasion when I attended a local village meeting where the *bale* informed us on the spot that the village had already decided to give us their bush. I made a little speech thanking them and saying that we hoped for full co-operation and that we would do all we could to work with the people of the village. In closing, I said that when we talked about the village we not only talked about the men, but the women as well. A great shout went up from the women present – there must have been about thirty or so – who clapped and talked excitedly, and the *bale* smiled and said that of course the women would get their share.

These *bales* could not do as they pleased. They were elected, the election rotating amongst families; not everybody could become the chief of the village. The *bale* had certain privileges and duties and if he was too rapacious or incompetent, or sometimes unlucky, the village would depose him. This meant disgrace and he would have to go into exile. There was an underlying grassroots democracy in these villages which could not be ignored.

Once we had established working successfully in Chief Seriki Fawehinmi's area, ONA 4, we were approached by the licensee of part of the area, ONA 1, north of Ondo town, which extended as far as the boundary with Ilesha. It was a rich bush; to reach it we first had to construct a bridge over a fast-flowing river. This took some time; we completed the work and began operations in ONA 1.

The forest had many mahogany and other desirable species in the north near the boundary with Ilesha. We wanted to work there in the dry season to take advantage of the weather and go back further south towards the town of Ondo in the rainy season, and pushed ahead making a road towards the boundary. We came across one totally deserted hamlet to be told that it had been wiped out by smallpox. Our guide insisted we walk around it and not through it. 'Smallpox,' he whispered in awe, 'SP.' It was clear there had been no farming for several generations and the forest was equally thick on the other side of the boundary. It was our intention to negotiate with the Ilesha licensees if there were any, or with the Ilesha chiefs, to work there in future.

However, as our men began to fell, they were attacked by a gang of Ileshas who came with matchets and other weapons and drove them away. We complained to the Oshemawe of Ondo and asked him to clarify just where the boundary was and whether there was any good reason for the Ilesha people to oppose our operations. The Oshemawe assured us that this was part of Ondo and his domain and brought out old maps prepared by district officers which showed that this area had been demarcated as part of Ondo Province after a dispute which had been settled by the district officer.

Neither we nor the Oshemawe opted to stop the Ileshas by force from driving our workers away. Instead, we decided to approach the Ilesha council and chiefs. They claimed that the area in which we were working was not part of Ondo but part of Ilesha. We pointed out that we had been shown old maps clearly defining this part of the province as being Ondo. They would not accept this and our work in the northern part of ONA 1 came to a halt. We approached the Ilesha people once again and pointed out that there was no farming in the area, that nobody from Ilesha had claimed ownership, and we wondered why they were suddenly making difficulties. They repeated that it was part of their land and that any trees felled would have to be paid to them and not to Ondo, who of course disputed this strongly. We then suggested that we continue to work while the dispute between Ilesha and Ondo was being settled one way or another, and that we pay the fees for the trees we were felling into an escrow account where the money would be held until the dispute was resolved, and then collected by whoever was given the area. The chiefs consented and Ondo reluctantly agreed to this, but in the meantime weeks had passed and some wild Ilesha people had gone to the forest and set fire to many trees to discourage us. We pointed out the folly of such action and eventually they demurred but not before many trees had been badly damaged by fire, some to a point where they were useless.

An old man told us that many years ago there had been a clash between Ilesha and Ondo hunters in that very bush and one man was killed. He was buried on the spot, a monument was erected for him, and peace was made over his grave. We brought the story to the attention of Ondo and Ilesha, and other old people did in fact remember that this had happened. There was no written record but we were shown the grave on which stones had been heaped in the middle of the forest.

We had a similar dispute in Ogoja Province, where a rare and valuable small *Afrormosia* forest was destroyed by fire.

Boundary disputes were not uncommon in any part of Nigeria, the more so as the forest areas were never sought after except to burn for farming. It was only when the timber rush started in the early 1950s that the towns and villages became aware of the value of this land.

9

Logs: from manhandling to mechanization

F ar away from urban civilization, the hardwood tree is felled in the tropical forests of Africa, Asia and South America. It ends up as furniture, shop fittings, decorative veneer, and many other things, often thousands of kilometres away. How does it reach its destination?

We may hate a lovely tree one hundred and more years old being cut down, but we love beautiful furniture to adorn our houses – much as we don't think of the lamb covorting in the field being boiled in our pot. These are emotive and understandable reactions. Like it or not, working wood is one of the oldest human occupations.

Before describing the progress of the tree from forest to port, let me make clear that I am talking of the tropical hardwood trade. Timber as a business falls into two separate categories: the hardwood and the softwood trades. A hardwood comes from a deciduous tree; the wood is not necessarily always 'hard'. Softwood comes from a needle tree, and is not necessarily always 'soft'. By and large, hardwood is used for selective applications, while softwood – which accounts for around 90 per cent of all wood manufactured – is used for the general run of timber work.

The hardwood trade was, and still is, much more fragmented and dependent on individuals with experience and flair, people who, at the top end, are not unlike the art dealer with his specialized knowledge. It considers itself superior to the common cousin in the softwood trade, even if poorer; it belongs to a small fraternity with wide international ramifications, insiders who know each other however many miles and continents apart.

A figured tree will attract buyers from every corner to be inspected, valued and bid for; it may then be shipped from Africa to France for specialized slicing into veneer and sold on to Japan or the USA.

The loggers engaged in the trade are roving and restless characters working in Nigeria today, Brazil next year, and the Philippines the year after that. They are at home in the tropics where men – black, white or yellow – and conditions vary little.

When we began working in Ondo with Chief Fawehinmi in the second quarter of 1948, only manual labour was used. We had neither mechanical saws nor tractors and lorries. The chief had already started work in the area recently allotted to him with a gang of some seventy men hauling the logs to a tributary of the Oni river which flowed into the lagoon. He floated his rafts to Lagos for sale in the open market where one of his sons disposed of them. He was limited by financial constraints but did not want the bush to lie idle. He was afraid that the concession would be taken away from him if he did not work it, thus depriving the native administration of expected revenue. He was therefore looking for a company to join him. When Bill Reeks's firm dropped out he was happy to conclude with us, fully realizing that we did not have the clout of an established UK company; however, we were expatriates and (in the view of the times) therefore bound to command money and expertise. A lone Englishman had operated the bush before 1914, cutting mahogany on a very selective basis; on the outbreak of war he went home and was lost when his ship was torpedoed by the German navy. Otherwise it was virgin forest.

Sandy soon returned to Kajola to acquaint himself with conditions and settle on a working plan with the chief. Fawehinmi convinced him that one small gang could not do justice to the potential; this should be brought up to full strength of 100 men, and a second gang also engaged. It meant that our monthly wage bill would more than double almost immediately. We thought 'in for a penny, in for a pound', and agreed.

87

These gangs were recruited east of the Niger amongst the Ibos to an established pattern. One selected an Ibo 'headman' known or recommended who would travel home to pick the men. One had to give him money for transport and a small advance. He was to return within a month or two.

These Ibo villages were poor and overpopulated. A tradition had grown for young men who could not find employment to seek work outside. They would know the headman and follow him in groups, together with friends and other youngsters. It was understood that they would 'sign on' for at least six months and generally for a year. They trusted the headman to take care of them; he was their boss, who had himself started as an unskilled labourer in similar fashion years ago. It meant they would earn money and see something new.

Arrived at their destination, they would live in the heart of the forest in U-shaped labour camps, composed of huts of mud with thatch roofs. In the centre of the camp a larger building would serve as an assembly and recreation place and as a church on Sundays. The service would be taken by one of the seniors or the occasional visiting priest. They were all nominally Catholics. Kerosene lamps would light their rooms, and water would be fetched from the nearest stream or collected in buckets from the rains.

Nigeria lies a few degrees north of the Equator and daylight varies but little over the seasons; there is a difference of perhaps twenty minutes either way in the year. It gets light around 7 a.m. and dark around 7 p.m. – a factor which must influence the habits of the population.

Most of the men did unskilled work hauling logs; the more capable ones would advance to become tree fellers, crosscutters and eventually foremen. Each gang would have a few very young boys to act as cooks and do other light work. Only the headman and the foremen would have their wives in camp.

There was no female company; the local village girls would have nothing to do with these men who spoke a different language and did not have much money. For all that, life was orderly and unrest or desertion was rare, although the work was hard, of course. In the evenings and on Sundays, the men would get together to sing or talk and wash their clothes; they would also go 'hunting' to find additional food, which included the giant snails and any small animal which had some meat. Now and then they might buy some palm wine in the nearby village. They were careful with the little cash they had.

The pay was 2/6 per day, of which they could draw monthly an advance of sixpence per day; the balance would be received at the end of the six-months period. This represented their savings. Most stayed one year before going home. Many would come back for another year and some, more especially the skilled men whose pay was better, would remain for several years, going home each year to put their money into their post office savings' bank. Workers who became foremen could pay the dowry for a wife and bring her back.

At the top of the pyramid stood the contractor, in our case the chief. He would employ a clerk, under whom two or three junior clerks would serve. They would be locals as a rule and always Yorubas, and would detail the daily work through the headman. He in turn would allocate so many men for each particular task. In addition, the contractor would take on tree-finders, often local hunters, to mark the stumps to be cut.

Once the camp was established, the daily routine could begin. The tree-finders would have marked the stumps to be felled days ahead, and would accompany the fellers to guide them to the location. Many trees like mahogany had huge buttresses which it would have been wasteful to cut through, so the fellers would build platforms to reach the trunk proper. On these they perched, armed with 8lb axes, and began accurately to break into the tree: first cutting a wedge on one side – the side on which they wished the tree to fall – and then going to the opposite side to continue wielding their axes. Four would be so engaged, working in teams of two for about an hour, and then relieved by the other two.

Depending on the size of the tree and the species (as well as climatic conditions on the day) this could take several hours – sometimes even more than a day. As the tree was about to fall it would make a noise – it would 'sing', the workers said, though 'cry' might have been a better expression. One of the fellers would jump off the platform to watch and the other would give it the *coup de grace*. Down it would come, crashing on to the ground, a giant of the forest in all its majesty laid low, an exciting and sad sight. After some seconds all would be quiet, a few leaves floating slowly to earth, torn off as the tree fell. The fellers would leave to proceed to the next tree. They had a daily task set by the contractor's clerk and would normally finish work in the early afternoon.

The fallen tree would be inspected to make sure it had not shattered, and then marked for crosscutting into logs by a team of crosscutters with long saws operated by two men, one on each end. The stump number would be scribed on each log, then a serial number added and recorded into a book. The stump number was the forestry's permit number. If all had been done according to the rules, a forest guard would have inspected the tree before a permit had been issued and he would again be called to hammer each log before it could be moved. These forest guards could be capricious and time-wasting individuals, and the chief made sure to keep on their right side.

Once hammered, the logs could be hauled to the waterside. They had to be prised apart; iron wedges, so called 'timber dogs', with rings attached were then driven into the logs on each side, through which $\frac{1}{2}$ or $\frac{3}{4}$-inch wire rope was threaded, long enough at each end for forty men to get hold of and pull. To ease progress over the uneven terrain, wooden rollers lubricated with palm oil were laid in front as the men pulled. This was the job of the cooks who ran about with primitive brushes and kerosene tins full of oil. As soon as the log had passed over the rollers they would rush to pick them up and replace them in front once more. Palm oil, of course, even of inferior quality, could also be used for cooking. To avoid pilfering the headman, on morning parade, would urinate into the kerosene tins in front of all the men to discourage bad habits. One of the less romantic aspects of the operation.

The distance to waterside could be up to three miles and, according to the weight and distance, three logs on average per day would thus be dumped into the stream. The men, as they pulled in unison, sang rather like the Volga boatmen, encouraged or cursed by their foreman.

Orderly as the men were, they could be roused to fury if they were not paid on time or felt cheated of their wages. There could be nasty incidents. We heard of a case where a small contractor repeatedly failed to pay his men their balance; one day he mysteriously disappeared after going to his camp to mollify his labourers and ask them once again to wait and meanwhile to carry on with their work. By the time he was reported missing by his family, the camp was deserted and partly destroyed, and all tools gone. His men had presumably killed him and buried him somewhere in the bush and then made their way home, taking such tools as they could lay their hands on as compensation. Nothing more was ever heard of the contractor, nor could his men be traced.

The contractors had developed mean little tricks. They would set the daily task too high and then deduct money for non-fulfilment. They would charge each man a shilling for an exercise book in which his records were kept, when in fact they used only one sheet of paper. And so on. We soon suggested to the chief that we take over all direct financial responsibilities and did away with these petty chicaneries. He more than made up for the loss by increased production on which he collected his commission. We also did away with the custom of the headman collecting 'his debts' from the labourers through the clerk paying out, or paying an absent man's wages to him or to some 'brother'. We eliminated dead souls.

Such timber extraction had been going on for many years, I would say generations, but was superseded in the early 1950s by increasing mechanization. The gangs singing as they haul the heavy logs are no more. The axes and crosscut saws have gone. The young boys and the kerosene tins holding polluted palm oil have vanished. No loss to humanity that!

In those early days Sandy and I were called 'the managers'. This was common practice. In the background there was always assumed to be 'the company', some far-off mighty organization of which little was known. The idea that we could also be 'the company' took time to sink in. It was assumed that we were managers who had to report to home office, from where we got our money and our instructions. A bright clerk working for a rival then trumped this by calling his white man 'the director'. This was a serious blow to our prestige and we soon let it be known that we, too, were 'directors'.

One heard some weird tales. The Ibos would come and go in groups but occasionally a man would have to travel alone – perhaps he had been ill or was summoned home by some urgent message. I was told that group travel had its origin in the old days in the fear that a lone man might run the risk of being kidnapped and used as human sacrifice during fertility rites. I asked the old chief if there was any truth in this and he replied that he had never heard of it but it may have happened.

I was stuck once in Kajola during one of these festivals and it was an eerie experience. As darkness fell and the consumption of palm wine increased, there were strange processions through the village, men and women chanting and seemingly transformed by a religious fervour as they prayed to the old gods. A few hurricane lamps moving up and down at the hands of their carriers added to the air of mystery as goats and sheep were sacrificed. It went on for hours. I kept indoors. Next morning all was normal again; the people's composure and sense of humour had returned. (Human or animal sacrifice and cannibalism are barbaric and incomprehensible to the refined and cultured West. To be civilized, you have to produce and use the atomic bomb which kills tens of thousands at a blow or murder *en masse* in gas chambers.)

The Ibo workers were never lighthearted. They were a solemn and broody lot, made this way, no doubt, by the hard environment of their existence. But from both peoples – the Ibo and the Yoruba – there grew the next generation, better educated and looked after, a tribute to the parental sense of responsibility and the ambition which has done so much to change the face of Nigeria for better and (sometimes) for worse.

~   ~   ~

Mechanization loomed large and could no longer be ignored.

92

The dull rhythmic thud of the axe cutting into the tree at a regular beat had to be replaced by the constant high-pitched whine of the mechanical saw.

The road to Ayesan and Bragg's two Albions started it. If you have lorries you need petrol and oil and spares and heaven knows what. You also require drivers and somebody who can repair a fault. You have to transport the fuel to the camp. You have to store it. Drivers are not unskilled labourers: they demand better accommodation. Logs have to be loaded on the lorries and secured; they have to be off-loaded. Two ex-Army lorries are found wanting; you buy a new one to make it three, then four, then five. Then you switch to heavy trucks.

To load five lorries by hand takes too many workers and is too slow. You buy a tractor for the job. Then two tractors, in case one is off the road. You still haul logs to the gantry by men pulling them out of the bush but they find it hard to feed the lorries. Do you take on more hands? No, on the contrary: you buy a crawler; each crawler replaces at least fifty men. Then you buy another crawler.

You need more spares, more skilled hands. You branch out into the bush far away from the stream You must make roads, you need a grader and you require tippers to carry gravel for the road. You must transport your workers, and need more tippers or other equipment to be mobile. And so it goes on – the circle ever widening, the face of the logging operation changing, and with it the people engaged in it. Not to mention the extra money to pay for all this.

Your starting point is still the forest and its trees. But an approximate knowledge of its composition and a few tree-finders will not suffice. You have to become more precise and plan well ahead. I have already touched on that in my sketch on forestry.

You are looking at a new concession. Enumeration has been well advanced and you know where you would work the next three years and the approximate tonnage you expect to extract – if all goes according to plan.

The management team must decide what the operation requires to meet the target. Where will the camp be located?

How many men will have to be accommodated? How and where will they find food? Where will the workshop and garage be placed, and the stores and office? How many crawlers are to be procured, how many trucks, lorries, small tractors and graders? How much personal transport? How many tippers? What quantity of spares should be on hand? How much fuel will be consumed monthly? How many miles of extraction road will have to be constructed to reach the nearest convenient highway? What promises have been made to local villages to connect them?

A memorandum would eventually be drawn up. We would study it under a magnifying glass. Before we signed up the new concession, Sandy and I, with the help of the accountant, Bill, had of course already calculated what funds would be required for what equipment. We had walked the bush, but invariably the detailed plans of the management team put in charge of the new venture would exceed our figures. They allowed for floods and droughts and collapsing bridges and all the hazards they could imagine in order to get as much equipment as possible. We would sit down with the manager and go over it all once more until we were in agreement. We had to be. We did not want to hear later: 'I told you so.'

We also had to be of the same mind on staffing; how many expatriates would have to be recruited or transferred? What would be their precise function and who should it be? How many senior Nigerians, how many mechanics, clerks, etc? Most of this had already been determined when we took on the concession but it had to be gone over again because a man may have fallen out or could not be spared for one reason or another.

On the other hand, the accountant was a suspicious character who always felt that people asked for more than they really needed, and he tried to cut down on principle. On balance we would rather have too much than too little – if we could afford it, that is.

Certain fundamental principles guided the choice of a campsite. There must be an adequate supply of drinking water all the year round. One had to rely on local knowledge for that and it was generally a safe bet to build the camp near a village. Mistakes could occur. A village of one hundred souls may find the water supply quite adequate but it would not suffice for a labour force of double or treble that number in addition. One would not like the camp to be too far away from the working areas, nor too far away from a road, which would make communications slow and expensive.

Being near a village had the added advantage that food supplies could be secured more easily, provided the villagers grew enough to spare. If they did not, however, their enterprise would soon extend their planting. Even if the camp were to rise some miles away the benefit would be felt, and in any case a road would have to be built to extract the timber. Such roads could be used by villagers to take their produce to market and when the company left, the permanent fixtures constructed by the logger would be handed over to the village free of charge.

The construction of the camp would be given to a local contractor. The labour accommodation which had originally been primitive, build of mud and thatch, was much changed as the new type of worker was more skilled: cat operators, drivers, mechanics, demanded a higher standard of living. Their quarters were built of wood with corrugated iron sheet roofs. They had more modern sanitation, although only the larger camps were wired for electricity. All had communal facilities and some of the employees had their wives and children living with them. There were first-aid posts staffed by a nurse.

When we first mechanized, our resources precluded buying heavy crawler tractors and large lorries. We went in for Fordson tractors with strong winches attached and five-ton Bedford trucks. This meant that we still had to hand haul the logs from where they had been felled to a gantry, a pit into which the lorry drove, or a ramp onto which the logs were hauled. We soon found that to be competitive we had to buy crawlers and later huge-wheeled tractors – Caterpillar and International Harvester were the preferred makes. They hauled the whole tree from the stump to the lorry loading point. From the five-ton lorry we advanced to the twelve-ton lorry and later to the thirty-ton trailer truck.

We would need tippers for throwing gravel on the rough roads to ease the passing of the lorries and to carry the workers to the area in which felling was taking place. We would need mechanical saws, Land-Rovers, the more common spare parts, a workshop to undertake urgent repairs, and stores. We would also need a place for keeping petrol drums or a petrol/diesel pump, and a generator to provide power and light.

The ordering of spares was a constant bone of contention. The man in charge of operations would always request what seemed to us an unreasonable quantity and it was difficult to argue. If the spares were not on the spot, many days, and sometimes weeks, would pass with a unit out of action. At the same time, it was not possible to keep spares of everything; as often as not the one spare required was out of stock, encouraging the manager to order enough for every eventuality.

When a model was scrapped, one was left with spares almost impossible to dispose of. On the other hand, a cat or a truck off the road for a week could lose more than the cost of spares one never needed. One had to keep a fine balance, and it was better to err on the side of generosity.

Whilst all this was going on, a unit would move into the area to map out roads and mark trees so that once the camp was ready no time would be lost. One aimed to commence work in November or December when the rains were over and extraction could go ahead full blast. All this had to be done regardless of the hazards of the market, with demand swinging up and down, sometimes violently. Logging was a long-term business.

Ordering the equipment presented challenges. We had certain guidelines. We preferred to buy from suppliers who were well represented in Nigeria and we tried to standardize. More easily said than done. Models changed without warning. Nothing was manufactured in the country, everything was imported. We would come up against unexpected technical troubles.

In the 1950s we were going through the boom of post-war reconstruction and development, and the equipment manufacturers were working to capacity. Delivery was tight and even if promised much delayed. There was a scramble for limited supplies, and I can say that in handling this situation we were very much on top and got more than our share. There were good reasons for this.

We were known to be on the spot and always accessible. People respected our attitude to hard work. We knew most of the characters involved: some were our friends. We stuck to our undertakings and never cancelled at the last minute. If goods were on order, we would be in and out of the distributors' offices day and night to find out when they might arrive to be sure they were not diverted. On the contrary, the sellers would divert in our favour if another purchaser did not turn up in time – or even if he did turn up in time. And, last but not least, we were known to pay as arranged. In those days we bought lorries for our contractors at the rate of around twenty a year, in addition to what we required for our own operations.

We would sometimes accommodate the sellers by taking equipment they could not move off their hands; I remember once buying four lorries fitted with Perkins diesel engines nobody wanted to touch and the agent offered them to us at a seemingly keen price. Chapman was his name, and I said, 'Look, these lorries have too long a wheelbase; that's why people are shy of them. And, besides, their engines are new here. I think we can fit them in but we do also need six Bedford lorries of such and such a type, can you supply?' Delivery was six months and we got them in six days. His four lorries did actually turn out to be unsuitable and gave trouble; we took it in our stride. Our star was in the ascendant!

I have described our first purchase of the two Albion ex-army lorries at auction. When it later came to buying new lorries, we concentrated on Bedfords which were very suitable for our work and well represented by UAC. Spares were available and, most importantly could be found in almost every little town. When we switched to twelve-tonners we decided to go for Albions, a British make manufactured in Scotland and also represented by UAC.

The first batch of four Albions behaved adequately. We ordered a second batch of four for another operation and ran into trouble. The crankshafts seized up one after another, putting the units off the road. There were no spares in the country. Nor could the sellers find out what might have caused the problem. It was suggested by the manufacturers that we had used the wrong oil and we could prove that this was not the case.

We urged the agents to fly out new crankshafts. The manufacturers thought this to be too great an expense; they flew out one and shipped the others by sea. Nor would they accept responsibility until they had seen the defective crankshafts and analyzed them. UAC were embarrassed but could do little to help. We were outraged. We were in dire trouble and had to switch equipment as best we could to keep the operation going.

It happened that an Albion representative was visiting Nigeria and we took the matter up with him. He was an administrator, not a technician, and at a loss to know what had gone wrong. Our invitation to him to come to the bush and have a look at his lorries was politely refused. He could not see what good that would do. The company eventually replaced the crankshafts free of charge but never told us what the defect had been. I assume they were a batch manufactured to the wrong tolerances.

At about that time, a new German dealer had opened up in Lagos representing, amongst other items, Krupp lorries. The man in charge was a Mr. Weber. He called repeatedly to interest us in his Krupps which he was anxious to get into the market.

'We don't like to experiment, Mr. Weber. There's no track record of these lorries. You're new here – what about spares, service, and so on?'

The German industry was beginning to find its feet again; they were hungry, and Weber was a keen type. He offered to come out to the bush to see the use the lorries would be put to; if he thought his Krupp could do the work he would give us one for three months free of charge to test it. 'If it's suitable you can pay when you like,' he added, an offer we could not refuse.

He visited the forest, said he felt certain that his lorry would be up to it, and sent the lorry out. We found it extremely good. When a part to be replaced was out of stock, Weber had it sent out by air. We were impressed. For once a supplier was running after us, not the other way round.

We ordered four more units. In time we switched to Krupp and never regretted it. Nor did Weber regret his ploy. Our Krupps were on the road, our engineers and drivers praised them, and within three years you could see Krupp timber lorries all over the country. Weber sold hundreds of them – more than thirty to ourselves.

Krupps' marketing approach contrasted strongly with Albion's and, I regret to say, that of other British manufacturers, who preferred to do their business with the large conglomerates, talking to them in their London boardrooms, ignoring medium and small concerns as not worth bothering about. Checking their product in the field did not suit them. It was no surprise that German industry soon overtook the British who should have collared the markets; instead, they fell to their German and other competitors. In 1950 over 90 per cent of all vehicles on the road were British; by 1980 less than 10 per cent.

Let us return to our trees.

At daybreak the tree fellers would set off, guided by the tree-finders. They would have a task set them of cutting a projected number of trees. A team consisted of three men: the tree-finder; the sawyer, who cut; and his apprentice, who carried the saw and other tools like files, and also food.

Once felled, the tree would be collected by the caterpillar within a couple of weeks, the forest guard having first hammered and recorded it. The same tree-finder who had directed the feller would guide the cat and its team to the stump. The cat would come noisily through the bush, assisted by workers brandising matchets to help clear a path, and manoeuvre into position to secure the tree. This could be destructive – the cat could not always avoid damaging or knocking over smaller trees. Its winch would drag a large skid made of solid iron slightly raised in front and on the sides, about four feet wide and four feet long, on which the butt of the tree would be placed by pushing the skid under it; it was then dragged through the forest to the assembly place or 'gantry', as we kept on calling it. Later we employed logging arches which raised one end of the tree a couple of feet in front so that only the other end would touch the ground thus speeding its journey.

The ideal distance to haul was half a mile; anything over one mile was reckoned to be uneconomical, but still happened. Therefore rough roads for the lorries to pass would have to be made about one mile apart, which was the job of the cat, also used to construct feeders to the nearest main road. The cat had a blade in front for cutting roads and a winch at the back for hauling.

Extraction and road-making, however, would not be even all the year round. During the rainy season, progress would be much slower and in certain circumstances we would halt work altogether for a month or six weeks to reduce the wear and tear on the equipment and to give us a chance to overhaul it. The thicker the bush, the lower the cost of extraction. For an average bush, two D6 cats normally coped with the task on hand. We later switched to heavier D7 models. In an operation scheduled to yield 8,000 tons a year, 37 tons had to be hauled daily. 37 tons meant three Krupp loads, sometimes four if the logs were of an awkward shape. A lorry normally managed one trip per day which meant we required three lorries. An extra stand-by lorry was also advisable.

At the gantry the tree would be inspected and cross-cut into log lengths. No log under 12 feet long would ever be taken out of the forest, and as they often split where cross-cut it was a general rule that the minimum length be 13 feet unless the log had a very large diameter. Few users liked logs over 30 feet long; on average a tree would yield two or three logs of between 16 and 24 feet. Very large trees were a headache all round, for the logger and for the buyer, whose equipment might not be able to accommodate too large a log. Nor would every ship or port be able to lift it.

Each log would be measured for length and girth, and its

volume and weight established. Loads would be made up by the clerk i/c gantry and piled on the lorry with the help of a Fordson tractor, or later with the help of a front loader, a mighty machine which could lift weights of 20 tons and more.

Creaking and swaying, the lorry would take off to its destination. It required experience to be a timber driver and it was a well paid job. The first part of the journey on the rough makeshift roads was the most hazardous, more so if it had been raining. Many a time a lorry would get stuck and have to send the driver's mate to call for help; a Fordson or even a cat might have to be sent to haul it out of the mud.

The destination would be either the nearest waterside, where the logs would be dumped and made into rafts to be floated to port; or, in the east, the millside; or, in the Cameroon, sometimes to a railhead. The shorter the distance, the less costly the evacuation; hence we tried to restrict distances. In some countries trucks would travel 200 miles and more each way and their lorry requirement would be double or treble ours for the same weight of timber. Nigeria is blessed with waterways which cut down the cost of transporting logs considerably, although this took longer and had other risks such as a raft scattering, getting grounded, or being attacked by marine borer. One had to know what one was doing.

We floated on the Cross River to Calabar; we floated from the Cameroon to Calabar, rafts being towed by hired tugboats or our own tug, Nina; we floated on the lagoon between Lagos and Sapele, again mainly using tugs once the rafts were in safe water; we rafted also in Rivers Province, later Rivers State, to Abonnema; and briefly and unsuccessfully on the Yewa River from Badagry to Apapa, Lagos, where floating grass clogged up the waterway.

Not all species float; some such as iroko and afzelia, sink like a stone. Fortunately the sinkers were relatively limited in our early felling programme, rarely exceeding 5 per cent. Such logs were a headache: to float a sinker it was positioned between two floaters and physically secured in the water by timber dogs and wire rope.

In a quiet corner of the river the boys assembled the rafts of between 40 and 60 logs. A small hut would be built on top of the rafts which became the waterboys' home for a few days. Occasionally, one or two logs would cut loose and be lost. During the rainy season, when storms could be encountered, it happened that a raft was pushed against the banks and broke, scattering the logs which had to be collected again – painfully, one by one.

Our waterboys were splendid. One had to marvel at the ease with which they handled these huge logs in the water, how quickly they managed to assemble the rafts, and with what skill they steered them through calm or turbulent rivers exposed to the elements. They could swim like fish. A raft would be manned by three or four boys; when a tug towed more than one raft, only one crew would remain, positioning itself on the last raft of those joined together. Most came from the Niger Delta and were of the Ijaw tribe where it is said children learn to swim before they can walk.

In the Cameroon we loaded on the railway at a small town near our concession area, from where the train made its way to the grand timber port of Douala. When, at a later date, a road was built near our Cross River concession to Calabar, we used it to carry logs all the way to our millside or to port for export.

Once the raft arrived safely at its destination – say Lagos foreshore – it was taken over from the rafting boys by the waterboys working on the logging beaches, mainly at Ebute Metta on Lagos mainland. Here the rafts were taken apart, timber-dogs and wire rope removed, and each log rolled up on to the beach to be inspected and treated.

This rolling up was undertaken by gangs of workers of between ten and fifteen men under a headman who acted as independent contractor. After rolling up the log, it would be marked for dressing with adzes to eliminate obvious defects and to make it round. The work was heavy and hot in the sun but relatively well paid.

This dressing of logs seemed a custom peculiar to Nigeria. I never came across it in other West Coast timber ports where logs had been cross-cut in the forest before transport and shipped as they were, the bark protecting the wood against the sun. I don't know how this dressing habit arose. Possibly its origin lay in the old days when logs for shipment were squared, something that had practically gone out by the time we began operations. (Squaring the logs was meant to cut out waste in sawing and also in loading on board, but as many logs were used for peeling it did not make any sense.) Later we replaced the gangs with a Fordson tractor and winch, and in the end we eliminated dressing altogether.

Certain norms were laid down internationally for the grading of logs, but up to a point grading rested on the interpretation of the individual grader: no two logs are alike. Disputes between seller and buyer would arise on a parcel and sometimes led to arbitration.

We were strict in our grading, preferring to downgrade a dubious log at our end rather than wait for the seller to complain, and soon built up a reputation which stood us well when the markets turned down. Even so, we met occasional claims which had to be handled by our London brokers, or by ourselves when the broker was not involved.

Absolute rejects would be sold to local sawmillers for what we could get. The government-owned sawmill at Ijora was our largest buyer, but had the worry that it lifted logs slowly, and one would have staff hanging about their mill for weeks or even months awaiting their turn.

Advice would be received that the designated vessel was due, and the rafts were taken by our waterboys to a fixed point and made fast to await the shipping company's tug to be towed alongside. The station was about two miles from our principal beach. A primitive hut served as store for spare wire rope, timber dogs and other essential tools, and two or three working canoes would be available to accompany the raft to ship.

The shipping company would alert us that the vessel had arrived and that a tug would be sent to pick up the raft, preferably when the tide was turning, since the waters could rush with uncomfortable speed, making the tow that much more difficult.

The tug would turn up, sometimes punctually, sometimes late, according to the ship's working progress. Our boys would secure the raft between 30 and 60 feet behind the tug which would then slowly move off, a canoe in tow, for the boys to paddle back in when loading was completed, bringing with them their tools, timber dogs and wire rope. They would travel on top of the raft going out.

The ship might lie at Apapa wharf or more often in midstream where it could pick up the timber on both sides. Securing the raft alongside ship was a delicate operation requiring a cool nerve, plus, of course, the co-operation of the ship's crew. They would throw down ropes to make fast at both ends, the tug standing by until this operation was successfully completed, with the tide running fast by now. The raft would bob up and down alongside. Once the ship was ready to start lifting, a stout wire would be thrown overboard, the end of which had a strong hook. Our boys would get hold of this hook, pass it under the log near its centre, and signal the ship to tighten its wire. They would knock out the dogs holding the log and gesticulate for lifting to begin; up would go the log, slowly to disappear into the ship. Once on the ship's hook, the log became the ship's responsibility. If it slipped and dropped away, it was 'lost overboard'. The insurance company would be liable.

Great care had to be taken not to knock out more wire than essential for fear of breaking up the whole raft. Such loading would take place day or night in most weathers. The timber dogs were often lost when they were knocked out, but the wire rarely. Our men used heavy axes which they had to swing standing on the raft, never still in the water. The log thus lifted would have to be stowed by the ship before the next one could take its turn, and loading would take many hours.

Sometimes we would load two or three ships at the same time in the same port; only on very rare occasions would we fill a whole ship especially chartered. The ships averaged 8,000 tons and were not exclusive timber vessels, but carried general cargo. Loading completed, the waterboys would return to base in the canoe.

Logs: from manhandling to mechanization

Our tree was on its way to its destination.

~   ~   ~

We had rolled up our first logs, the mahogany bought for the USA, on a beach behind the police station on the Iddo causeway. We were now looking for more permanent facilities.

We had engaged a beach-master, John Stolom, who took us to a beach at Oko Baba in Ebute Metta which had a front of about 100 feet and a depth of about the same size. In the centre stood a small tree. There were many such beaches along the foreshore of Ebute Metta, tidal and therefore not of much use except for loading and discharging canoes and for rolling up logs. Outside the tidal limits were pit-saws and then the houses of the street running parallel to the beaches. We met the proprietor of this beach, Mrs. Akinremi, and arranged to rent it for an agreed monthly payment.

Many years before, the area had been settled by refugees from Abeokuta who had been given certificates of occupancy by the government. There had been fighting between Ibadan and Abeokuta, many of whose inhabitants fled to Lagos.

Within a couple of years, we had five beaches in Ebute Metta to accommodate the logs delivered by water and lorry; not all came from our own production in concession areas. We bought in large quantities from different sources. As the supply of logs increased so did the number of headmen contractors handling them. The labour engaged in this task reached several hundreds, some in regular employment, others casual hands.

Women traders attached themselves to the beaches to sell food; blacksmiths came to sell timber dogs; all sorts of people came and went and these beaches were like beehives from morning to evening.

We checked measurements and quality and made sure that our staff took rolling up in turn and showed no favours (for a small consideration) to a particular supplier. We got a name for fair dealing – no sharp practice was allowed. Hard as the work was, the atmosphere was friendly and congenial. We became a major local economic force and from time to time were called in as arbiters when disputes arose between the gangs or between men and contractor. We saw to it that the men got their money in time, that the money was adequate by the standards then prevailing, and that there was no cheating.

Either Sandy or I would be on the beaches by 7 a.m. every day. The traffic in those days was light; it took us no more than fifteen minutes to drive from home to beach. We even bicycled on occasion. We would repair to the little office we had taken in one of the houses nearby to check the accounts of the previous day and pay what was due. We had no telephone – we could not get a line until 1950, by which time we were the largest log exporters in Lagos.

Whilst Sandy had started his timber career working for an established logging company, I had come into it fresh. My approach to the small Nigerian timber contractors was without prejudice and I quickly built up a good rapport with most of them; I took them as I found them. Meeting them, listening to their problems, real or pretended, something very familiar struck me which at first I had difficulty in analyzing. I finally realized that the stories and pleadings for support, the hazards encountered with their competitors and the authorities, the family troubles, and the obvious attempts to plead for money under one pretext or other – or in the face of real problems – mirrored the stories my grandfather had told me of life in the small Polish town in the south-east of Galicia, then part of the Austro-Hungarian Empire.

He had been a man of substance and dealt intimately with the peasants and small traders who brought their goods to market. He told us many tales of the comings and goings of daily life, of the cunning and attempted cheating, of the confidence placed in him as a fair-minded elder, of the sense of responsibility he felt and accepted without falling for every trick. All of that had ended when, during the First World War, the town became a major centre of hostilities and he had to flee from the advancing armies of the Czar, never to return.

These tales came back to me, almost subconsciously, and helped me greatly to understand the ways and motivations of the many contractors who brought their logs for us to buy on the foreshore of Ebute Metta and who asked us for advances to bring more logs. Sandy felt that we could not trust them and stood to lose our limited reserves. I, on the other hand, argued that whilst some might run away, we stood to gain if only we could convince them they would make more money by being honest, bringing logs, selling them for prompt cash, and going off to bring more logs once again. Some did disappear, but others played the game and soon became bigger contractors. As the word spread around that B & R would help you financially and buy at reasonable prices, more and more came to us and the turnover snowballed.

Many of our competitors thought we were mad; they never gave advances and when buying logs delayed payment as long as they could to keep their funds until they had shipped and been paid, which often took many weeks. By the time they woke up to our dealings, we were streets ahead. As my grandfather had advised: 'Treat them well and as business partners; let them make a profit and they will stick to you.'

Not all of these advances came back. There were natural hazards like rafts being swept out to sea or scattering in a hurricane, or low rainfall leaving the logs high and dry. There were contractors who diverted their logs to third parties and pretended one of the natural hazards had overtaken them – we soon found out when this happened – and there were contractors who never had any intention of felling wood and ran away with the money. That they could do only once.

I reckoned that if these losses did not exceed 15 per cent of the total advanced we would be on the right side, as indeed we were, except when the market turned against us and we had to accept logs to recoup advances although we could not sell them at a profit. On the other hand, when we had a boom, as we did during the Korean war in the early days of our operations, we were very successful and got a large proportion of all logs offered on the open market. It laid the foundation of our financial success which we would exploit without having to go to the banks for badly needed funds to underpin continued growth.

There were operators who delivered logs not to port but to a waterside like Agbabu in Ondo Province/State where timber companies would establish buying stations. Once again some of these contractors were in need of finance, and we pioneered the system of advancing not money but lorries, which we bought new for them, to be repaid from delivery of timber. We also bought lorries to operate nearer Lagos and let out these lorries to the occasional contractors who had gone into the timber business riding on the boom though knowing very little about it. These lorries ran between Ibadan and Lagos, between Akure and Agbabu and their branch roads, and in Ahoada.

If a man came to say he had logs and wanted us to buy them, we either did so on stump, after inspection, or hired the lorry out to him for a fixed rate to be deducted from the sale of the logs so transported. On the whole it worked well. Over the months the occasional dishonesty was discovered, as when a contractor persuaded our drivers to take the logs somewhere else and to come back to us to claim that they were inaccessible. Invariably such drivers were betrayed and sacked on the spot and the contractor struck off. It was easier for the drivers to say they had been stopped by police for overloading or bad tyres, and had to pay two or three pounds to be able to proceed. That, of course, we could not check, and it was known that the police practised such blackmail.

Albert Akinshade was our head driver. He had been the first to drive the Albions purchased so painfully from Elias at the army auction. We made him supervisor and bought him a motorbike to check on the lorries.

Our strategy of buying high paid off. The news of the way we handled these local purchases spread like wildfire, encouraging contractors with limited means to turn to us. We were not too popular with our competitors who accused us of trying to monopolize the trade by buying at high prices. A futile argument, as I pointed out: our policy did not only benefit us, it also benefited the small man working in the forest, generally near convenient waterways on which to float the timber to market. And there were many more of these than of the casual shippers who had sprung up to take advantage of the continuing demand. For every one who objected to us there were ten to support us, although the objector was often a more sophisticated person able to make his opposition known. In the end they had to follow suit, and when the war boom ended in 1951 they left the trade. We carried on, if under great difficulties, until business picked up again a couple of years later.

The policy of advancing either cash or equipment was built up over time. It was a question of personal recommendation by staff or friends, checking up on past performance in general (not necessarily timber work) on finding out where the logs were to come from, and, of course, on our judgement of the market: could we sell these additional quantities at a profit?

One species especially, abura *(Mitragyna stipulosa)*, was widely offered by contractors; it grows mainly near swamps and water and does not lend itself to mechanical extraction, nor is it usually to be found in concession areas. It is a smallish tree of a neutral light-brown colour and became popular in the UK as a substitute for beech. Rafts of abura arrived in Lagos and other ports seasonally, after the rains. The trees had been cut just before the rains got heavy; then the waters rose and the logs could be manhandled into deeper channels and thus eventually floated to their destination. Lagos, Warri and Abonnema were the three most common markets for this wood, although we also saw it in Calabar.

From our point of view, the caprices of the market were somewhat cushioned by the policy of working with smaller producers and contractors. If a downturn was in the wind, we would give limited advances and thus receive fewer logs. Limiting advances could be effected either by reducing the amounts given to individuals or by cutting out a certain number of contractors altogether. Either way there was pandemonium.

One day I was phoned in Lagos by Festus Ekotie Eboh, the Minister of Finance, to say that I must come to see him urgently. I rushed to his office in Tinubu Square where a special lift took me to the top floor of the building to the minister's private office, a very large, well-furnished room.

The minister sat at his desk and in spite of my presence people came and went with papers and files, the telephones ringing incessantly. We had known the minister well before his present appointment and had a good rapport with him. As I took the seat offered me, I wondered what weighty business the minister was going to discuss – would he want to consult me about matters on which he thought I was particularly qualified to give an opinion?

But no; he complained that we had failed to give his brother in Abonnema, of the same name, the expected advance of £250. 'You really must not fail him – how is he going to carry on?'

I explained that trading conditions had taken a downturn and that we did not want to receive too many logs at this time. 'But of course, Minister,' I added, 'as he is your brother we can at least be sure that he will not default and we will make the advance available.'

'Thank you, Mr. Brandler. I knew I could count on our old friendship and thank you for sparing me your time.'

We exchanged a few more pleasantries, enquired after the health of our respective families, and I took my leave. An array of important looking callers were awaiting their turn to see the minister as I went down in the private lift. For all that, he was one of the most effective ministers the country ever had.

It was more difficult for us to reduce our own production with its long-term planning. The small producer, cut off from the source of his finance, would simply stop felling. Local requirements were limited but would then absorb what was left. Only in a severe recession such as we had to face in 1952 and again in 1961 would really calamitous losses be made by all engaged in the industry and many a shirt lost.

10

In Search of World Markets

The logger who is cutting trees in a concession area can produce only such wood as the forest contains. When he signs his agreement he believes that he will be able to market his product satisfactorily.

We soon discovered that the hardwood trade is fashion conscious. At times mahogany furniture was all the rage. When homes became smaller, the mode changed to lighter woods and mahogany prices weakened. Other sentiments, too, influenced the choice of wood which the architect or furniture designer preferred.

However, contrary to preconceived ideas, the bulk of timber production in West Africa is/was no longer for fine mahoganies or their cousins like sapele, but for the production of plywood or cheap solid planks. For every mahogany log shipped there would be at least ten of obeche, abura and others which did not offer themselves only to the high class consumer. It was the abundance of such species which made the trade take off spectacularly after World War II.

Few of the ultimate consumers would buy their requirements direct from the producer. Only the very large ones who could plan well ahead could afford to do so. The trade was in the hands of importers, merchants who would have large timber yards in strategic positions in many locations depending on the size of their undertaking. They would have their depots near ports where they would stack the logs high. It was to those merchants that our brokers, Cobbett & Co., as a rule sold our

111

wood. We could not really produce to order; we had to sell what we produced. But by keeping in close touch with the markets we could speed up or retard production or evacuation to fall in with the agent's ability to sell.

Early on we would ship only against contract. As we grew and handled large quantities, we would at times ship 'on consignment': that is to say, load without a fixed order. This happened if, for instance, during shipping famine we were offered space at short notice because another shipper had fallen down on his booking and the ship then in port was anxious to load its quota. We never refused such offers; we would load if we had the stock and cable the broker to sell. We kept in the good books of the shipping companies, an important factor.

By that time we were strong enough not to be taken for a ride by buyers thinking they had us at their mercy over what was called a distressed parcel: i.e., unsold logs close to destination or after landing. As we tried to accommodate the shipping companies, so our buyers would try to accommodate us by taking the parcel off our hands even if they had no urgent need of it. They understood our reasons. Sometimes such a parcel fetched an even better price than normal because a buyer was desperate to lay his hands on it; it could also happen the other way round.

Once the temporary ban on the import of hardwoods into the UK was lifted we took off rapidly. The Korean war boom came and we could not go wrong. Prices rocketed and we had to follow suit, but the margins increased in our favour. Although demand outstripped supply in those boom times we took no unfair advantage. We continued to grade logs according to standard; we kept to our contracts even if the price by the time we shipped had gone up by 50 per cent. If we were unable to ship on time we would alert the brokers well ahead to warn the buyer that we would be late.

We pressed the brokers to cultivate new markets to widen the field. They demurred at first, pointing out that they could sell everything we had to offer in the UK. Why bother going elsewhere? We knew that selling outside the UK meant they had at times to share their commission with other agents but we were adamant.

'Twig,' I said, 'there will not always be a boom. The more buyers we have the more likely we are to survive a slump. Now is the time to get into new markets when buyers are crying out for wood. If you don't want to sell outside the UK we shall have to do so without you.'

The point was taken and acted upon – it saved us when the markets collapsed at the end of 1951. Out of the seventy shippers in Lagos in 1950, only four were in business by 1952.

Everybody went into timber in those days. Lack of knowledge or lack of scruples meant that many of these shippers loaded rubbish, sometimes substituting one species for another. London agents came out in droves trying to find shippers and signed contracts with all and sundry without finding out if the shipper knew what he was doing. Nigeria got a bad name in the international trade. Non-delivery, poor quality, and fraudulent supplies knocked her reputation, and that poor name lived on after the fly-by-night shippers had long vanished from the scene.

Towards the middle of 1951 I became uneasy. Over a drink I said to Sandy, 'Look, we've done well, it's going our way, but this can't last forever. Sooner or later the market will take a dive and if we get caught we shall cough up most of what we've made. Let's rein back. Let's warn the contractors that we are reducing our buying to make sure that we can place what we are producing ourselves in Ondo.'

He was surprised. 'Why do you say that? It's going great guns.'

'It always happens, Sandy. It's a question of timing. If we cut back now we may not make as much as we could, but for certain we won't lose everything we have made.'

He wondered if we should consult the brokers.

I disagreed; 'We are their main source of income and they may gamble on the timing. But we're the ones who are going to take the consequences if things go wrong.'

We did reduce, and some of the contractors rushed to other shippers. For a few months we looked foolish, and then the crash came. Prices dropped by over 50 per cent, so that sometimes one could not even recover the cost of freight. My training had paid off. Not that we got away scot free, but our losses were minimized and we could carry them easily.

'How did you know?' I was asked by some of the people who had been badly hit.

'Ah,' I would reply, 'I listened to my grandfather's tales of what happened to his father after the Franco–Prussian war in 1871, and then to him after World War I.' That, I thought, and my years with Lister in the 1930s who had taught me so much. This action of ours, at first derided and frowned upon even by our overseas friends, put the seal on our reputation.

Cobbett & Co. had started off by selling our goods in the UK to the hardwood importers mainly concentrated in London and Liverpool. As we became shippers of consequence we kept personally in touch with the buyers. Sandy and I travelled to London where we were taken around and introduced as 'our shipper'. Their principal meeting ground was the Great Eastern Hotel at Liverpool Street and a nearby wine bar, the Capitaz.

They were a friendly lot, some representing very old, established companies, others of recent repute. It was a trade not overpowered by huge corporations – that came much later. In these places one discussed common problems and exchanged views, followed by a good lunch, perhaps next door at Gows, a famous fish restaurant. One would also call on buyers to negotiate contracts or settle disputes, or simply to keep in touch.

To introduce my wife Pam to the trade (we had got married in April 1954), and as a public relations exercise, George Cobbett gave a party in the Savoy Hotel in London. It was a grand occasion and we invited all the senior Nigerians in the UK we could get hold of. Among those who attended were Dr. Nnamdi Azikiwe, later to become president; Ernest Ikoli, the doyen of Nigerian journalists and the London *Times* correspondent in Lagos; and a number of others whose names I cannot remember – I think Bode Thomas was one of them. For our numerous English guests it was an eye-opener to talk to our African friends and perhaps vice-versa. Seeing the

Africans, some in their flowing robes, pass through its portals was for the Savoy Hotel a novelty and a curiosity.

Later we expanded our visits to take in Germany, Holland and Belgium where the atmosphere was much the same when we called on the importers, but subtly different when we met the actual producers like veneer or plywood manufacturers. These seemed sharper, more inclined to test their wits against yours, less willing to make allowances for the other side's problems.

France had many African timber-producing colonies and we sold only selected logs there, shipped to Le Havre where a couple of internationally famous experts dominated the market for top veneers, figured logs, and such. One was a M. Noel, who was a real artist and had an eye for a log like no other man I ever met. In time we also found a buyer in Marseille for similar selected logs.

Cobbett's did not want to touch Italy. They felt that the credit risk was too great and many buyers too unreliable. 'They claim before the timber is even loaded.' It was an opinion widely held in the trade at the time. Nor did they want to sell in Spain.

We were approached by an Italian firm and asked Cobbett's if they would not re-consider their policy; these people were sending inspectors out to look at the logs they were buying which at least should eliminate the risk of claims, but we could not move them. So we decided to deal direct and they became one of our best connections. Once we had established mutual confidence and met the principal in Milan we did not even insist on letters of credit, a procedure Cobbett's considered highly unwise. The major shareholder was a most cultured man by the name of Usuelli, who was said to be an ultra left-winger in politics. This contact led to other connections in Italy, of less importance but equally correct in their dealings.

Much the same happened in Spain where we found a first-class agent, Juan Lang, whose principal buyers were at Valencia, the centre of Spain's timber trade. When I first visited Valencia, Franco was still in power and I had strong reservations about the country. Politics notwithstanding, our agent also represented the timber interests of the USSR which made large shipments of Russian softwood to Spain.

The atmosphere in Valencia and Madrid surprised me. It was much more liberal than I had imagined: the bookshops, for example, displayed works by many left-wing European authors. It was the time when Spain was developing her tourist industry and could not appear to be too intolerant. Business in Spain under Franco was pretty bureaucratic and slow, and a fair amount of corruption could be detected.

We also handled the Eastern bloc ourselves. My visits there were less exhilarating. The Eastern bloc countries were poor and their mills out of date. One dealt with a central buying body which had specific requests to meet from its manufacturers; this made closing contracts protracted and troublesome. Once a deal was agreed, however, all was plain sailing. I called only on the Poles and East Germans, the former in Warsaw, the latter in Berlin, and they would take me to their factories to acquaint me with their requirements. Their behaviour was correct and civil but no close personal relations developed. We sold also to Hungary and Czechoslovakia in small lots, and once to Yugoslavia.

We never got into business with the USSR which at the time – I am speaking of the 1950s and early 1960s – preferred to buy its African hardwoods from Ghana; they purchased her cocoa as well. They cultivated relations with Kwame Nkrumah, then head of the government of Ghana.

In the end we also managed the USA direct. We appointed an agent, Randolph E. Valensi (or Randy as we came to know him), who was well connected in the trade – a very likeable and imaginative man. Not only did we do considerable business with him, but our three families also became close friends.

In the UK over the last twenty years many of the smaller independent sawmills cutting African logs have gone out of business; sawn wood is now being sold from Africa. The sawmill industries in Ghana, the Ivory Coast, and many other West African territories have established themselves, as they have done in Nigeria where, however, the export of timber is at present very much restricted. Logs are still being shipped for cutting into veneers and making plywood but here too there have been many changes. Several countries have banned the export of logs to encourage local veneer and plywood industries.

~   ~   ~

By the end of 1950 we were strongly advised to turn our partnership into a limited liability company. In January 1951 Brandler & Rylke Timber Company became Brandler & Rylke Limited. Sandy and I were the directors, with myself taking the chairman's rank, and our holdings were in the old proportion of two to one.

A young Englishman working for one of the large companies had been helping us in his spare time to keep books. We had not been asked for any tax returns, but Bill thought it would be only right and proper to offer them and had come up with a liability of over £10,000 for the year 1949/50. We were dazed.

Bill explained that a partnership had to pay taxes on the same basis as an individual, that the tax laws in Nigeria were identical with those of Britain as far as expatriates were concerned, and that these taxes could reach something like 95 per cent progressively. The taxes of a limited company were, on balance, very much lower once a certain profit stage was reached. Why people willing to risk their fortunes in business should be taxed much more heavily than an anonymous body I never understood, but there it was. If we wanted to expand rapidly as a partnership we would have to borrow. So we turned the business into a limited company.

Not that tax-collecting was pursued with much energy or diligence. Our Syrian acquaintances who ran their businesses as private affairs were surprised at our concern. 'Taxes are imposed on the big companies and their employees, on government officers and such like. They collect head tax from the rest if they can get it. As for people like us, they accept our figures.'

We complied with the formalities, assisted by a lawyer:

appointing auditors and a secretary; keeping a minute book; holding annual general meetings; etc.

I must digress for a minute. I had been brought up with the idea that to owe money, to be a borrower, had a stigma attached to it. To save was a virtue; to spend money you did not have and thus become a debtor was thought to be immoral; you did it only *in extremis*. You saved money to buy a house or a car and lived within your means as you went along.

Before money economies became widespread, you became and stayed rich by having serfs working for you. Serfdom disappeared as money economies spread; money was made by manufacturing goods. You had to encourage people to buy these goods and the more they bought the richer you would get. If people could not afford to buy, you gave them credit. A man who owes money is not a free man in society; he is a modern serf. In the second part of the 20th century many households in Britain live in debt. Now it may be more acceptable to live in debt and have all the amenities of modern life than to feel free and do without them. Nowadays governments encourage you to borrow to keep the economy buoyant. I will not argue about the merits of this, since perhaps I have a naive way of looking at it. Be that as it may, I had a horror of borrowing.

I realize that I am contradicting myself in that we went to Cobbett's to borrow for the road to Ayesan; life is full of contradictions. But let me say that even as a 'company' we felt personally responsible for what we owed. This attitude in the end did us little good, I must confess. One must act within the system. Morals have changed. If you fail as a limited company, it is not quite the same as if you personally go bankrupt. That too was made clear to us by Bill when he recommended that we change to a company.

On formation, we invited a Nigerian, E. A. Sanda, to join the board. It was a most unusual step to take in those days. I don't think there were a dozen Nigerians on the boards of expatriate companies: I certainly knew of none.

Our affairs were very much geared towards co-operating on level terms with the Nigerians; we were looking for a board

118

member who knew something about forestry, was well connected in the Western Region, and was himself a man of consequence. Sanda, an Ibadan businessman, answered all these qualifications. We had met some time before and he had since been appointed a member of the Ports Authority, proving that others, too, appreciated his worth. Unfortunately he died within a few years and we replaced him with my old friend, Bank-Anthony, with whom we had lost touch because the timber business was quite outside his sphere of interests.

Between 1948 and 1965, the business made steady, and often spectacular, progress, as I will describe later in other sketches. For years we kept a low profile, as much by circumstance as by design, because we were so busy and had little time for social activities. For all that, it soon got around that we were dealing in large figures – of both men and money. Our circle of acquaintances, business friends and official contacts widened. We became known.

With expansion arose the need for management staff. We suggested that Bill leave his company and join us as our accountant. He agreed. I met by chance a chap I had known briefly in the army – Ted Smith – who was also working for one of the large companies and he came over to us. We replaced Bragg with an engineer named Davies recruited by our brokers in London. By the time we joined the US Plywood Corporation we had eighteen expats working for us in various stations. Some stayed longer than others, some were more suitable than others. Most were British, though others were Dutch, German and Italian, and one was Chinese. Then USP brought over their Americans.

We recruited by word of mouth, by answering applications, and by advertising in the trade press in the UK. Cobbett's would sift through the replies and we would visit London to interview the candidates. In spite of the international make-up of these men we did not encounter animosities or strife based on their varying backgrounds. The nature of the work soon drew them together. Some brought out their wives, often young women who, posted to small localities, seemed to enjoy the experience. It was new to have servants to take care of the chores, to be of some importance, and to be married to a man who was in command of a sizeable operation. The latter point did not mean so much in Lagos, but apart from ourselves only Bill and one other would normally have been resident in the capital.

Every expat had two or three senior Nigerian understudies attached to him. Wherever possible they would replace the expat as time went on. To bring them up to standard we sent one or two suitable candidates each year to England for training.

'How about Francis?' Sandy said. 'Good man. He could do with a few months attachment to a London shipping agency.' Francis was in charge of the loading of vessels.

We called him in. 'Francis, how would you like to go to England for half a year?'

'Sir?'

'You heard. We want to send you to London for a few months for further training.'

Francis was speechless. 'Sir?' he repeated.

'You are in charge of shipping. It will help you to understand the problems at both ends.'

He knelt down. 'Thank you, sirs.'

'Do please get up. We're not Ondo Chiefs.'

As we had started in Ondo, most of our original staff had been engaged there and had risen in rank; therefore many of our Nigerian seniors came from Ondo. We recruited mainly by personal recommendation. If a man misbehaved we could go back to his sponsor. These Ondos has been sent to us by the chief, by the Oshemawe, and others like them.

Before he flew off, we gave Francis a farewell party attended by staff, his friends, and his young wife. There was music and I danced with her.

'Thank you for sending my man overseas. I know he will be all right.'

And he was. When we broke up, he became manager of one of the largest shipping companies in Lagos. To have worked for B & R was a good recommendation. Many years later Francis sent his children to college in England. This shows how the country had raced ahead in one generation.

To see this in perspective, one must know that Francis came from a small town in Ondo Province, Okitipupa, had attended a local secondary school, and had had no opportunity to see much of the world. There were no cinemas or libraries and TV did not yet function. What he knew was what his teachers had taught him, and what he had been taught he had learnt well. Such were the men who helped us build our business. They came from all parts of southern Nigeria where forests grew and timber meant something. They were eager, they responded to leadership, and you could rely on them provided you knew what you were doing and they knew that you knew. If you eased off they would take advantage; there was no loyalty to the abstract idea of the company.

Of the men sent abroad (there were some women too) only two failed to measure up to expectations. One sank under the burden of his wider family's unreasonable demands on him for money. Another was taken to the cleaners by admiring females; to satisfy their appetites he had to put his hand into the till. If you had been overseas it was felt that you must be a big earner.

The graph of success did not shoot up in one straight line. There were setbacks. Within our first year we were nearly knocked out when the UK Timber Control placed a ban on the import of tropical timber. There had been an oversupply, and there was a shortage of foreign exchange. As Britain was our only buyer it meant we would be ruined if this ban were to continue for long. It was lifted after ten weeks and during that period we had our stock of logs sawn, and disposed of the planks to get our money back. Builders and furniture-makers took it off our hands.

Later, during the Korean war boom, there was a great shortage of shipping space and the timber contractors complained to the Government. An inquiry was set in motion, and I remember one of the officers of the Ministry of Trade and Industry buttonholed me at the Polo Club one afternoon saying, 'Do you know, Joe, that your company is the biggest shipper of logs in Lagos?'

'Are we really?'

'You are, by far. Don't you have any difficulties in getting shipping space?'

'Of course we have.'

'Why didn't you sign the petition then?'

'Nobody asked us to!'

'That's strange,' Morris said.

'No,' I pointed out, 'it isn't. The trouble is, most of the shippers are occasional. They book space and when the vessels arrive they can't load as often as not. When we book we have the cargo. We never fail the ships so we have some pull.'

'Yes. They complain that you get preference.'

It was an awkward situation for us. Everybody had gone into timber and of course it was a haphazard affair. They had either the logs and no space, or space and no logs; some bright sparks booked space to sell it to some desperate shipper, and in the end the shipping companies got fed up and supported their regular customers.

The complaint to the ministry had been that the shipping companies supported the white shippers. As we were by far the largest of those, the complaint really was pointed at us. I guess anything is fair in love and war and in business too, and the Nigerian shippers – who were really not timber traders but general traders jumping on the band wagon – waved the flag of colonialism, and the ministry had to take notice.

The takeover by the Americans effective at the end of 1965, followed by the Civil War, changed the character of our company. It was the end of an era for us. For almost twenty years we had been active in timber. The business grew and we got older, so we did not run about as much as in our earlier days, but we were still with it and of it.

We represented the hewers of wood and we liked it. It was a man's life. The idea of sitting in a stuffy office in London, Hamburg or New York did not appeal to us at all. Ours was not the art of making money by being smart, by shuffling papers. Ours was the excitement of walking and judging the forests, battling with the elements, looking after thousands of men, planning roads and equipment, bringing the timber to port or mill; yes, and watching the market and the currency fluctuations imposed on us by the city slickers. But for men like us who needs agents, bankers, huge edifices in the cities? It was not a view that carried much weight then, nor does it now.

Our Nigerian friends quickly saw the equation and preferred to be agents and bankers in their huge edifices in the cities. One must admire their acumen, but it was not our scene. We did achieve something, however: we produced and we delivered, and if we reaped personal benefits we knew where they came from.

11

Moving House

Late August 1949 we were sitting in the office in Docemo
Street when the messenger came in. 'A Mr. Mohammed
to see you, sir.'
'Who is he? What is his business?'
'A moment.' The boy came back. 'He says he is an estate
agent.'
'An estate agent?' I never knew such existed here. 'Well,
please tell Mr. Mohammed we have no need of his services.'
By that time Sandy had moved out with his family to a
newly completed apartment block in Macarthy Street, leaving
Docemo Street as the office and my living quarters. During the
evening of the same day, my steward came to say that a Mr.
Mohammed had come to see me. I was a little taken aback, but
many people called after hours on business and I asked the boy
to show in Mr. Mohammed. Mohammed was really a northern
name; at least I had not met any local Mohammed, and out of
curiosity I wanted to see him.
In came an elderly fellow in native dress, not too impressive
on first sight.
'Yes, Mr. Mohammed, what can I do for you? I understand
you are an estate agent, but we really have no need of such.'
'Sir, I have a very fine house for you.'
'But as you can see I have accommodation.'
'This house is very fine. You will like it when you see it.'
'Where is this house?'
'On the racecourse, sir.'
'On the racecourse? Are you saying you have a house going

124

on the racecourse?'

'Yes, sir.'

I could hardly believe it. This indifferent-looking old man was offering me a house in one of the best locations in Lagos where houses were few and far between and where most belonged to the government. I felt suspicious.

'Do you have an office, Mr. Mohammed?'

'No, sir.'

'Could you show me the house you are talking about?'

'Yes, I can do that any time.'

'Who are the owners of the house?'

'Dr. Abayomi, sir.'

I had heard of him. He was an eye specialist, and one of the few practising Nigerian doctors.

'Come now, Mr. Mohammed, are you saying that the doctor has a house on the racecourse and that he wants to let it? What is the actual address?'

'The address is 64 Campbell Street, and it is close to the racecourse.'

That was a little different, but I arranged for Mohammed to call the next afternoon, and to go to see the place.

I was shown a house which was almost at the very end of Campbell Street, practically overlooking the racecourse at one end, opposite King's College, with a large playground in between. The house had obviously just been rebuilt, and was not quite finished. To one side was another compound followed by the last house in the street, the HQ of a building firm, and to the other side, an older-looking house built in the Brazilian style with a winding staircase on the outside – rather attractive. That was No. 62.

There was a whole Brazilian quarter in Lagos, so called because the repatriated Brazilian slaves were settled in it in the previous century. Many of them were craftsmen and they built themselves houses in the style they had seen in Brazil. Not a few of them became eminent, or their children did, and names like Da Silva, Da Rocha, Viyera, etc. were not uncommon. The Brazilian quarter was some distance away, but their way of building had spilled over into other areas.

I was taken with the house at once. 'I really would like to live here,' I thought, 'away from the hustle and bustle and the noise of Docemo Street. Can this old boy really be the agent for it?'

'The house is very fine, Mr. Brandler, it has just been rebuilt at great expense. Don't you like it?'

'Yes, not bad. How much rent does the doctor want and what do we do next? I may be interested. Or rather the company may be.'

'I will see the doctor and come back to you.'

'All right, Mohammed, I will wait until I hear from you.'

Next day I took Sandy to the place and he, too, could hardly believe that Mohammed could offer this accommodation. A few days later Mohammed returned to the office. 'The doctor says he is ready to let the house at £350 p.a. three years in advance.'

A fortune!

There was no way we could take that amount of money out of the business at that time. 'All right, Mr. Mohammed. Thank you. We will contact you soon.'

Sandy and I liked the house. If we took it we would have the office on the ground floor and I would live on the first floor. But the rent was high, more than double what we paid at Docemo Street, and three years' advance could not be managed.

I went to see Bank-Anthony. I explained to him what had happened and asked him if he knew the doctor. He said he knew him well. So we asked Bank-Anthony to intercede and negotiate to see if one year's rent would be an acceptable advance.

He came back to us and it transpired that Mohammed had had no contract to negotiate. He had seen the house being rebuilt and, putting two and two together, very cleverly came to us to say there was a house, then went to the doctor to say he had a client for the house. He did not know the doctor or us. Nor had we negotiated any fee or commission with Mohammed. When I had asked him what his fees were, he had said. 'I leave it to you.'

We met Bank-Anthony and the doctor, and agreed to pay one year in advance and that, all being well, we would pay two years after the first. We signed an agreement and the rent was paid – which the doctor needed to complete the building. We gave notice to Issa Williams and moved into Campbell Street on 1 December 1949.

It was very pleasant for us all. We had two large rooms as offices, and a wide corridor which led to yet another room with bath to be used as a guest room or whatever. Upstairs there was a bedroom, dining-room and lounge overlooking the street from which one could see King's College and to the right the racecourse, in the centre of which was the cricket pavilion.

At No. 62, the Brazilian house, lived Mrs. Manuwa, divorced wife of Dr. Manuwa. She was born Phillips, a daughter of the first Nigerian Anglican bishop and a very grand middle-aged lady. She later turned it into a nursing home for expectant mothers. At No. 66 lived the caretaker of the secretariat and his large family. Diagonally opposite were the old quarters of Barclays Bank's expat mess used as a nurses' home (the General Hospital was nearby in Broad Street), and next to it lived Mr. (later Chief) Okunowo.

As commission Mohammed suggested 10 per cent of the rent. We paid him £50 for his trouble and resourcefulness and he was very happy.

Before the first year was out, Dr. Abayomi was knighted. He needed money to go to London to receive the honour and to live in better style now that he was so important, so he approached Bank-Anthony and asked him if he thought we would like to buy the house.

Bank-Anthony came to us. He explained the circumstances and urged us to negotiate.

'How much does the doctor want?' we asked.

'He wants £18,000.'

'We will think about it, Bank. That is more or less fifty years' rent!'

But much had happened in that year. We had profited by the Korean war boom and were in funds. The country seemed to be doing well. We felt property was a good investment. So we went to see Mr. Irving, who was the number one when it came to real estate in Lagos and asked his opinion.

'Yes,' he said, 'not a bad property. I would say worth about £5,000.'

'Why,' we cried, 'he is asking over three times that!'

'He must be crazy and so would you be if you paid more than £5,000.'

Irving was a colonial whose father had already been active in Lagos. We always took the opinions of the old colonials with a pinch of salt and we were nervous lest Mr. Irving would find another client and rush to the doctor to make an offer. He had, after all, no obligations towards us and was indeed most surprised that we had been offered the deal.

So we went to Bank-Anthony and said, 'All right, we will buy and pay cash if all the documents are in order.' He gasped, and one could see his quick brain working – there must be somewhere I can come in – and why not?

It took only a month to complete the formalities and we handed the doctor a cheque for £18,000. We had no qualms. We knew we had paid a high price but we now had our building and we had taken a gamble on the future of the country. Many people, when they heard of it, thought we were crazy, but we were not, as will be seen. Indeed, when we got the documents it transpired that the doctor had bought the house for about £2,000 only a couple of years before we moved in, had spent perhaps £1,500 doing it up, had received a year's rent, and had now enjoyed a profit of around 450 per cent.

Within a couple of years, when the Korean war boom had collapsed, the owners of No. 62 approached us through Bank-Anthony and also offered to sell. The Phillips needed the cash to send one of their sons to the UK to university, and in any case felt that if they could get the same as Sir Kofo it would be a good deal. We pondered the matter.

By then we had expat staff in rented quarters. Our business had expanded rapidly and although the market had collapsed we had been prudent, or lucky, enough to foresee it and were not badly affected.

We bought, and put our English accountant in the house to

live upstairs. We used the ground floor as a store for 'minor produce' (pepper, ginger, etc.) in which we had started to dabble. A sharp odour permeated the house.

Soon after we were allocated a plot in Ikoyi, in Milverton Road, where we planned to build for ourselves. Sandy had met a young Polish architect, Borys, whose family he had known in Poland. He designed a lovely duplex for us, quite different from the norm in Lagos where houses were built to a standard originally laid down by the PWD.

Since Bank-Anthony by then was on our board, he was in the picture. He had persuaded a new Italian firm of contractors from Turin to come and set up business in Nigeria. At that time they had received just one commission, to build a large garage and workshop in town, and Bank-Anthony persuaded us not to go to tender over the Ikoyi property, but to give the contract to his new friends. Borini Prono had appointed Dr. Camino to run their new Nigerian concern and had made Bank-Anthony a director.

Borys was doubtful (or had his own friends in the building industry) but we decided to give the contract to the new people as they impressed us and as Bank-Anthony was connected with them. They did build two very fine houses, although their lack of experience in the country told; it took them a year longer than expected to complete. The ground was swampy and the rains that year were heavy. The foundations sank and had to be reworked. They completed in April 1954 which suited me. I had got married that very month and in May moved into my side with my new bride, the Rylkes having moved into their side the month before.

Our houses were quite Californian in style and much admired. They had an internal gallery and wood was prominent everywhere. We furnished by Maples of London – my wife, Pam, had selected our requirements before we returned and the ship bringing it all arrived more or less with us in May.

There was a large verandah and a sizeable garden on each side with many palm trees. Wild monkeys still visited the compound, attracted by a tame female we kept in a large cage in the garden. Palm wine tappers, under an old custom, were allowed to come into the compound and tap the trees. At the back were six boys' quarters with kitchens and showers.

The plot had been leased us by the Crown for ninety-nine years. Milverton Road had been reclaimed from swamp and was low-lying. Later the whole area was raised by two feet when new and major reclamations were ordered. The raising caused us much trouble and flooding which the town council eventually took care of. A young Nigerian officer was involved who later became distinguished not only as a town engineer but also as a writer. He was Mr. Tim Aluko who wrote *'One Man One Wife'*, one of the first publications by a Nigerian, followed by other books dealing with the changes in Yoruba society. Aluko was, if I may presume to say so, a particularly good author, representing that short era when everything seemed so promising to the progressive and liberal-minded. He was a British-trained engineer, who put his skills to excellent use and carried on from where the best type of British administrator, technical or professional, had left off.

Borys was a junior partner in Nixon & Borys. They had been commissioned to build the cathedral in Onitsha and, whilst Nixon took care of that, Borys opened a small office in Lagos. He was very original and enterprising and made rapid progress. Our houses had been a good advertisement for him and for Borini Prono.

In 1955/56 we pulled down the two houses in Campbell Street and built the first modern office block in Lagos. It was as tall a building as any in the capital – equal in height to the new Secretariat nearby, also just completed, both having six storeys – and only the third to have lifts. The building consisted of three blocks connected by open passages, with two courts between the blocks to give light and air. It was a clever design by Borys. We called the building Kajola House after our first timber camp.

Kajola House took on an international complexion in the early sixties. We housed parts of the British High Commission, the German and Swedish embassies, Reuters, the *Herald Tribune*, *Time* magazine, ourselves, and Faltas an Egyptian concern. Eventually, the British High Commission took over almost the whole of the building. It was not ideal for that purpose and most of the staff disliked it, but they hung on until the end of 1975 when their own building had been completed. It was an interesting time because we knew our tenants and were often friendly with the officers.

On the staff of the British High Commission for a time was Prince William, the eldest son of the Duke of Gloucester and a cousin of the Queen. He often came up to have a coffee and a chat. His home in England was in Oundle, not very far from where we had our house, and as it happened his parents, when visiting Ethiopia in the thirties, had called on my in-laws in Harar where Clifford Henry Fitzherbert Plowman, CMG, OBE, was British Consul. William was a pleasant and charming young man, very keen on flying. He died in a flying accident in England, a great tragedy.

The *Herald Tribune* was in the charge of one Garrison of a well-known American family of journalists, and *Time* magazine was run by a Canadian scholar. Both were well informed and of the old school which insisted on reporting what they saw and knew, and not what they thought their editors or the public wanted to hear. Reuters were factual and much less intellectual, which did not save them from being closed down and expelled by the Nigerian government during the Civil War.

We lost Kajola House in 1975 when the Nigerian government took it over by compulsory acquisition, a sorry tale I shall relate elsewhere.

12

Abonnema: the lone riverain settlement

One afternoon in 1950, Sandy turned up in the office carrying a man and his broken bike in the back of the kitcar. 'We had a slight collision and I brought him here to help repair the damage.' He introduced me: 'This is my partner, Mr. Brandler.'

'Good afternoon, sir. My name is Emmanuel Shegbone and I work for UAC Transport.'

'Sorry about your bike, Shegbone. Please have it repaired and let us know the cost.'

'Oh, don't worry sirs. It was as much my fault as anybody's. I will attend to it myself.'

This protestation came as a surprise. Who was this young man who would admit to a mistake and not make the most out of having been knocked down by a white driver, no matter who was to blame? Well, he was a very smart fellow who saw at once that this unexpected acquaintance could be worth a lot more than a cycle repair bill.

We mended his bike and he called several times to tell us about the new timber paradise of Abonnema where his father was prospecting; a lot of logs were coming down the rivers and many more could be arranged if there were timber companies to buy. At present only a couple of small concerns were operating there. Abonnema, in Rivers Province, was also known as New Calabar. The settlement had been founded by migrants from Old Calabar further east, who had been at loggerheads with their neighbours.

Sandy went to Abonnema with Shegbone to meet his father

and look around. He flew to Port Harcourt, and thence to Abonnema wharf to pick up river transport. Old and over-crowded boats with outboard or inboard motors left when they were full, their timetables elastic. The trip to Abonnema took around three hours, depending on the speed of the boat and the tide: at low tide she could take a short-cut through Buguma; at high tide the bridge at Buguma would not allow boats to pass under it. The boats went westward along the creeks and ended up in the Sombreiro River near Abonnema. Buguma was an isolated fishing village approachable only by water, about half-way to Abonnema. Its 'royal' family were the Amakiris or Amachrees; a scion of that family, Godfrey Amachree, became in time attorney-general of the (British) Cameroon and then one of the four deputy secretaries-general to U Thant, Secretary-General of the United Nations in New York. Isolation is relative.

Sandy came back and reported favourably. 'There are pos-sibilities if we can man the station. Timber seems to be com-ing down the Engenni River from an old reserve, except for the abura; I don't know where that comes from. The town is a bit of a hole, without communications, but there is a large oil palm crushing plant run by UAC, a bank, and two ship-ping agencies. It must have seen better times. I met two log-ging firms, one run by a Dutchman, the other by two Irishmen, both fairly limited in scope. Abonnema is surrounded by water and unless you travel via Port Harcourt you reach it via the Ahoada Road end – leaving your car and hiring a canoe to cross to Abonnema if you can find one willing to make the trip across fairly rough water. That alone takes about ninety minutes. Old Shegbone seems to know his way around although he is not a native; he would make a useful contractor. But who could we put in charge? That's the question.'

'How about offering Basil Ashford the job of going there to open up shop?'

Basil was a young Englishman who had been sent out to Africa by his uncle, who owned a timber business in the Midlands. He was a bright and good-looking fellow who had joined the RAF at the tail-end of the war after passing 'A' levels at his public school. He had flown a few operational missions as a navigating officer, been demobbed, and joined his uncle, who had sent him to Nigeria. His company decided that Nigeria was not in their line and he was to return to England.

Although he was quite inexperienced in business in general, and Africa in particular, we liked him very much and he had taken a liking to us, amazed at the informality, the rough and tumble of the timber business as he found it in Nigeria, compared with what he had seen at home. We felt he could soon learn – after all, Sandy had been a regular cavalry officer all his life until he ended up in the forests of Nigeria.

We offered Basil the job as manager of Abonnema operations. We suggested he spend a few weeks with us in Lagos, go to Abonnema to have a look at it, and then make up his mind. He agreed, wrote to his uncle of the proposition, and received the latter's blessing.

In due course I took Basil to Abonnema, where Shegbone had been alerted and prepared the ground. Within a few days Basil accepted. A house was found for him, a reasonable building with old ships' cannons lying around the compound; a cook was engaged and a steward; a small office was rented, and one of our more experienced clerks from Ondo seconded to him. A bank account was opened. The show was under way.

It was all new to him; suddenly to be 'The Manager' in a far-away place like Abonnema was not only a challenge he accepted gladly, it was a new way of life altogether, where so much depended on personal judgment and relationships, on making quick decisions, on being the boss. He took to it like a duck to water. All the restrictions and limitations imposed on a young man in England had little meaning now. One acted as one's common sense and conscience dictated.

The wife of a chief very soon found a lovely girl for him: she was still at school, warm-hearted and amusing. He could have her if he promised to look after her – and any baby that might come along. They put that in writing and he signed. (I don't think we would have approved had we known.) He helped her with her lessons, and living openly with a woman who at once looked up to him and treated him as a man gave him a sense of self-respect he had clearly never known before. Affection is the one thing many Europeans are starved of, and Basil found it in Abonnema. It also helped him incidentally to become very familiar with what went on in the town.

On this first visit, Shegbone proposed that I take a trip up the creeks to a place, Nko, 'where abura was growing like in a plantation'.

'Have you been there, Shegbone?'

'No, we will go there with a guide. It will take us about five hours each way by canoe so we had best leave early in the morning.'

We set off next day at 5.30 a.m. It was still dark. Two oarsmen either side paddled the canoe carrying Shegbone, myself and the guide. Being an important person, I was supplied with a deckchair. By 6.00, with Abonnema fading in the background, it began to rain. It kept on raining for hourse until we reached Nko (or was the place Soku?). My deckchair was the worst possible seat because water collected at the bottom.

It was midday before we reached our destination, only to find that the place was deserted. There had been a big fight in the vicinity, and when the canoe was spotted with a white man inside the villagers assumed it was the district officer come to investigate and perhaps make arrests. They vanished. The district officer in charge was Bill Newington, an old colonial with a very tough reputation. Months earlier he had personally helped to demolish a juju house to put the fear of God into the locals and stop the bloody fighting that kept on breaking out sporadically over fishing rights between the Kalabari and Okrika tribes which lived there.

An old woman, too frail to run, was spotted and she was assured that I was not the district officer and that she had nothing to fear. 'Ask her for some gin,' I told Shegbone, 'or I will die of pneumonia.' She brought some native gin spiced with herbs; I bought a few bottles and drank one myself.

There was not one abura tree in sight. The guide said we would have to move further to find them. 'Do they exist?' I asked Shegbone.

'Who knows,' he replied, 'but if they do we will now surely

135

get them. The news of our arrival with the white man will spread quickly enough.'

So we returned the way we had come, along endless creeks and rivers. A lone fishing canoe was seen; a fish eagle circled overhead; tell-tale blue smoke rose out of a hut near the bank – a still distilling native gin. The banks were lined by mangrove swamp, their weird roots growing upwards. Small villages had their fishing nets out for drying on frames, which looked romantic as we paddled slowly by. Big fish could be seen jumping out of the water pursued by bigger fish. The people were sturdy and of a very dark complexion. It was a memorable journey. Within a few years, outboard motors replaced the paddles, and near Nko, Shell drilled its first crude oil well in Nigeria, which was to change the future of the country so very much.

I spent some time with Basil, got to know the chiefs, the bank manager and the shipping agents – all of whom became Basil's good friends and drinking partners. Abonnema had a twin village separated from it by some 200 yards of water: Degema. It was here that the magistrate had his quarters, along with a few other government officers, and where the inevitable club was situated. One crossed by canoe. The club sported the figurehead of an old sailing boat, the *Shotton*, on its wall – the ship had been a wooden trading vessel anchored off Abonnema for years until it rotted away. Its cannon were lying around the ground of the club. The magistrate was Uranta, a witty fellow who was bored to tears with his position, as was his wife who had been an Alakija.

Under Basil's dashing leadership, Abonnema became a very important part of our business and in its best years shipped 30,000 tons of logs. All the timber came down the rivers: abura from the Niger areas. This should really have gone to Warri port but the contractors preferred the longer route to Abonnema where, they explained, there was less harassment from officials and, of course, where they found good buyers like B & R. Ocean-going vessels sailed up the river to load midstream. Such vessels called every other week and entertained their shippers on board, a welcome diversion for all concerned.

The oil palm mill closed in the mid-1950s, a serious loss of jobs for the locals. Before World War II there had been a large sawmill in Abonnema run by UAC which was closed, to be replaced after the war by the modern plywood and sawmill in Sapele. The log business substituted for these vanished industries and kept the place humming for some years. When the log business too disappeared, the town became ghostly and the young people went off to find work elsewhere.

For years Sandy and I took it in turns to visit Abonnema/Degema every few weeks for a couple of days. In 1952 we even got George Cobbett to come along and he enjoyed himself greatly. Basil's girl, Fine, by then a sophisticated young lady, did the honours and looked after the important guests. It was a far cry for George from the City. He stayed one night in Basil's house as the launch laid on for him to return to Port Harcourt failed to show up. Twig had come along, too, and so had I. 'If my friends in Moorgate could only see me now,' he laughed. And yet, wasn't the City living and earning its keep basically because there were places like Abonnema?

We also found a fair volume of mahogany, which we branded as 'Degema mahogany'. This was sold mainly to the USA where Randy Valensi established the mark. The texture was not as fine as the Ondo species; it had a slightly different colour and sold at a cheaper price. It took time to persuade vessels sailing to the USA to call at the port of Abonnema, but we succeeded in the end and pioneered Degema mahogany.

Banking activities, however, ceased in Abonnema when Standard Bank decided to transfer all its activities to the much larger centre of Port Harcourt. As most of our business was done on a cash basis, it meant that Basil had to travel to Port Harcourt once a week for money, which he kept under his bed until he decided to buy a safe.

Basil remained in Abonnema for many years, going on leave every twelve to eighteen months, but always returning. We offered him another posting – he had become a senior and respected man in the company – but he preferred Abonnema until eventually he became our GM in the Cameroon. Sadly, he died quite young of cancer at the age of about thirty-eight. He had left us by then to become MD of a rival group about the same size as ours, also in the Cameroon. By 1960 Bernard Perry had replaced Basil Ashford in Abonnema. He was an older man of experience, slightly built and socially active. Keen on football, he organised a B & R team which did well, and he employed staff on the strength of their powers in the game. More suave and less tough than Basil, he became popular and had many friends. His remuneration included a commission of tonnage loaded, a deviation from the norm; we usually paid a bonus on results reflected in the accounts.

By then we were the kings of abura, most of which we collected in Abonnema. 1960 was a good year – we shipped over 20,000 tons of that species alone – and 1961 promised to be even better. Perry gave out advances in the first half of the year for logs to arrive in the last quarter.

As the year progressed, there were ominous signs that the market was turning. We had to send a signal to Perry to stop advances and to collect from the contractors only logs to the value of his advances when the rafts arrived. He protested. If he had given an advance he must accept all the logs the contractor brought; that had been the rule and he could not see it being changed. 'It will spoil our business for the future and play into the hands of the competition.' He thought he would get at least 50 per cent over what was owed, which would be normal. He had a point.

We cut the price and urged the brokers to sell for November/December shipment. We could see trouble coming. They placed several thousand tons at the best price they could get, and for this season at least the abura market was ruined. Worse was to come.

The market went dead. The logs came pouring into Abonnema and Perry bought. A man scheduled to bring, say, 150 logs turned up with 350. Perry bought: B & R never turned down logs from its suppliers. Sandy went to Abonnema to find out what had happened; where did all the logs come from? The explanation was simple: our competitors had stopped buying and their contractors gave their production to ours – either selling them cheaply or just entrusting them to their friends for later settlement. By the end of November we had 5,000 tons of unsold abura logs in Abonnema!

'Whatever you do,' Cobbett wrote, in late 1961, 'don't ship them. We couldn't give them away and there is no room anywhere to store.'

Bernard Perry came to Lagos in despair. 'What am I to do with these logs?'

'Load them,' we said, and he did on two vessels, 3,000 and 2,000 tons respectively.

I went to London to see how we could dispose of them. 'My God,' said Twig, 'we told you not to load!'

'My friend, what are we to do with them?'

'You will lose your shirt.'

'Look, Twig, anyone can sell on a rising market; only the really good agents can sell on a falling market. We played the game with our buyers, now they have to play the game with us.'

'That's a load of balls,' Twig said, 'we can't even sell these logs for the freight. How much do they cost you f.o.b?'

'About £3.10.'

He arranged lunch next day with one of the major buyers of abura who had had prompt and good deliveries. I told him that he would be hard put to get any abura next year. 'Maybe,' he replied, 'but where am I to store them, Joe? And how much do you want?'

'Make us an offer.'

In the end he took 3,000 tons on the first vessel which was about to land in London, at £3 per ton.

'That was a miracle,' said Twig, 'but what about the remaining 2,000 tons which are due in a week's time?'

'Tell your friend that he had better take them, too. Otherwise they'll be sold for £2 and ruin his deal.'

And that is how we got rid of the abura with a black eye. Eight months later the price was £5, and when I met our friend from the company involved – London and Eastern – I ventured to suggest that they must have made a killing from the deal. 'Not at all,' he replied. 'I cut the lot up into sawn timber and sold it off as best I could. We made some money but no more than our regular margin.'

I thought of the petty contractors felling trees on the Niger and other riverine areas. I thought of our own efforts, our clerks and managers, our waterboys loading these logs, of all the effort it took to get these raw materials to the English market, and here in London it was just another commodity. I voiced that view to a buyer and he replied, 'Well, when the going is good you squeeze us, when it is bad we squeeze you. That's how it goes. No good being sentimental about it.' The market has its own logic.

Perry later took a job with an Italian builder in Port Harcourt where the Civil War overtook him. He stayed on, one of the few expats who did, and, when the town came under siege by the federal army, organized its water supply. He did more; when it was about to fall, he collected many of the Ibo girls stranded and in danger from the soldiery and stuck them into the hotel where he himself took refuge. When the federals entered, he handed his charges over to a senior officer and they escaped the worst. Nor was he molested. We would not have thought him capable of such courage.

13

Cross River

I t's the same old question, Sandy, isn't it? How far do we
want to get involved?'
Sandy had run by chance into Rosevear, the Federal
Chief Conservator of Forests. He had reminded Sandy of our
visit to Ibadan when he had recommended we look at the eastern forest reserves on the Cross River right up to the border
with Cameroon. They were vast and had never been worked by
a timber company, only by a few pitsawyers.

We had called on the Chief Conservator of Forests a few
months previously to enquire, tentatively, if we could negotiate for any government forest reserves which, with their
twenty-five year leases, would give us a more solid base than
the short-term concessions and local arrangements which we
were working. Rosevear had then told us that there was really
nothing of any size available west of the Niger. 'Why not look
at the eastern reserves? They are isolated, yes, and the species
now popular are thin on the ground, but you must look ahead.
Times are changing.'

We had heard of them, of course. We knew that many timber
men had taken a look and that nobody to date had established
there. One of our Greek competitors, Pappas, had tried his
luck felling in a few free areas and floating his logs down river
to Calabar. His rafts got stuck on the Cross River and never
reached port. When we mentioned this to Rosevear he dismissed it. 'You would have to take a long term view, build a
sawmill and all that. My department is keen to get something

141

going in the east and will support any firm opening up there. Today these forests don't look enticing but it will look different in ten years' time.' It was clear he was riding his hobby-horse.

'In Poland,' Sandy said to me later, 'all the timber merchants got rich and most sawmillers periodically went bankrupt.' We had left it at that. How could two chaps like us look ten years ahead? This was 1955, and if we looked back ten years we were in the army, not knowing what the next day would bring.

And yet here we were, doing well, becoming a force in the tropical timber world, and being talked of as the men of the future. If we wanted to establish something more permanent we would have to expand. It need not be the remote Cross River reserves; one could investigate the Cameroon or the Ivory Coast or even Liberia – all within reasonably easy reach. But then we were already in Nigeria, being courted by a senior government officer there, and perhaps we should try his proposition first? After all, we need not commit ourselves if we did not care for what we saw.

Arrangements were made for us to fly to Enugu, where we met the Eastern Region Chief Conservator, March, and his deputy, Efiom Okon. They showed us their detailed maps and their enumerations and echoed Rosevear's vision of the future. They made several points: we should concentrate our interest on a group of reserves called the Cross River Reserves, about 420 square miles lying astride the river, and forget for the moment the very much larger Oban Reserve which was at this time too inaccessible. These reserves had fair stands of obeche which we could almost immediately export by floating them down the Cross River. Lastly, they knew that the railways had a very substantial demand for sleepers and that the species predominating were ideally suited to cut them: a railway contract could keep a medium-sized sawmill going for a long time.

We reminded them of our Greek friend's disaster. We enquired after communcations.

'Yes, the river is tricky and seasonal,' said March. 'It's in flood roughly between May and November. Carting sleepers across the river to be delivered to the railways would be cumbersome. You won't make a fortune in a hurry but road extensions are on the drawing board and possibly a bridge. There's potential here if you can hold out.'

We thanked them, said we would think about it, and that we would return to walk the forests should we want to take things further.

Back in Lagos we contacted Rosevear: could we count on his support in negotiating with the railways? He made an appointment for us to see the chief engineer, a Scot. His requirements for sleepers in the east were indeed substantial: replacements were essential as little had been done since the war, and supplies in the east were limited to pitsawyers. He was ready to give large contracts if satisfied that we were serious. He showed us his list of acceptable species which matched much of what grew in the east. His specifications were demanding, but the price he could offer was not unattractive. Delivery would be made to the nearest railway station, Afikpo Road, and payments made monthly in Lagos against receipts signed by the station master and countersigned by his accountant.

We wrote to Cobbett's in London and to our agent in New York, Randy Valensi, to send us quotations for circular sawmills suitable to cut the heavy wood we had talked about. We then set off for the east once more, to look at the scheme on the ground. March had detailed a forestry officer and his team to meet us at Obubra on the east side of the Cross River. It was the administrative centre of the areas we were to prospect, in the charge of a District Officer.

Straight away we saw the physical difficulties we would encounter. There was no road from Calabar to Obubra, only the river communication, and we had to drive from Enugu to Abakaliki well to the north, and then via Afikpo to a point where we had to leave the Land-Rover and walk two miles to the ferry – a long journey.

It was market day in one of the principal villages and the roads were crammed with people walking with heavy baskets on their heads, carrying foodstuffs for sale or which they had bought. The young girls were clothed only from the waist downwards. In due course the government, under Dr Nnamdi Azikiwe issued a decree forbidding women to walk about half naked. There were protests: who will marry us now? It was the single young girls who walked about with their breasts bare. A roaring trade in imported second-hand clothing resulted in this decree, which was in the end obeyed, much to the delight of the missionaries. What the young men thought of it must be left to the imagination. The birthrate, however, did not decline.

On the Obubra side, we climbed up a steep embankment to the forestry office. A road connected Obubra with Ikom to the east, close to the Cameroon border, and Ediba to the south – another ferry point – running from nowhere to nowhere, so to speak, as far as contact with the western side of the river went.

We spent five days walking the Cross River Reserves, which were divided into four separate units. The country was sparsely populated: fishermen lived near the river, and farmers lived inland in tiny villages.

The forests were magnificent. Large trees in abundance for mile after mile were interspersed with small settlements which would obviously be no hindrance to timber operations. There was much wildlife – water buffalo, elephants, monkeys, hogs, antelope and birds – as yet undisturbed by human interference, except for the occasional hunter. In the river were families of hippopotami. It was the Africa of old times with the mist hanging over the forest in the morning and people living in primitive conditions. This part of Nigeria was one of the last to be pacified by the colonial regime. The natives had very different origins. Some were said to be of Bantu stock who had migrated down the Cross River and settled. Others had come up from Calabar. They spoke different languages and could not understand each other.

Once we got lost for hours and had to find our way by wading a stream until we reached a spot known to our guides. It was awesome and adventurous, but could we work there? One of the reserves had obeche close to the river, and a few other species which would lend themselves to floating down to Calabar for export. There were also other floater species like ilomba, in profusion; these were not currently in demand, but most of them were of the heavy type suitable for sleepers. One cannot of course really judge a forest in a few days' walking, but what we saw, coupled with the figures available from the Forestry Department made it clear to us that a sawmill and a railway contract were a *sine qua non*. Even then the logistical problems would be formidable.

Where would we place the sawmill? How would we get the equipment across and now much of it was required? Where would we find the labour and accommodate it? How long would it take to make deliveries once the timber was cut? Who would be in charge? When would the proposed road linking Calabar with the area be built? It would ease matters considerably. Above all, how much money would we have to find and when could we hope to break even, let alone show a profit? It was a challenging and exciting prospect, but could we handle it and would it get us anywhere? We would have to consider all this before reaching a decision.

March met us at Ikom; he had laid on a canoe trip down river to Itu, complete with a luncheon basket. It was a large canoe hauled by eight paddlers and we had a fascinating journey. We came across many hippos; every now and then we spotted a little village on the banks. Approaching one of these, we saw two-and three-storey buildings in the distance. 'Where are we, and why do the people here build these large houses?' We were nearing Akunakuna and thereby hung a tale. Young girls of Akunakuna by tradition or long practice went off to Accra on the Gold Coast (now Ghana) to become ladies of pleasure; they spent a few years there, saved some money, and invested this in building these houses when they returned home. The name for a prostitute in Accra was 'Akunakuna', originating from this small lonely town on the Cross River.

We went back to Lagos and began working on projections. We called in Kenneth Cooper, an old hand in Nigeria, and asked if he would join us and take charge of the proposed new enterprise.

'Yes,' he said, 'I would like to join you. I once visited the eastern forests and came to the conclusion that they were not very encouraging; but if there's a railway contract and we are prepared to wait it could be worthwhile. Of course,' he added, 'the whole thing may be a ghastly failure and you could lose a lot of money. I suppose you appreciate that.'

'Let's have another look at it.' I took a second trip to the area to make enquiries about the river and its peculiarities. I was also introduced to some of the chiefs, without whose co-operation we might find it hard to work satisfactorily. All of them sang the same song: we badly need development, we must have work for our young men, we must have better communications, we want to earn more money. They would welcome us with open arms. There would be no obstacles from their side.

In Ugep I met Chief Ofem, who invited me to his house. 'We must celebrate. My wife had twins yesterday, a boy and a girl. If this had happened in the old days, we would have killed the twins and perhaps the mother as well. That was our custom. But now Cow and Gate baby milk takes care of that.' (Those twins, now in their late thirties, are still our good friends.) The chief also mentioned that he remembered cannibalism in his early youth. The odd stranger from the west side of the river would be caught and put in the pot. 'We look on all that now with abhorrence.'

After months of discussions with the railways, with government, and with accountants, and after a host of financial projections, we decided to take the plunge and sign up the Cross River Reserves, realizing full well that it would be a long haul before we would see any return. Our reasoning was that 420 square miles of forest would be turned into an asset if we could survive long enough. We would have a base in which to put up a larger manufacturing plant and grow.

I went to Enugu to meet the Council of Ministers of the Eastern Region to sign the agreement. The government was headed by Dr. Azikiwe ('Zik'), who was away: his deputy, Ojike, presided. Dr. Okpara, who became premier after Zik left, and several other ministers were also present. Each minister wanted the industry established in his constituency, whereas, of course, only one could have it. I confirmed that the mills would be situated to the east of the river or not at all. This was accepted.

We planned to start export logging in six months, and to complete the sawmill within a year. We ordered the logging equipment; we bought an American type circular saw and all the other items required for the mill, which included a power house of Lister generators. Cooper went to and fro laying out the site, recruiting staff and labour, and preparing for the operation to take off on time. He hired two Scots to run the sawmill, Cramb and Duncan, who took over from Cooper when he became seriously ill and returned home. Pleasant living quarters were constructed for expats and Nigerians, and although the nearest town, Enugu, was many hours' drive away, everybody liked the posting to Obubra: it was a happy station. The actual mill site was at Appiapum, a few miles distant from Obubra town.

The local ferry could not carry the heavy caterpillars; we had to construct our own pontoon made up of 44-gallon petrol drums and almost lost one of the tractors. An American came out to help with putting up the sawmill. We dug a deep well for water, only to discover there was a spring half a mile away. There was much coming and going, and much excitement in the villages, with new prospects for the locals being eagerly taken up, providing labour and supplying food and drink for 350 people. By now we were familiar with the excitement generated by a timber operation about to set up in remote and hitherto isolated country – except that this place was more remote and more isolated than anything we had tackled before. The Ogojas were well-built, friendly, pleasant and reliable workers. The fishermen of Appiapum made excellent water-boys and knew their river intimately.

Within six months the first raft was despatched to Calabar where we had opened a shipping station. Within a year the first logs were sawn, and the first sleepers produced. We cut timber for local demand and sent selected lumber by rail to Port Harcourt for export to the UK and the USA in small quantities. We lost only two rafts when we took a chance too late in the season – against advice – and paid the penalty. The river dropped suddenly by ten feet.

The investment had been heavy, the going hard. The profit from export logging was more than swallowed up by the deficit of the sawmill. The sleeper contract turned out to be of minimal value. The specifications were too rigid and the yield down to a third of the volume of a log; the falls had to be cut into flooring and similar sizes, for which the market was limited and low in price. To make matters worse, sleepers soon had to be delivered to Enugu, many miles further than Afikpo Road station. There had been cheating by the station master in cahoots with a number of contractors, or vice versa. The loaded lorries arrived, receipts were issued, and the lorries then went out again, still loaded, and came back for a second, third and fourth receipt. On stocktaking, the railway found itself short of thousands of sleepers.

We opened a station in Enugu, the capital of the Eastern Region, and Sandy and his wife spent much time in the house we had rented. We kept in touch with Chief Ofem and his large family in Ugep, where once I met Zik electioneering and we had a beer together – it was one of his less popular constituencies.

White men resident in the neighbourhood were taken to be either administrative officers or missionaries; our German engineer was surprised when his girlfriend in Ugep, after an enjoyable night, applauded him with 'Thank you, Father.'

The mills were visited by the then Governor of the Eastern Region, Colonel Ojukwu, and his entourage, which included the Minister of Education, who did much of the talking. When they left, our headman, Mathias, whom we had transferred from Ondo and who like all other senior staff had been presented to the august party, commented drily, 'Look at that minister, so much talk, and what ministry has he got? Education – an empty ministry he can't make a penny out of.'

Our undertaking in Obubra district became the catalyst for much other activity in the area; one benefit was the opening up of a grammar school in Iyamayang which soon flourished, and is still going well to this day – the local council had the good sense to save the royalties accruing from our felling of their trees for this purpose. We put up a subsidiary sawmill in

Agoi Ibani twenty-five miles from Obubra to utilize the stands of opepe species, increasingly popular as construction wood. This little mill was run by an old steam engine which took a month to crawl to the site. We worked on land agreed and approved by the Forestry Department with which we had good relations. The villagers were co-operative and there was little friction; they were too aware of the benefits the new industry had brought them.

This peaceful atmosphere was shattered late in November 1964. I was on a visit to the Cross River, and the headman, Mathias, asked to see me privately.

'Sir, there is recruitment going on in the camp for union membership. One of the foremen is union secretary and collects money from the workers. I don't like it, there will be trouble.'

'Does Mr. Dockrell (the GM) know about it and have you discussed it with him?'

'Yes, I have talked to him. He says it doesn't matter.'

'Well, Mathias, if the union is registered and our men fall into the category of the union, it is quite legal. In fact you may find that it will make life easier negotiating with a union rather than with individuals.'

He shook his head. 'I know my men, sir. They don't understand unions and all sorts of promises will be made to them to catch their subscriptions. These union people look after themselves. They will mislead our men, there will be trouble.'

'What trouble?'

'I don't know what trouble but there will be trouble.'

'Well, thank you. I'll talk to the GM later and we'll meet again tomorrow.'

That evening I brought the subject up with Dan Dockrell. 'What's all this about a union?'

'Yes, I have heard about it. It seems a Union of Agricultural Workers has been set up and they're trying to rope our men in. It doesn't worry me.'

'It worries Mathias. He's been to see me. Is the union registered?'

'I don't know if it's registered; we'll find out. They haven't

149

approached me yet and I prefer to leave it at that. Mathias is old-fashioned; he is afraid that his influence over the men will suffer. I heard he had been to see you. Let's play it by ear.'

Next morning I was told that the union secretary wanted to meet me. I gave him an appointment and called in Dan and Mathias. He was one of our logging foremen, a young man. He explained that he was not the union secretary but an unpaid official representing the union. The secretary was one Ebony, who was not on our payroll and did not live near the camp but in Enugu, although his home was in Iyamayang. He did not know if the union was registered with the Ministry of Labour, but thought so.

'Sir, we are to protect the rights of the workers. We want your help. The union will co-operate with the company and expects the company to co-operate with the union.'

He went at length into various matters of procedure, priority being given to their urgent demand for the company to introduce the check-off system. It was a coherent presentation, and must have been well rehearsed. The check-off system meant that on payday the company was to deduct from all its workers the monthly union fees and hand the money over to union officials. It presupposed the workers' agreement. Mathias objected strongly and countered that to his knowledge only a few men had joined the union and that he was quite sure that none of the employees would agree to have union fees deducted. The meeting closed. We asked the official to bring the union registration to confirm that it was an official body, and said we would then sit down to discuss its rôle in the affairs of the company.

The unionists then went about telling the workers that the company would not accept the union, that it was exploiting the workers and was afraid of the union, and that the men must stick together and fight for their rights. One knew the arguments but they sounded strange in the midst of the African forest. The check-off system was not mentioned.

Suddenly the men went on strike. It took us by surprise. We called on the foremen, who were themselves bewildered, and we also called on the elders of the village to talk reason to the men and their wives. Mathias was very active. He damned the union rep and said all he was after was money through the check-off system which nobody had heard of or understood.

After three days the matter was settled. But this was not the end. A month later I was called to come to Obubra urgently. There was new trouble with the union. The secretary, Ebony Okpa, had appeared in person, and much agitation was going on.

I met him. He was a youngish man, very well spoken, who had been trained in the Soviet Union, had visited China, and then returned home to organize the workers as a first step to a political or union career, or both. He had picked on our company to show his mettle. Ebony was a man of considerable talent, a good public speaker, and a cunning politician. He knew his onions.

The scenes which follow and are described in some detail may sound bizarre and unreal to many readers but are related almost verbatim. Ebony had attended seminars in the Communist world which specialized in educating Third World potential in Marxist philosophy and action. He talked like an editorial from the *Daily Worker* and was, I think, a committed Communist to whom any privately owned company was *ipso facto* an exploiting machine of capitalism, more so if it was a foreign one. He had all the familiar patter at his finger tips; the condition of the working class in Africa was fertile ground for his agile mind.

'We must have the check-off system' he insisted. 'Without it the union has no funds and my ignorant countrymen will not pay their fees regularly.' He was quite open about it.

'Mr. Ebony, we have no right to deduct money from wages unless we have written consent from each man agreeing to this. We must also have agreement from the ministry and we must in the end feel that this will be to our advantage and to the advantage of all workers concerned.'

'That is capitalist talk. You are colonial exploiters.' He corrected himself. 'You are neo-colonialists and we shall fight you to the end. The workers are with me and I will prove it to you.'

I was not prepared to give in to threats, although I was not in principle opposed to trade unions. If Ebony seemed very aggressive and offensive, I ignored that. The discussion was attended by our union men as well as the secretary; we felt that they would have a better understanding of our problems than the outside secretary.

'We are prepared,' the GM announced after we had reviewed matters, 'to put the issue to arbitration with the Ministry of Labour in Enugu and abide by their decision.'

Ebony had to accept this or lose the confidence of his followers. So we went to Enugu and had two long meetings with an official of the ministry appointed as arbitrator, where it was agreed that the company would deduct union fees from anybody who consented in writing to this procedure. It was a considerable success for Ebony, and for the ministry.

We returned to the camp, and a mass meeting was called to pass the good news to all workers.

'You had better tell the meeting what has been agreed, Mr. Ebony.'

'I cannot do that. The agreement must have the ratification of the work force. It is not for me to speak first, but for the director.'

So I got up and briefly gave the news of the agreement, and then invited Mr. Ebony to speak.

Mr. Ebony must have been a prize scholar in the USSR. 'You have heard what the director has said. Fellow workers, you have heard what the foreign exploiter has said. I never agreed to any terms; it is for you to agree. I am your secretary and will do your bidding! But if you ask me if these are good terms, I must tell you they are not. Without the obligatory check-off system we cannot look after your rights. But it is up to you. Are you really going to agree to these terms dictated by management?' It was a deliberately confusing statement. He was gunning for a fight.

I was dumbfounded and saw that I had fallen into a trap. Of course a loud shout went up, 'No! No! No!' in unison. Fists were raised. Ebony turned to me and said, 'We had better sit down and discuss new terms or there will be a strike.'

I did not answer him. White with fury, I left, walked straight through the mass of men, and back in my quarters gave instructions for my car to be prepared to drive to Calabar.

'There can be no further discussion,' Mathias and Dan agreed. 'Let them do their worst. Go to Calabar and make sure we load our logs ready for shipment. After that we shall see. The strike here won't harm us much – we are at the end of the season – but allowing the logs in Calabar to rot would be a serious loss.'

It must have been mid-month when this happened. In Calabar all was quiet; we despatched the rafts without interference, although a messenger from Ebony turned up after some days asking the station for their support. Ebony, however, was a stranger to them and they carried on working as normal.

The strike in Obubra was solid, and no work was done. When at the end of the month no wages were paid, there was a riot and the police had to intervene. The GM, now very much in Mathias's tow, gave notice to all workers that their appointment would be terminated unless they returned to work within two days. The men began to feel the pinch: there was little money to go round and about half the shifts came back, although there was much intimidation as Ebony saw the strike slip from his grasp. In the end the strike petered out and about two-thirds of the complement were re-employed. No check-off system was introduced and slowly life returned to normal.

Sandy and I were greatly upset. Our wages were the best in the province; we had brought new industry and employment; we always felt we looked after everyone working with us. Why had they picked on us?

But we could also understand why, and Ebony's reasoning. Find a vulnerable company, one run by whites, but not too powerful. Find one that may not be able to stand the risk of sinking through a strike. Show the contrast in conditions. Make the workers feel their power and promise them better wages in a short time if only they will follow the union secretary. Use class and colour in order to rouse resentment.

153

Ebony, however, had not done his homework well enough. First, we could withstand the mill closing down for some weeks; our concern was rather with the perishable stock in port. Second, we would have had to lay off men seasonally in any case. Third, and not least, the feeling of the population at large was not with him. This new mill had changed the face of the villages on which it rested, and even if wages were not enormous they were good by local standards. Several hundred men had jobs and used their earnings to look after their dependants.

This Moscow-trained unionist was out of his depth and had lost touch with the realities of his own country. He was carried away by his own rhetoric. There was a case to be made out for better working conditions in the country, and room for worker representation and even pressure, but it had to be in the context of the general development of the ex-colony. Ebony could hardly have expected to start a social revolution in the middle of the Obubra bush with a following which looked no further ahead than tomorrow. I met him from time to time in later years, still active in union affairs but much sobered up, pursuing the art of the possible.

The Cross River operation lived on hope. It barely broke even for years and the investment turned over slowly, but we persevered and in the end were proved right when it became the springboard for the large timber complex we erected in Calabar in partnership with major Nigerian, American and British interests.

These two mills played only a minor role once Calabar Veneer & Plywood Ltd was formed and took them over. They did not deserve the sad fate which befell them during the Civil War when both were burned down and utterly destroyed, the quarters looted and damaged beyond repair. It was a great loss for the company and much more than that for the local community.

14

A Move to the Cameroons

S anda called. 'Chief Akin Deko has lost his seat in the
elections,' he said. He was referring to the regional elections held in 1958.

Akin Deko was at the time the Western Region Minister for
Agriculture. We had negotiated with him over many months
for the Ofosu Reserve in Ondo Province. His home town was
Idanre, the mountain village between Ondo and Akure, high
up on a rock. He was a very aggressive and go-ahead man and
we never knew how it came about that he lost his seat in the
Western House Assembly, but he did.

'Who has taken his place?'

'Chief Akinloye, a lawyer from Ibadan.'

'Does that mean we have to start negotiations all over
again?'

'Yes, but he is a friend of mine and you should have no
difficulties.'

We negotiated with the new minister. All was agreed and his
Calabar wife came to the office in Oko Baba to tell us.

A month later we were told that the reserve would have to
be gazetted again; the minister explained that he was not fully
satisfied with the proceedings and wanted to show everybody
that all was open and above board.

'But it is, minister.'

'I know it is, but does everybody else know that?'

'We will not apply again, minister.'

'But you must, gentlemen, and you seem best qualified to
work the concession.'

155

However, word reached us that a Mr. Asaboro – a progressive Nigerian who knew little about timber – was strongly in the running and that we would have little chance against him. We wondered if we should get in with our rival to discuss the matter, but thought better of it.

'Asaboro,' I said to Sandy, 'is the brother-in-law of Professor Thomas and he at least is riding high. It's a straw in the wind and our friend Sanda is too ill to fight for us. We know Asaboro can never run this forest; let them find out for themselves. You go to the Cameroon and see what you can find there. They say they have wonderful obeche stands.'

Under the Berlin Treaty of 1885, the Cameroon had been allocated to Germany. On her defeat in 1918 she had to surrender the colony to France and Britain under mandate of the League of Nations. Britain, who got the smaller part, attached the southern Cameroon to Nigeria for practical purposes of administration and appointed a high commissioner to be in charge of the territory.

Sandy went and came back: 'All the accessible forests have been allocated to one firm. I saw the chief conservator and he confirmed it.'

'Who is he?'

'Hussey.'

'What of John Field? He is the High Commissioner.'

'I didn't meet him. Maclaren is milling around there, talking to the Cameroon Development Corporation who have some timber workings.'

'Did you talk to any Cameroonians?'

'I met Tamajong, who is a junior forestry officer and some of the local politicians, but they don't seem to have much say.'

'Did you meet the chap who took the concessions?'

'No. He's named Heb Leman and seems to have all the money he needs.'

'Well,' I said, 'It's no good chasing the minister, he's already failed us once. And I don't think we'll be in the black in Obubra for a long time; it's going to take all our cash. Who is this Leman?'

'An English timber bloke. As I said, I never met him.'

We left it at that for the moment. The Ofosu Reserve was gazetted again asking for bids and after much thought we did not apply. Word was relayed to us that the minister was expecting our bid.

'Tell the minister that we are not bidding.'

'You mean it?'

'Yes, we mean it. He only wants our bid to cover himself.'

'Why don't you go to the Cameroon,' Sandy suggested 'and see what's cooking?'

I flew to Tiko and took a taxi to Buea, the seat of the government of the southern (British) Cameroon, where I put up in the Mountain Hotel which was a pleasant lodging place built by the government to attract tourists, nestling at the foot of Mount Cameroon. I ran into Maclaren there. 'Hey,' he said, 'what are you doing here? There is nothing to find that's not already allocated.'

'What are you doing here, Mac? Whatever it is, I will do the same.' I called on John Field, the high commissioner, whom we knew because his wife had worked for us as a private secretary. 'It's true, Joe,' he told me, 'that Hussey gave all the forests to Leman. He was so anxious to show some results that he signed up in a hurry.'

'But Leman can never have the finance to run all this, John.'

'I understand that the London bankers, Brand, are behind him.'

'What of Maclaren then?'

'I think he is going to work the few areas under control of the Cameroon Development Corporation.'

John's residence/office was in the schloss built by the German governors when they ruled the Cameroon until 1918. It was a pseudo-castle, Gothic and imposing. I took my leave after a drink or two. 'Let me know how you get on,' John said, 'we would like to see more companies established here.'

'Where do I find this Leman?'

'I think he rents a chalet in the Mountain Hotel.'

'Thanks. I'll keep you informed.'

I called on Mr. Leman. He was middle-aged, a little stout,

157

and extremely astute. He told me that he had come to the Cameroon after he had been involved in the BOAC crash in Kano which killed his wife and left him with two broken legs. He had found the forests very interesting, and had signed up all that was within reasonable distance of the port of Tiko from where he was shipping. We talked.

'You know,' he said, 'several timber men have been snooping around here lately, including Maclaren. Not one of them had the courtesy to call on me. They think I'm not good enough for them, but I will see them in hell.'

'I won't intrigue against you, Leman.'

'It won't do you any good, although I hear you're a friend of the commissioner's.'

'Forget that.'

We had a lot to drink that evening. 'What are you after, Brandler?'

'Look,' I said, 'you have all the forests within easy reach of the port, but even with Brand's help you can't run them. Sooner or later you'll meet opposition. Sometimes half a loaf is more than a whole loaf. You've got few friends and many enemies – you must know that.'

'I know.'

'So why don't we combine and run the forests together?'

'Go to hell,' he said.

'Think about it, Heb. You can find me in the main block of the Hotel.'

'Go to hell,' he said again, and then, 'Have another for the road.'

I bided my time. I went to meet Cameroonians of standing: Kale, Dr. Endeley, Mbile, and others. I went to see Hussey. I went to see Maclaren's friends in the Cameroon Development Corporation.

The third evening, coming back to the hotel in the late afternoon, I found a note from Leman. 'If you are free, please come and dine with me tonight.' I went.

There was a third party present, his English secretary, a young, well-dressed woman. Gossip had it that she was more than his secretary, but that was in no way evident. A man like him was bound to attract much gossip. We had a splendid dinner washed down with champagne.

'Have a brandy.' At that point the secretary excused herself and disappeared. 'I've been thinking about what you said, Joe. Not that I can't hold all this – you know Brand's are behind me. What's in your mind?'

An idea had formed in my mind and I explained it to him. 'Brand or no Brand, you can't hold all this. You'll be scratching the forests, and politics will come into it, and you'll be harassed from morning to night. Let's share the areas, exploit them together, make roads together, and have some real clout when it comes to talking to government. They regret having given you all the concessions, you must realise that.'

'I know.'

I got out a map showing the demarcations of the various areas. I drew a line and said. 'That for you, that for us.'

'You must be joking.'

'Think about it, Heb. Adjust the map and I'll look at what you want.'

'I have got what I want.'

'You will have to hold it too, Heb. Think about it. Don't rely on the bankers. Together we'd be strong. You need allies.'

He looked at me hard. 'I've never had anybody talk to me like that,' he said. 'You've got a point, of course. It's been worrying me for some time – you devil.'

'Let's sleep on it.'

'Let's.'

We made rapid progress over the next few days. I calculated that we would need much finance for the proposed deal and wondered where we could raise it. I reported to the commissioner and then a snag appeared. 'We want to have Maclaren here as well.'

'You must be joking.' It was my turn now to use the phrase.

'No, Joe. These are vast concessions and all the advice I have tells me that it will need at least three good timber companies to run these areas efficiently.'

So that crafty Glaswegian had been busy. 'I can't see Leman

agreeing to work with Maclaren, who has been bitching for weeks.'

'I can,' said John, very much the High Commissioner. 'And you'll have to act as the catalyst if you wish to get anywhere. I hear you want to have the government as shareholders.'

'We do.'

'Then split the areas into three and you'll have our full support. Let me know.'

After a lot of discussion, we reached an agreement in principle. Leman would retain 40 per cent of the areas, and Maclaren and we would take 30 per cent each. After much wrangling, we fixed demarcations and signed a letter of intent. Leman was bitter but realistic. 'The old school tie wins again,' he said.

'There's no school tie about Sandy and me, and there's certainly no old school tie about Maclaren. He must have left school at fifteen.'

I went back to Lagos with the draft agreement, cock-a-hoop. 'Where are we going to get the money from?' Sandy asked. 'This is a huge undertaking.'

'In the last resort,' I answered, 'the banker Brand. But first we'll approach Price & Pierce.'

I went to London and saw Anthony Benn and his financial director, Robertson. 'We need funding,' I explained, and showed them our plans and, as we saw it, the prospects.

'What about your agents, Cobbett & Co?'

'They'll have to join you in order to run this show. And if you can't do it we'll have to go elsewhere. We think this is a very good deal all round.'

'We will send out our Mr. Robertson and Mr. Eric Dennes of our Company,' said Benn. I did not know it then, but Robertson was a brother of Sir James Robertson, the governor-general of the federation.

Robertson called on his brother, then we set off to Buea. Robertson was introduced; he saw John Field and John Dudding, his deputy. They met all and sundry, including Maclaren and Leman.

'You have friends at court,' said Robertson. 'They seem to

think that with your participation the protectorate will stand to gain in this business. I'll recommend it to the Board. Can you give your personal guarantees?'

'If we could, Lindsay, we wouldn't need you, would we? We will pledge the shares if you wish, but we wouldn't like that.'

'What if you got killed?'

'You could attend my funeral, Lindsay.'

The deal was struck. We organized the best logging operation seen in West Africa. Maclaren got his finance and Leman took more money from Brand. It was a marvellous success. For the second and third year, we declared a dividend of 100 per cent, so that the government doubled their money in a short time. We were able to repay Price & Pierce, and still do well ourselves – all in spite of political upheavals when Western Cameroon voted to secede from Nigeria and join Eastern Cameroon in the newly independent Cameroon Republic.

The political friends we had cultivated had been in favour of staying with Nigeria and were out. Only Foncha, for whom we had given a party at the Mainland Hotel in Lagos, remained. At that party he complained, 'You see all these boys here – they are mainly servants. Our people haven't got a chance in the federation.' It was true in a way. Most of the elite southern Cameroonians had been educated in Nigeria and were pro-Nigeria. But the great mass of their nationals in Lagos were cooks and stewards and common labourers.

We ourselves had a cook from the grasslands of Bamenda, a first-rate chef when not drowning his sorrows in drink because his wife kept on delivering female children – he had no less than five daughters. One early evening, as we returned to the compound from visiting friends, we came upon a great commotion. The cook's eldest girl, aged eleven, had been violated by a neighbour's gardener. The culprit had been caught and had summoned his pals to help him settle the matter by offering pecuniary compensation.

As we arrived upon the scene, heated negotiations were going on, with the father unable to make up his mind whether to accept the money or call the police. White man's logic demanded that the miscreant be arrested and face trial for his foul deed. My wife would have been outraged had any other action been taken. The gardener was handed over to the police and spent such money as he and his pals could raise on lawyer's fees; he ended up with a gaol sentence of several years. It transpired that the man was propelled by an old superstition that his VD would be cured were he to deflower a virgin; the poor girl had to have treatment and I felt then, and still do, that he fully deserved his punishment. The cook was not so sure that this had been the right way to go about it. It benefited neither father nor daughter that the man was in gaol when they could have squeezed the last penny out of him to the advantage of the family.

The forests were fabulous. The terrain was very hilly and required heavy extraction tools – caterpillars and big lorries – but the trees were large and of excellent quality. The Cameroonians were very disciplined labourers and performed well.

The port of Tiko from which we shipped – it had been built by Elders & Fyffes as a banana loading point – was the hottest place we had ever encountered. The three companies co-operated in making roads and securing spares and materials. Our headquarters were in Muyuka, half-way between Tiko and Kumba, as were both Leman's and Maclaren's.

To operate in the Cameroons we had formed a subsidiary company, Brandler & Rylke Cameroons Ltd, and invited a Chief Martin from Victoria to join its board. Chief Martin had had a distinguished career in the (Nigerian) Civil Service until he retired.

Once the Southern Cameroons became part of the Republic of Cameroon this business had to be hived off from the Nigerian-controlled concern. A new entity, Cameroon Forest Products Limited, was established, with registered offices in Buea (or it may have been Yaounde). Two other Cameroonians joined the board, one of whom was Nfon (Chief) Victor Mukete from Kumba. Mukete had been engaged in Nigerian politics and by 1960 had become a federal minster. In spite of this he advocated reunion with the new republic and resigned his ministerial position in Lagos to return to the Cameroon.

In the plebiscite he threw his weight behind reunification. Highly regarded, he maintained his prominence. Amongst many high appointments he held the chairmanship of the Cameroon Development Corporation in which the Commonwealth Development Corporation (an official British body) had a considerable financial holding.

Independence in the Cameroon was not followed by the aggression and free for all witnessed in Nigeria. The French became predominant, or remained so, and did not let go as the British did in Nigeria. The transition was much slower, for better or worse. Our Cameroon directors did not immediately demand Mercedes cars and mansion accommodation. For all that, a new middle class rose up and the country prospered.

The end of this story is rather sad. We sold out to Maclaren when our American partners in Calabar put pressure on us. Maclaren sold to some Germans. Leman's empire collapsed as his bankers closed in on him, and he committed suicide shortly after marrying a very charming new wife who bore him a son. He had once told me, 'Joe, I have been broke many times but never poor.' This time he could not face it.

~   ~   ~

I took time on my many journeys to the Cameroon to see something of the country.

Its principal town in the south under British Mandate was the port of Victoria (now called Limbe) which lies on a wide bay circled by mountains. It was of modest size. There were the inevitable two banks, Barclays and Standard; there was a Kingsway department store, part of UAC; and there were two or three petrol stations, a hospital, schools and churches. There was also a fine botanical garden laid out by the Germans, who had left their mark generally, although they had been there for only about twenty-five years.

Going north from Victoria, the next town was Kumba. The road rose all the way; one travelled first through huge banana plantations, then through rubber plantations, and finally through forest. Buea lay off that road, to the west, some 50 kilometres from Victoria.

To reach the eastern (French) side of the Cameroon, one had to branch off at a village called Tombel. However, as a wartime measure, the road had been made almost impassable – the Vichy French had been in the saddle – and even after fourteen years nothing had been done to repair the surface.

One could see the nonsense of colonial boundaries. British Cameroon was totally cut off from Nigeria by a large mountain range; the road from Ikom to Mamfe was narrow and poorly served, and operated a one-way traffic except on Sundays. Supplies for Mamfe were mainly carried by water on the Cross River which was navigable for only five months of the year. The port of Victoria had few facilities, and much the same applied to Tiko; but Douala could not be used because it was French and even then road connections, as already mentioned, were very poor.

In Victoria I came across an old Chief, Williams, who proudly showed me his *pickelhaube* – a pre-1914 German army helmet which had been given to him by a German administrator. Williams still spoke good German, as did many of the older Cameroonians.

The people were orderly. There was less asking for 'dash' than one was used to in southern Nigeria. Cameroonians were also much slower on the uptake, not having engaged in trade which had sharpened up their Nigerian brothers. Whether by natural inclination or by severe German training, one could not help noticing the difference in attitudes of the inhabitants. It was seen not only on the British side of the Cameroon, but also on the French.

In this seemingly quiet atmosphere, one of the tribes which felt themselves badly treated by the British government suddenly rebelled. The administration took 'emergency measures' and called for a battalion of the Grenadier Guards from the UK. On the road to Kumba the odd pot-shot was taken at cars but nothing much happened. The ringleaders were rounded up and interned, and branded as Communists, a familiar label all over Africa whenever people protested against their masters. Whatever else Lenin did for the liberation of the continent, he certainly gave a convenient explanation for all protests.

The hilly forests had large stands of timber on terrain that was bisected repeatedly by streams and rivers. When it rained – we could have as much as ten inches in a day – these streams became torrents for a few hours and then subsided again. I never visited the grasslands much praised for their beauty, but then I think all of Cameroon is a beautiful country, surprisingly little known to European and American tourists to this day.

After Dr. Endeley had been defeated, and Foncha and his party took over the government of the Western Cameroon, the emphasis changed from English to French. First, driving on the left was changed to driving on the right. This went off surprisingly smoothly. Then the currency was changed from pounds sterling to CFA. French was taught at the schools although the country remains bi-lingual. Most ambitious Cameroonians learnt French, as the capital was in Yaounde on the French side, which held most of the population.

Thus, within a span of less than fifty years, the western Cameroonians had been governed in three different languages. They seemed to have taken to it easily, and of course most of them spoke their native tongue when at home.

Once unification was well under way and the roads improved, the port of Tiko was no longer used by us and we went instead to Douala, loading our logs onto the nearest railway station at Loum. Other logs we took by road to Mbonge, where they were dumped into the waters and towed to Calabar, a journey of many days. Mbonge was situated on a forlorn creek at the end of one of UAC's large palm oil plantations. It was real old Africa; endless waters and swamps, hardly any habitations, and crocodile in great numbers.

There was a superstition amongst the locals that people could turn themselves into crocodiles, wait for their enemies, and kill them. Some fishermen certainly did get killed but I should not think that these were men turned into crocodiles. Another theory advanced was that fishermen would train crocodiles in some mystical way and then command them to kill their enemies.

I remember a retired policeman telling me how he had been detailed to get to the bottom of these stories when two or three men had been killed in quick succession. He said he lived with the locals for months, going from one fishing village to another, even marrying (i.e. having an affair with) one of the Chief's daughters, to find out their secret. However, he never discovered anything and went back to his station to report failure.

'Do you think there was ever anything to report?' I asked.

'Well, sir,' he replied, 'it was common knowledge among the locals that such things existed but perhaps it was just a trick to make people afraid.'

I once made the journey on a launch from Mbonge to Calabar through these wild swamps, then across the Rio del Rey estuary, where oil has now been found, and into the port of Calabar. Flying from Calabar to Tiko in small planes at about 2,000 metres, I twice saw large flocks of flamingos below me in the estuary of the Rio del Rey – a pink cloud disturbed by the drone of the aircraft.

Our logging station near the Rio del Rey was a lonely place for our staff. Even the forestry people hardly ever went there, preferring to inspect the rafts nearer civilization. On this Rio del Rey, however, the Germans had had a station for loading produce; the river could take ocean-going vessels, but the station was closed and our attempt to re-open it as a loading port was not approved. It was feared that such a place would become a centre for smugglers unless there were customs, police, harbour officials, etc, all of which would have been too expensive.

At that time, our HQ was still in Muyuka; we later shifted it to Kumba, some sixty miles north. This was a tragic move for those of our staff who lived close to Muyuka. One of the clerks met with a fatal motor accident visiting friends. The chief clerk was given a Land-Rover for his colleagues to attend the funeral. On the return journey a large tree fell on the car as it was moving and killed six occupants who were sitting in the rear, although the driver and the man sitting next to him escaped unscathed.

Within a few days we lost seven of our office staff, all good men of some years' service. In this emergency our agent, Ted Smith, enrolled his cook as office staff; he turned out to be a minor genius and rose quickly in rank. He had taken the job as cook to be near his family when nothing else was available. How good a cook he was I cannot say, but his clerical talent was considerable.

Kumba was a medium-sized town lying at the crossroads between west and south-west Africa. It had a buoyant market which included currency transactions. Once, when I was dining in the boardroom of the Chase Bank in New York, one of the senior Americans there asked me how the dollar was trading in Kumba. He explained that it was one of the international indicators they followed.

15

Liberia

We failed in Liberia. We were defeated by the very problems we prided ourselves on being good at overcoming: logistics, physical obstacles, communications.

We found ourselves operating in the far eastern corner of the republic. There were no road communications except inside the county. No truck could bring supplies from Monrovia or the Ivory Coast. They had to come by sea, be reloaded into lighters, and brought to the small port of Cape Palmas, alias Harper. The ships called infrequently and never when they were expected. We would run out of fuel, or would receive fuel when our tanks were still half full, leaving us the problem of where to store it. Spare parts had to be flown in – expensive and sometimes physically impossible. In consequence we tended to overstock them.

There was no telephone connection with the outside world. The radio in the harbour master's office was always out of order when we wanted it, nor was there any guarantee that our message would ever get to the party it was meant for even if it was relayed - and vice versa.

The ship we were expecting to load our timber might by-pass Cape Palmas because of bad weather or because the captain did not fancy calling there – it was rarely a scheduled stop. Alternatively, a ship would appear out of the blue when we were not ready for it, which gave the port a worse name still.

We required cement: none was available in the town. We ordered well ahead - it either did not come or we received a double quantity. The local labour had no sense of urgency; absenteeism was chronic because the men would go off for days without prior notice to help on the family farm. Every mile of road required a culvert or bridge, the construction of which had to be supervised by senior staff. Malaria was rampant, for all our urging to take prophylactics. Everything that could go wrong seemed to do so at the same time.

You may well ask: did we not know all of this before we let ourselves in for the undertaking?

We certainly did, and had faced similar circumstances before: on the Cross River, in the Cameroon, and so on. What beat us in Liberia was an error of judgement. Previously we had always begun in a limited way, building up each operation as we went along, sometimes very rapidly. In Liberia we took over an organization not designed by us, conceived on a grand scale from the start, and, as it turned out, badly conceived. We thought we could put it right, and probably would have done had we been given more time.

We had been alerted by Swedish friends to the forests of Liberia. A consortium of Swedish and American steel companies had signed an agreement with the Liberian Government to exploit an iron ore mountain at Nimba in the north of the Republic. To bring the ore to port, a railway 250 kilometres long was under construction and our friends had obtained the contract to supply the sleepers for it. They had brought over a portable sawmill and were felling trees to cut the sleepers as they went along. They informed us that there were large forests untapped except by small producers catering for the limited local market. They wondered why no timber company had established itself to exploit the stands freely available.

Vague as the information was, and in spite of Liberia's poor reputation as unreliable and underdeveloped, we could not resist the temptation to have a closer look at what might be on offer. We engaged an experienced logger, Bob Ball, and sent him to Liberia. His brief was to prospect the forests, communications, ports, and labour situation, and to form a general opinion of the country, its administration, and its potential.

Over the next few months his reports came in at irregular

intervals. All had much the same refrain: the country was poorly organized and communications were sparse. American influence was strong, underlined by the huge investment of the Firestone Rubber Company which had large rubber plantations all over Liberia. The population was split between the Americo-Liberians and the natives. The former were the offspring of the liberated slaves settled in the country in the 19th century when the American and other navies intercepted slave ships and rescued their victims or brought back slaves already landed in the USA. Their origin had not been Liberian. These Americo-Liberians had adopted American habits and spoke with a southern drawl. They were the rulers, spoke only English, and kept themselves apart from the natives whom they despised as barbarians. They did not speak any of the native languages and had no social contacts with them, but were very much in the minority. President Tubman and his entourage were omnipotent but 'accessible'.

Ball had met many people, local dignitaries as well as expatriate and Lebanese businessmen. More to the point, he had walked through forests in the centre and west of the country. All had good stands of timber but the species were mostly unknown on the world markets and might be considered unattractive. He suggested one of us come out to Liberia in order to evaluate the position.

I flew to Monrovia. I was met by Ball at Robertsfield International Airport, a modern complex built by the Americans as an air base in World War II and handed over to the Liberians when no longer required. By contrast the immigration and customs facilities were dingy, and the officers manning them were rude, slow, and full of their own importance. This was compensated for by the long drive into Monrovia through one of Firestone's rubber plantations, the trees standing in line like soldiers on parade, mile after mile, interspersed with neat labour camps and offices. Tarred roads led off the main highway at regular intervals.

I walked some of Ball's forests and had to confirm that they were an uncertain proposition. I paid a courtesy visit to the British Embassy. The officer I saw was not very complimentary about Liberia; he opined that it was full of nepotism and corruption and dubious commercial practices, with plenty of red tape and bureaucracy.

Our next call was on the Chief Conservator of Forests, Saye, an exception to the rule that only Americo-Liberians were in charge. He was one of the select band of natives picked by the administration to be educated. Tubman realized that the Americo-Liberians were too small in number for the country ever to become a more modern state, and initiated a programme of widening the range of people to be called on. He experienced much opposition to this policy from his caste. He was also persuaded that Liberia needed a modern Army; no self-respecting Americo-Liberian would serve in the Army except as an officer (the same applied to the police), and so all other ranks were composed of natives who had to be schooled to a minimum standard to be of any use. This dilemma in the end cost the Americo-Liberians dear.

Saye received us cordially; he was anxious to develop the timber industry. On our comment that the forests seen so far were not encouraging in their composition, he advised us to go to the east of the country, Maryland County, and its capital, Cape Palmas, where we would find what we were looking for. He had recently signed an agreement with a German concern to exploit some of the eastern forests. There were no road communications between Monrovia and Cape Palmas, so we would have to fly there.

We visited Mr. Wishnant, a lawyer, whose offices were within the presidential compound and who had the title of 'Social Secretary to the President'. He was a well-spoken, dapper little man who talked at great length. He impressed on us that his country was opening up, that foreign investment was welcomed and protected, and that there were many opportunities. 'Don't only consider timber; there is much else. We have, for instance, a thriving diamond trade here. Form a company and you can do what you like. I would be happy to assist you with the formalities.'

'I didn't know Liberia mined diamonds.'

'We don't mine them. They're smuggled from next door,

Sierra Leone, and once they're in Liberia they are quite legal. We have buyers coming from all over the world.'

'Fancy that', I thought. Instead of felling trees weighing tons to be carried on heavy trucks for miles, we could buy a few diamonds and stick them into our pockets. However, I kept my counsel. (I might add here that this diamond racket got so bad that the South African Oppenheimer Organization, which controls world diamond distribution, opened an office in Monrovia to syphon off as many of the smuggled diamonds as possible and so keep a measure of control on the trade).

I met some of the other friends Ball had made and got a fair idea of how things were managed, but the crux of the problem remained unanswered: could we find the type of forest we were looking for?

Should we despatch Ball to Maryland? Would there be room for two companies if the Germans really had signed up? We had heard of this affair on the grapevine. The firm involved was a veneer company from Lemgo in Westphalia owned by the Moehring family who also ran veneer mills in Canada. We knew them well, they often bought parcels of logs from us. Their head was Karl-Heinz Moehring. They had dabbled in tropical forestry before and had never succeeded in making a go of it. Were they about to try again?

I asked Ball to mark time and said that I would ask Sandy Rylke to come out to get a second opinion. Sandy went to Monrovia, followed more or less in my footsteps, and suggested that we ask Ball to proceed to Maryland, and in particular to track the Grebo Forest lying inland, which had been recommended by Saye.

Weeks passed until we heard from Ball again.

Yes, the Germans were established in Cape Palmas and had brought in much varied equipment. The Grebo Forest was more interesting than what he had already seen, but the terrain was hilly and intersected by many small streams. Also, in order to reach it, we would have to bridge the Gi River, which was wide and fast-flowing. It would take two to three years to get going and required a lot of capital. There were no port facilities. Cape Palmas harbour could only take small boats and seemed to have been built for the convenience of the president's yacht – Maryland was his home county. Loading would have to take place in the open sea. Nor were there any telephone or cable communications; all that would have to be channelled through Monrovia by special runner. But, he repeated, the Grebo was enticing. He asked for instructions.

Sandy flew out again and came back confirming Ball's views: 'Great possibilities and great hazards; it would take a fortune to establish an operation in the Grebo. You go and have a look.'

Off I went, flying to Cape Palmas with Ball, walking the Grebo, looking around, and then returning to Monrovia. Ball and I went over it all again. I came to the conclusion that, interesting as it was, we would have to borrow a great deal of money to establish a logging operation. This would be a gamble, and the risks were simply too great. 'We'll send you official instructions shortly, Ball, and I think we can offer you a job in the Cameroon. Hang on for a week or two.'

I had put up in the Ducor Palace Hotel, newly opened, and that evening in the bar met an elegant American. He asked me what I was doing in Monrovia. I explained my mission. 'And what are you doing here?' I asked.

He said he had come to have a look around. He was connected with a bank in Washington, DC, which owned a Liberian bank, the International Trust Company of Liberia. It had been formed by the late Stettinius, at one time a prominent politician in the USA.

The present head was General Olmsted. Stettinius had negotiated a monopoly with the Liberian government for the registration of ships wanting to sail under the Liberian flag of convenience. It was a very profitable business which had led to other banking activities. It was his first visit and the managing director, Conway, had told him that they were under pressure from the president to invest in industry if they wanted to keep their monopoly. They had not found anything suitable. The timber industry was traditionally a field of interest to American banking. 'Maybe we could find something in common. Come and have dinner with us tomorrow.'

I accepted. Conway had met Ball briefly and was informed of his activities. In such a small town a good banker would know everything that went on.

'If you have a proposition to develop the timber industry here we'd be glad to know more about it,' he said.

I told them of the conclusion I had reached, but promised to keep in touch. As we parted, my bar acquaintance gave me his card. He was Sumner Gerard and lived in New York. 'Please call on me when you visit America.'

Next morning I flew back to Lagos. Sandy was keen to hear my conclusions: 'We've been to Liberia four times, not to mention Ball's prolonged presence there. We've spent a lot of money and can't go on dithering. Yes or no?'

'The answer, Sandy, must be no. It's beyond us financially, and the risks seem to me to be greater than the possible gain. I've seen Moehring's show and I doubt if they know what they're doing. We must recall Ball.'

He concurred. 'By the way, Joe, did you get my message about Moehring?'

'I received no message. Anyway, he wasn't in Liberia. What was it about?'

'I have no idea. He sent a cable that he wants to meet us.'

'He can do that when I fly to New York next month. I shall be going through London. Let's reply to that effect.'

We cabled Moehring in Germany to see me for lunch in London on a given date, and he replied affirming the arrangement. When we sat down he came straight to the point.

'I know that your man, Ball, has been milling around Liberia for some time, and that you're looking for concessions. I can save you the trouble – take over my company, the Maryland Logging Corporation. We've invested a lot there, but it's not clicking. I can't cope with these Africans and their way of doing things. Nor can I spend enough time there, I have too much on my plate. You and Rylke know a lot about tropical logging and can make a go of it. My terms would be easy.'

'You've only just gone there and you want to get out already? What's wrong?'

'I told you – I'll stay if I have to. Mine are the best concessions in Liberia and I can have the Grebo, too, if I want it. But this logging business is not my game. Think about it. Send out Ball to our place. He'll have the fullest co-operation. We'll show him everything.'

We talked some more at length. I said I would contact Sandy and we would respond as soon as I had returned from the USA in a couple of weeks. I sent a cable to Sandy in Lagos to await my news and wrote a long despatch setting out the points raised by Moehring. I mentioned that an idea had formed itself in my mind: if the International Trust Company of Liberia were willing to buy the Maryland Logging Corporation – provided we found it in reasonable shape and could recommend the purchase, and provided the government gave it the Grebo concession – we would undertake to run the show as managing agents, and, as proof of good intent, could take up a minority interest in the Company. In the meantime Sandy should ask Ball to remain in Monrovia.

In New York I called on Gerard. I met him and his brother and his old father. They were clearly people of substance with interests in real estate, crude oil, and banking – the Liberian affair was a minor matter. Gerard also had political ambitions and was later appointed American ambassador to Jamaica, his career cut short by the downfall of Nixon, to whom he must have been close.

I mentioned the Moehring development to him. 'Sounds interesting but of course it's up to Conway, the man on the spot. Have you advised him of this?'

'We will as soon as we have more facts.'

Thus the Liberian adventure took a new turn.

At the time of which I am writing, the early 1960s, Liberia had a population of around 1.5 million. Monrovia was the seat of government and commerce of the country; it had schools and an embryonic university. It had a port, which took ocean-going vessels to 10,000 tonnes, and a small airport (as opposed to the international one at Robertsfield.) It sported a couple of cinemas, several restaurants, some small, efficient hotels owned by whites, and the Ducor Palace Hotel, which became a centre of social activities. Here the upper crust of the Americo-Liberians met for a drink: big men and women speaking in loud voices with American accents. They were educated people who mingled with the visitors from abroad. The men dressed in suits with watch chains across their waistcoats and the women liked to wear hats, whereas the natives generally wore shorts and open-necked shirts.

We gradually got to know quite a few of them. There was Mr. Tolbert, the Minister of Agriculture, with whose department we had many dealings. He had a lovely secretary with the exotic name of Opral who was being courted by a Nigerian minister. They later married and Opral became a great social success in Lagos. There was Mr. Wishnant, the social secretary to the president. Tolbert's brother became successor to President Tubman and was one of those later paraded naked through the town by the revolutionaries to be shot on the beach. Tolbert himself died earlier in a plane crash.

These troubles came years after we had left Liberia but I must confess they surprised me. I knew of the gulf which existed between the natives and the Americo-Liberians, but I did not think that the natives would have the political will and organizational power to sustain a revolt originated by the lower echelons of the army. I suppose they had some allies amongst the Americo-Liberians, opposition figures brutally suppressed by those in power (or envious of them). I was even more surprised when in the late 1980s the whole country blew up in a three-way civil war after the downfall of Doe.

In our days Monrovia was peaceful and inefficient. It even sported one or two night-clubs and had its sailors' quarters where lonely deckhands could find temporary company.

The academics at the university were a motley crew: mainly Americans, some curious to get to know Africa, others enticed by good pay and low taxes. Its disciplines in those days were mainly technical – agriculture, the sciences, engineering, forestry. It must have been extended greatly over the years. It was run on American lines.

There were said to be quite a few American military and intelligence installations in the country, of which we knew little. Every now and then the US Navy would call to show the flag, a red letter day for the town.

Tubman was building himself a magnificent presidential mansion which on completion must have cost the total income of his government for several years, if he ever met the bills. One reception I attended demanded white tie and decorations which I believe was the usual form – etiquette was rigorously adhered to. This façade of grandeur and sovereignty was to be pulled down brutally by Doe, the army sergeant who led the revolt.

So there we were – we had commissioned Wishnant to form a Liberian Company for us to become partners with the Americans in buying out the Maryland Logging Corporation. The final bargaining could begin.

Moehring asked for three times more than our suggested figure, protesting that even then he would lose a lot of his original investment. With the Americans anxious to come to a conclusion, an amount was eventually arrived at which to our mind was too high, and we pressed that payment be staggered over a number of years. Moehring conceded this point, realizing that we were still hesitant in our attitude to the proposed venture.

We insisted on the Germans remaining until we were ready to replace them with our own staff. We took on one of their mechanics, a bright young man, who accepted our proposal to switch over. In spite of that, most of the Germans drifted away before we could replace them and there was an unnecessary dead period when practically no work was in progress. Poor security also meant that small tools and similar items were stolen by the labourers and farmers.

Ball was in charge of the logging operation, Christopher Rylke oversaw the commercial side, and we had an English chief engineer, a Chinese forester, an Italian mechanic, an English beachmaster and accountant, plus several hundred Liberians. We could not recruit Americans because they were too expensive. We brought over five Nigerians as foremen to train the Liberians on the job.

From the financial point of view our commitment was limited, but the time we had to devote to this new enterprise drove us to the limit; initially either Rylke or I were there for much of the time. Progress was slow. Our goal was to get into the Grebo – which had been added to the concession agreement – as quickly as possible. This included the construction of many miles of road and several bridges, one of which, over the River Gi, was a major undertaking. It would take us at least a year to be ready to work on the other side of that river, depending on luck with the weather and other factors.

Meanwhile, we carried on where Moehring had left off. The one aspect of the physical problems which was new to us was the loading of logs well off-shore. It was extraordinary to see the tugs make fast in the harbour area where the logs were assembled and then turned into rafts of between thirty and fifty pieces, well secured by wire rope. The log boys rode on these rafts and once out to sea were often hidden by the waves for several seconds at a time.

At certain times of the year, this was a stormy corner of the Atlantic Ocean; squalls could suddenly come upon the ships which were scared of drifting ashore. On one occasion the loading vessel lifted anchor and sailed away, leaving our tug and most of its logs to make its way back into harbour as best it could. I greatly admired the skill and courage of the log boys. Most of them were Kroo men from another part of Liberia. Depending on the conditions of the sea and the equipment on board, it could take up to six hours or more for a raft to be towed out and loaded, and for the tug then to return to base.

The payroll we inherited included the chief of police of Cape Palmas, who received one hundred dollars monthly for special services, the nature of which we never discovered. There were also some other individuals, retainers of the Liberian director, Willie Tubman, a relative of the president.

The little town of Cape Palmas had its quota of Americo-Liberians and a few expats. There were shops selling general merchandise, a hotel, a couple of bars. On the outskirts, by the sea, were two restaurants serving food and drink in pleasant surroundings. Up on a hill was the Roman Catholic mission in the charge of Dr. Poppard, a medical missionary whom we visited. On our first appearance he warned us of the very special type of mosquito prevalent which could give one a bad bout of malaria in no time at all. When I asked the good doctor which prophylactic he recommended, he replied that he could not say because he took none, leaving it to his daily intake of Irish whisky to do the trick. He had lived there for ten years and never had an attack.

Our own camp was ten miles north of the town en route to the forest. In a nearby river we saw dwarf hippos; leopards were reported as well. There were monkeys of different types and other small wildlife. The inhabitants were friendly. Outside the town they had their villages, round houses of mud and thatch. Ball and I once spent two nights in one of them as guests of the owner. They were surprisingly roomy and cool.

The country was sparsely populated. Going east a few miles one reached the Cavalla River which was the boundary between the Ivory Coast and Liberia. It had a hand-operated ferry crossing. We learned that in 1912 a French gunboat had entered the Cavalla and sailed many miles up this large river. I wondered why Cape Palmas had been established where it was rather than by the river where a good port could have been built. Nobody could enlighten me.

One gathered in the evenings at the sea-side bars: a few Americo-Liberians, a few whites. One of the local specialities was Liberian oysters: these were huge, as large as a soup plate, and were so tough that they took many hours to cook. Meat came from the miniature cattle – no larger than a big sheep – which were reared in those parts. They were resistant to the tsetse fly. Fish was plentiful. The proprietress of one of the bars told us proudly that she had three children at university in the USA.

Cape Palmas had a post office, a school, a court, and administrative quarters, all on a limited scale. It also had electricity. It had undertones of a small mid-western American town, which showed in surprising ways such as the merchandise the shops offered and the American accent and spelling of those who spoke English. Such cars as could be seen were all American, Chevrolet and Ford monsters which stood up well to the poor roads.

Once outside Cape Palmas, one was back in old Africa, with its large trees, early morning haze, people carrying their loads on their heads, naked children running about in the villages, and small-scale farms swallowed up by the surrounding bush.

American Peace Corps youngsters had been posted to Cape Palmas and attached to schools and administration, a few even going right into the bush. Men and women in their early twenties, they were bright-eyed, intelligent and eager. They often lived in the style of the native, learnt the language, and became closer to the people than the Americo-Liberians. They had harsh words to say about imperialist exploitation. If many of them left disillusioned after a year or two, it was due to their impatience and upbringing. One does not change the habits and outlook of people in so short a time. The seed was in the ground – some of it would shoot.

Our camp had a genial atmosphere. Young, our Chinese, had fought in World War II and drifted into the UK from where we recruited him. A first-class man, he had his wife and son with him. His son (whom we called young Young) did his schooling by correspondence course, supervised by a serious mother who insisted on strict timetables for his studies. He was about twelve. Mrs. Young was an experienced cook and at weekends would lay on lunch parties for all. Fish was a major ingredient of these meals. Young had textbooks in Chinese which he consulted much to everybody's amazement, my own included. Why one should be so surprised I don't know, after all there must be as many people speaking Chinese as English.

Our German was an easy-going fellow who chased the local girls, one of whom he made pregnant. The acknowledged fee for this was $300; once paid, this would settle the matter and the girl would look after the child, unless the father took an interest. Our German, however, refused to pay, alleging that to his knowledge the girl had also been sleeping with a Peace Corps boy. It was a mean excuse, even if she had had more than one lover, and there was disapproval at his behaviour. In the end Young paid and adopted the child there and then – a fine gesture. He took the girl back to England, and one must hope

180

that she grew up into a lovely woman.

Our Nigerians did not acclimatize well. They spoke their own pidgin English and could not understand the locals with whom they came into contact. They were to organize enumerations of the forest. They were well skilled in this task, but since it involved a lot of contact with the local people, the Nigerians were hampered by the communication problems they encountered. They were quartered well forward of the camp. The pay and a sense of adventure attracted them. The salary was in Liberian dollars – rather higher than in Nigeria with a lower cost of living, so they could save money.

The work was hard and justified all of Ball's doubts. The rains were heavy that year and the road to the Grebo fell behind schedule – a problem we were used to. The equipment stood up to the job but spares were hard to come by because neither trucks nor caterpillars were standard. If we found them, we bought all we could and the stores were overloaded; this made control more difficult and also led to an inclination to replace a part rather than to repair it. This may sound trivial but the sentiment spread to other areas of activity and led to looser work discipline than we favoured. It was not easy to eradicate this, the more so as the Liberians originally employed by the Germans had adopted this attitude.

We came across much pilfering, more than we were used to, and had to introduce strict security measures which opened up a battle of wits not conducive to the *esprit de corps*. However, we pushed on and would soon be ready to build the bridge over the River Gi to lead us to the promised land.

I was invited to visit the iron ore mines at Nimba and spent a couple of days with Swedish friends. There was a whole mountain of non-magnetic ore a few centimetres below the surface – one could pick it up with one's hands. It extended into neighbouring Guinea, in those days politically in the wrong camp.

The Swedes and their American partners had built themselves a little village with modern houses and all conveniences and kept the place in ship-shape order. They had radio communications, entertainment, food stores, and most of them had brought out wives and children. The same was repeated at the port of Buchanan, down the railway line, which they had constructed to evacuate the ore and bring up supplies and equipment.

When we had completed the bridge over the River Gi, we invited the president to open it in November 1962 and he graciously accepted. I had suggested to a friend, Daldry, then head of Barclays Bank in Nigeria, that he come along and see if it would be interesting enough to re-open their branch which they had closed a few years ago. We flew into Robertsfield with a few days to spare before the grand ceremony.

On our way into town, two Liberian police cars, racing to catch the PanAm flight on which we had just arrived, hit us head-on in broad daylight. It was an absolute shambles. I managed to crawl out of the car and shouted to Daldry to do the same. I was afraid it would catch fire but it did not – just as well, since the third passenger, an American from the bank, had been knocked unconscious. The driver, too, was knocked unconscious; and he never recovered.

We were in the middle of a Firestone plantation, unable to move until some kind samaritan in a car stopped and said he would alert the Firestone first-aid post which was only a few miles away. The crash had been heard by some of the rubber tappers who gazed at us, picked out of the debris what they could easily carry, and ran off. Within an hour or so we were taken to the first-aid post which was in effect a minor hospital, well equipped, with an American doctor on duty. They diagnosed that I had broken my hip and damaged my spine, that Daldry had broken all his ribs and his chin, and said we were to rest for a few days before being evacuated to our homes abroad. The unconscious American had no broken bones or internal injuries and recovered the same evening.

My first visitor, within hours, was a gentleman from the bank with a document for me to sign that the bank, in whose car we had travelled, was in no way responsible for the accident. Now there is efficiency, I thought: catch them before they die or before they are bright enough again to know what they are doing. I did not oblige him. However, I got the bank to send cables to Lagos for Sandy to come and replace me at the ceremony, to our London brokers to let my wife know that I was alive though badly hurt, and to my brother to expect me in a few days' time and to ask if the could arrange to get me into a hospital.

A few days later I was shipped out to London via Paris on an Air France plane. I was given a pretty Dutch nurse to take care of me. The first trouble was that the stretcher was too wide and, as the bearers tried to tilt it to get into the aircraft, I fell off. Once inside, the stretcher was placed across a number of seats and we took off for Paris, via Dakar. The other passengers out of the kindness of their hearts came along to see their injured fellow traveller, which I though was very nice of them until I noticed that whilst they enquired after my health they looked down the blouse of my Dutch nurse, gazing at her ample and firm bosom.

It was cold in Paris, where I was transferred from Air France to British Airways on their own stretcher, and even colder in London, where I was met by the St John's Ambulance Brigade. A stern-looking woman said she was sorry to see me injured but that surely I was too old to go skiing if I was not proficient. 'We get too many like you.' Fortunately my brother appeared and I was carried off to hospital.

Rylke flew to Liberia post-haste and got there in time to greet the president, who cut the ribbon and the bridge over the River Gi was officially opened. It was a real achievement.

I was in hospital for over three months and never fully got over this nasty accident. The longer I lived, the worse the after-effects became.

Rylke decided to send out Ted Smith to take over as GM Liberia, and he took along his American wife. At the end of March 1963, I came back to the coast and set off for a quick trip to Liberia; the markets had taken a down turn and Maryland was not sticking to its budget.

In Monrovia I called on the bank and saw the insurance man who had asked me to sign his paper and half in jest said, 'I am going to sue your company for a million dollars.'

'Too late. The Liberian police have admitted liability. You

can sue them if you live long enough, the case will never get on the lists - not as long as Tubman is alive.'

'I will let my insurance company handle that,' I said, and later told Conway what I thought of them.

'Joe, if we can escape a claim we will naturally do so. It wasn't our driver's fault, was it?' (The bank were agents for the insurance company.)

Those four months sobered us up. We realized not only that we were financially stretched, but also that if anything happened to either of us the other was overloaded. We had to re-organize in a big way or cut our commitments. If the latter, what was to go?

It was Liberia that had to go. It was too far away, absorbing too much of our energy, too long-term a prospect, and, for ourselves, too limited in its potential gain. We advised our American friends of our intention to withdraw and said that we would help them to find another party if they wanted our assistance and that we would tell our staff that they could remain with the Maryland Logging Corporation if they preferred to do so.

They did find a Dutch concern to take over; once more staff drifted away as soon as they heard of the impending changes and the handover was not as clean as one would have liked to see it. Later a Canadian firm took over and built a plywood mill nearby. We knew the Dutch and met them occasionally but never had any contact with the Canadians. I do not know what happened to the company and the Grebo, but I hope our bridge still carries trucks to and from Cape Palmas.

We felt that the Americans thought we had let them down and whenever I had pangs of conscience I reminded myself of Conway and his insurance wisdom: if we can escape trouble we will naturally do so.

~   ~   ~

'The Land of Liberty.'

'Towards the end of the 18th century the American Colonization Society was formed in the USA with the object of

184

granting freedom to Negro slaves and giving them the chance of starting a new life in Africa.

'The place which was chosen for the settlement was the region on the west coast of Africa which our ancestors called the Grain Coast. Here the free Negro Republic of Liberia arose out of the colony which had come into being under the Society's protection.

'The first band of pioneers landed near Cape Masurado but the actual founder and leader of the Colony was not a Negro but the fair haired white American, Jehudi Ashman, who was sent out to rule the young settlement. Under his inspiring leadership the Colonists were able to hold their own against the natives who tried to obstruct the settlement of their brothers from America' ('Liberia', *Trade Industry and Travel*: Number 5, 1959).

'In 1923 the Firestone Tire and Rubber Company began an investigation of rubber-growing possibilities in Liberia and finding the environment favourable, obtained a concession of one million acres of land in 1926. At the same time, a loan of five million dollars was arranged through the Finance Corporation of America ... Administration of the customs and internal revenue was placed in the hands of a US financial adviser, assisted by five fiscal experts, with certain powers over the Liberian budget and expenditures.

'An investigation by the League of Nations of forced labour and slavery in Liberia, involving the shipment of natives to the Spanish plantations in Fernando Po, brought about the resignation of President Charles King and Vice-President Allen Yancy ...(1931)' *(Encyclopaedia Britannica*, 1967 edition).

'Cultural and economic factors have long separated the Americo Liberians from the indigenous peoples. In 1944 a National Unification Program was inaugurated to speed the assimilation of the indigenous populace into the rest of the community. All citizens have the vote, but the natives take little part in political life. Liberian politics have generally been characterized by the single True Whig party rule with strong executive control. The Reformation party (formed in 1951) and the Independent True Whig party (formed in 1954) were both banned by parliament in 1955' (*Ibid*)

Let it be noted that both of the opposition parties mentioned above were also formed by Americo-Liberians.

Unlike the colonization of North America, on which the freed slaves tried to pattern their future, immigration soon became merely a trickle. The natives not only remained the great majority of inhabitants, but also the proportion grew in their favour in the 20th century. In 1967 the population was given at 1.5 million; no breakdown between natives and Americo-Liberians is available. At an unreliable guess I would suggest nine to one.

William Tubman became president in 1943 and remained in power until his death in 1970. He had to perform a fine balancing act between the need to bring at least some of the natives into the mainstream of the political and economic life of Liberia because of the shortage of manpower and the absolute determination of the Americo-Liberians to retain their hegemony.

The policy failed under his successor, Tolbert, whose regime was overthrown in a bloody Army coup in 1980 led by Master Sergeant Doe, a native. Doe ruled for ten years and was in turn deposed in a bloody coup which led to the disintegration of the state, the aftermath of which, unresolved, is still with us.

There was nothing 'African' about the Americo-Liberians except their black colour. They were foreign conquerors and behaved as such. They did not even look like Africans. Their family names were anglicized: Barclay, Clancy, Tubman, Tolbert, O'Connor, King, Moore, Sherman, Hodge. The capital was named after an American President and the names of other towns had similar connotations.

This situation opens a small window on the nonsense of the whole colour question used by whites and blacks alike for political reasons. During our activities in Liberia in the early 1960s, I became acutely conscious of this. The natives, whatever their tribal differences stoked by the Americo-

Liberians, looked upon their 'masters' as foreigners, generally as hated foreigners. If they had any preference they preferred to work for the whites rather than their black overlords. But in so far as the whites more often than not co-operated with their oppressors, they had little love for either.

During 1969 I met a black American female officer working for USAID stationed in Buea in the Cameroon. She was in her early thirties, American in bearing, dress and speech. It was at the height of the racial unrest in the USA when Angela Davies was much in the news and black power often talked about.

On one of my visits she invited me to her chalet for a snack and a drink. We talked about the emancipation of blacks in the USA, the injustice she felt there had been and still was, and the prejudices against her colour. She said that she felt much more free and less inhibited in the Cameroon. 'Here I don't have to apologize for my existence; the problem doesn't exist. In America my colour is always with me, even within my organization, which is really quite fair in principle.'

'Here,' I pointed out, 'you are a black among black, true enough. You represent a major organization disposing of a lot of money and the power to bestow it. But here, too, among black people, there are prejudices, tribal hatreds and discrimination. You are a privileged black, but there are many under-privileged blacks. You'll find little democracy in black Africa and much abuse of power. Take Tubman in Liberia – his Americo-Liberians treat the natives as inferior – they just happen all to be black. Are you condoning Tubman's regime?'

No, she was not condoning Tubman, yet she felt it was different. She could not explain that difference.

'Religious or political persecution,' I intervened, 'can be halted, at the worst, by the persecuted going over to the religion or political opinion of the persecutor. But you can't change your colour or your origin. So it's racial persecution you must condemn. It's a tool of exploitation and Tubman rules through racial persecution. You should protest as loudly against him as against the Ku Klux Klan.'

We talked until the early hours of the morning and, although she agreed with me in principle, she would condone Tubman but not white racists. It was a sad testimony to human instinct. She was an educated young woman in a foreign country whose language she did not understand and whose people paid respect to her because she had power and education. Had she been white she would have had the same respect; there was no obvious colour prejudice in the Cameroon as there was in the USA, and, being black amongst blacks, she felt much more at ease. But that did not mean that the Cameroonians relying on her patronage felt at ease. I conceded her point on the evil of colour prejudice, but she would not concede my point that if you are persecuted it does not matter whether your persecutor is black or white.

The need was, and is, not for the so-called 'natives' to be integrated into Americo-Liberian society, but the other way round: it would lift the whole plateau of that country's existence.

16

Wind of Change

As a prelude to independence in Nigeria in October 1960, the colonial government had divided the country into three zones or states.

The Northern Region comprised most of the land mass. The north was dominated by the Hausa – a loose conglomerate of tribes generally speaking the same tongue and largely ruled on autocratic lines by Fulani Emirs. The Hausa were Muslim with a sprinkling of Christians and Animists in the southern parts of the Northern Region, the so-called Middle Belt.

The Western Region, west of the River Niger running north to about 250 kilometres, was mainly Yoruba. Its Eastern Provinces were inhabited by minority tribes who later split away from the West to form the Mid-West Region.

The Eastern Region, east of the River Niger and again running north to about 280 kilometres well south of the River Benue, was dominated by the Ibos but again contained various minority tribes.

This is a rough description and meant only as a general guide to what follows.

Each region was to have its own House of Assembly and government, for which elections were to be held - a trial run for the general elections before independence. Three major political parties had established themselves in the 1950s:

– The Northern People's Congress which had its roots in the ruling classes of the north and was led *de facto* by the Sardauna of Sokoto, a powerful figure of great influence killed later in the first military coup in 1965. The NPC was a Muslim party representing northern interests.

- The Action Group was led by Chief Awolowo, a young lawyer from the heartland of Yoruba country. He had a meteoric political career after returning to his country from studying abroad. The Action Group was looked upon as a Yoruba creation.
- The National Council for Nigeria and the Cameroons was dominated and had been founded by Dr. Azikiwe (Zik) who came from the Ibos, a man who had become a 'national' figure through his early advocacy of independence. The NCNC had its strong base in the east and was considered to be dominated by the Ibos.

There were also small parties of little consequence.

These parties all had overspills into each other's territory but remained firmly anchored to their base. Their social programmes differed little. There were undertones of 'socialism' in the Action Group, lip-service to attract a few young intellectuals. The prime objectives of these parties were to secure regional interests and to avoid domination by the other tribes, although each party had a foothold in all regions where minority tribes could be induced to vote against the majority.

Voting was universal for men and women. It had been decreed that voters must produce tax certificates to be eligible. This caused consternation. Nigerians, like all other people, were loth to pay taxes if they could avoid it, even if these were often nominal; a small farmer or artisan was asked merely to pay 'head tax' provided he could be roped in. To be fair, it was often difficult for the widely dispersed population to pay taxes even if they wanted to because the nearest tax office was miles away. The principal individual taxpayers were the civil servants and employees of large companies where tax was deducted from pay.

We had by then between 400 and 500 hands working for us in Ondo, part of the Western Region, all of whom had been given tax certificates as we were obliged to deduct tax. The labourers generally kept their tax certificates to be able to show them at road-blocks (it was a source of income for the police manning such road-blocks; they would ask for tax certificates and would demand money if these were not produced). These forest workers, almost all Ibos from the east, were dominated by their headmen who had recruited them for the company.

I was on tour in Ondo, some ten days before the elections, and went to our camp in Kajola where I was approached by the senior headman, Mathias, who asked me if I thought they could vote in the elections.

'Mathias, as far as I understand the procedures, any Nigerian can vote in any part of the country if he has a tax certificate. I don't know if you also have to be registered as a voter or whether the tax certificate acts as a voting paper.'

'We would like to vote if we can, but we don't know where to do it.'

'The *bale* will know. You had better ask him. Haven't you had any political canvassers here to ask you to vote for their candidate?'

'No, we have had nobody here.'

'How then do you know about the elections and who to vote for?'

'We know,' he said, 'we hear so from home and on my radio.'

'And do your men want to vote?'

'They will vote if I tell them. Can we have time off for the voting?'

Being a staunch believer in Western civilization and democracy, I had to reply in the affirmative. 'I will leave instructions with the manager that he should give you time off to go and vote. In fact, my friend, it is your duty to vote.'

There were within a radius of fifty miles several timber camps manned by Ibo labourers. Their numbers must have run into several thousand, a sizeable number in the constituency. It was surprising that so large a body of voters had been ignored by the parties and that nobody had turned up yet to solicit votes; but of course these men were not only far away from the centre of political activity, they were also considered to be, more or less, foreigners in Ondo, of little consequence. It probably never occurred to the organizers that here was an untapped source of votes.

I wondered if our men were really going to vote – it was quite a trek to the nearest booth – or whether clever Mathias had seized the opportunity to get a day off work. On the other hand, perhaps he had received a letter from home, or a message had been passed round the camps, to vote for the NCNC, which as good Ibos they would almost certainly do.

When I came back to Lagos I said to Sandy, 'I wonder if our Ondo friends are aware of what might happen. They are so sure of themselves that Ondo is a safe Action Group seat but if all these chaps vote against them they may have a fight on their hands.'

The elections came. They were in those early days fairly well conducted; it was a new experience run on British lines and still supervised by the district officers. All candidates in Ondo were Yorubas, no matter what party they represented, but those standing for parties other than Action Group were almost considered traitors.

The result was a bombshell. Ondo had elected an NCNC candidate! A Communist elected in the stockbroker belt of the Home Counties could have caused no greater sensation. The result was down to two causes: many natural supporters of the Action Group had no tax certificates for whatever reason; and word must have passed round the forestry and other camps that the Ibos with their compulsory tax certificates should go and vote for the NCNC. The NCNC candidate could hardly believe he had won. The good citizens of Ondo had their faith in Western democracy badly dented. The result had dire consequences for them.

The Action Group had won an easy overall majority in the Western House and Obafemi Awolowo became Premier. He cut off funds for Ondo projects like water works and electricity. He also engineered the exclusion of the Oba of Ondo from the Western House of Chiefs (a kind of House of Lords). In his place the Oba of Araromi was chosen to represent the constituency.

Araromi was a small town which had had no road to it at

all until we built ours through it to Ayesan. Although it later increased in importance as an agricultural centre, it was at the extremity of the constituency's boundary. Its Oba had been a forestry officer, a good man we knew quite well who much appreciated the fact that we had connected his village with the outside world. He was, however, a minor figure compared to the Oshemawe of Ondo, who felt the set-back keenly. He had been a good friend and we, too, were upset by his misfortune. Nor, I suppose, could it be said that the elections truly represented the will of the Ondo people, if one excluded the great mass of migrant workers from the East. But under the system they were entitled to vote and did.

Awolowo, however, made a mistake in punishing rather than wooing the town for electing the wrong candidate. The Ondo are a proud people. They were once great warriors. Their men are fine specimens of the human race, strong and well-built; their women are beautiful and intelligent. They had little love for the NCNC but when the government in Ibadan abused its power by depriving them of services to which they were entitled, they resented it, and supported their man in the House of Assembly. It was a mean trick to delay tap water and electricity for years longer than necessary and not much of an advertisement for elected government.

On 1 October 1960, as the rain fell, the British flag was hauled down and a newly designed Nigerian flag took its place. Federal and regional elections had been held after a constitution had been approved in lengthy discussions. A House of Assembly was established in Lagos, the federal capital, and others on a regional basis in Ibadan, Kaduna and Enugu. A new democracy was born. Tafawa Balewa, a Northerner representing the NPC which had secured most seats, was made prime minister.

There had been no signs in Nigeria of violent opposition to British rule, no terrorist activities, no large political bodies clamouring for an end to foreign rule. Independence was talked about in vague philosophical terms by some of the intelligentsia, a relatively limited number of people in itself; it was a subject of conversation in restricted circles among budding politicians who had been educated abroad.

Some businessmen thought about it and wondered how they would benefit. On the whole, however, the independence movement made no impact on the generality of the people; it was, in my opinion, non-existent to all practical purposes and had to be imposed from outside. To do so, and to do so in a hurry, was a major exercise cleverly executed against the opposition of many influential bodies in the country, especially in the north, which even then feared southern domination.

It may be said that British colonialism in West Africa collapsed in itself through the inability of the colonial power to maintain its hegemony in the aftermath of the convulsions of the times, accelerated by the exhaustion of World War II and the fear of the spread of Communism.

From its earliest days the USSR had seen the people of colonial territories as its natural allies in her fight against the West. The Soviet Union's part in the victory over Germany in 1945 meant that her prestige rose and she became in a minor way a focus for discontented African intellectuals. Little of this was evident in everyday life in Nigeria, but the intellectuals' cause was advanced by the colonial sentiment of calling all opposition and criticism 'Communist propaganda', an error of judgement only slowly corrected. Communism apart, the Soviet Union as a powerful political force became a magnet for opponents of the colonial powers, and her influence certainly increased. To counter the possible spread of Marxism and the more real risk of Soviet penetration must have been one of the considerations in the West's opting to relinquish her physical rule over the colonial empires. The economic and political conditions necessary to keep the newly independent African countries in the West's camp were rushed forward, often allowing undesirable elements to gain wealth and influence.

The ties that were to hold the country together were economic. It was believed or hoped that by creating a class of men and women whose self-interest would coincide within the context of a federation (however narrowly based that class, provided it encompassed members from all parts of the country), a strong nucleus would arise from which in time a new nation would be born.

That class expected to get its initial impetus from a common dislike of the foreign colonial master whose yoke was to be shaken off, a sentiment it fostered and trusted would carry it forward for a considerable timespan. In spite of this - almost in contradiction to this - the new ruling body relied on the full support of the old colonial power to sustain it should difficulties arise. The two sets of interests were seen to coincide. Had that not been so, independence would not have been achieved without a bloody struggle. As it was, the handover was peaceful and by mutual consent.

The plunge had to be taken, no matter what the doubts. Whether Whitehall foresaw the military coup which followed within a few years of handing over I cannot say, but they must surely have realized the risks which the inevitable scramble for domination and power would generate. It must have been felt that it was an acceptable risk, and that there was no viable alternative from the British point of view.

17

The Consul

I have made an appointment for you with the Minister of Defence, *Alhaji* Ribadu,' I said to the Swedish ambassador.

'What do you want me to talk to him about?'

'When I met the minister I pointed out that Sweden had organized the Air Force of Ethiopia, that she had long experience in Africa, was non-committed which must surely be important, that she had supported anti-colonialism in the UN at all times, that she had an up-to-date aircraft industry, and that I felt there may be much in common. I therefore thought that you should meet him as soon as possible, provided of course that this meets with your approval.'

The appointment was confirmed and the first Swedish ambassador met the minister.

The minister, as I understood the discussions, explained to the ambassador that Nigeria was about to form an air force and was looking for suitable co-operation and support. He had heard what the consul had said and was happy to meet the ambassador.

The ambassador did not share my optimism after meeting the minister. 'We don't really set out to arm these new countries,' he explained. 'We think they should use their sparse resources to build up their economy and infrastructure. Besides, this minister seemed to have unorthodox ideas on establishing such an air force which we could not meet in any way. However, I will report to Stockholm.'

I had thought that at the height of the Cold War, with

Nigeria wishing to keep a neutral stance, she would jump at the idea of working with the Swedes. It seemed that neither party was enthusiastic. My logic must have been at fault. A country might be grateful for another country's sympathy in the UN and other international bodies, but when it came to financial matters a different logic prevailed. So the Germans rather than the Swedes got the contract to establish the Nigerian Air Force, to be supplanted later by the Soviet Union.

I had been appointed honorary consul for Sweden in 1958. The Swedish Trade Commissioner for Africa, Rune Ulfsax, had called on me to ask if I would be willing to become his country's honorary consul in Lagos, and to say that if this were acceptable to me he would put my name forward. He knew that we had trade relations with Sweden; there were no suitable Swedes resident in Lagos and he explained that the duties of a consul were restricted to looking after Swedish commercial interests, to take care of Swedes in Nigeria who might need assistance, to register Swedish ships calling on Nigerian ports and similar affairs, and to keep Sweden in touch with what was going on in the country. Expenses would be reimbursed annually. Visas could be issued after reference to the consul-general in London who would be my immediate superior.

The previous consul had been Carl Rasmussen, resident in Lagos for many years and now retired; temporary consuls had been found whose appointment could not be confirmed for one reason or another. Sweden, he added, often appointed prominent foreigners as their honorary consuls if their own nationals were not available, a practice common in diplomatic circles.

I was flattered by the approach, thanked him, and said I would consult my wife and get back to him shortly. Pam was surprised, but did not see any reason to refuse. I accepted the appointment, which I held for over twenty-five years.

I had to fill in forms stating my background and so on, which were forwarded to the consul-general in London and the Utrikesdepartementet (Foreign Office) in Stockholm. Before the appointment could be confirmed, the consent of Her Majesty the Queen had to be obtained. Any British subject wishing to serve another nation in an official capacity could do so only with the consent of the Crown. This consent was asked for by Sweden and came to hand in due course, received under the signature of Her Majesty; a further parchment signed by His Majesty the King of Sweden was also received officially confirming the appointment, in each case counter-signed by the respective Ministers for Foreign Affairs. It was duly gazetted in Nigeria.

The seals of the consulate and voluminous correspondence and papers were handed over to me and my name was added to the list of foreign representatives accredited to the colonial administration in Nigeria. We were but a handful of career and non-career consuls in Nigeria dealing with commercial and personal problems as they arose. We enjoyed the protection of the Vienna Convention which lay down the duties and privileges of our position. We were under the jurisdiction of our countries' London embassies. Nigeria was part of the British Empire; London dealt with its problems and London delegated responsibilities.

My work as consul was never very onerous, much of it routine. I mailed periodic reports on economic and political developments. Occasionally a sailor would get into trouble and had to be bailed out and sent home. Once a ship ran aground which meant an official enquiry had to be instituted. Another time a Swedish woman was arrested in Douala, Cameroon, and I was asked to intervene; this fell geographically outside my competence and cables went forward and backward to give me the necessary authority to act. The good lady had slapped a *gendarme* who had detained her African lover in a police cell and there was quite a rumpus because in the end she refused to leave unless her man was also freed. My offer to send her home, on instructions, was turned down, penniless as she was. The more than generous Swedes eventually agreed to let her man sail to Sweden with her at public expense.

Following independence in October 1960, my appointment was re-confirmed directly from Stockholm, and a new parchment was received from Her Majesty the Queen of Britain and His Majesty the King of Sweden and once more published in the Nigerian gazette; I became a member of the Diplomatic Corps. A year or two later Sweden opened her own Embassy in Lagos and my duties were much reduced; I became answerable to the resident ambassador. My knowledge of the country, my contacts and experience helped to smooth the way for the establishment of the embassy. I met all the ambassadors and most of the junior staff and would walk in and out of the embassy as one of their own.

After independence, diplomatic missions accredited to the newly independent state were opened in the capital, Lagos. Slowly at first, then with increasing momentum, foreign countries sent their ambassadors to Lagos: Western Europe, Eastern Europe, North and South America, and the Far East, to be followed by other newly independent countries in Africa. All felt it necessary to be represented in Nigeria, the most populous African country.

To set up and maintain an embassy in Lagos was an expensive matter and some countries must have felt the cost keenly; a few only could expect to defray even a small percentage of the outlay by issuing visas and stamping the odd document. The initial rush caused great logistical problems. Embassy buildings had to be rented, bought or built, and the staff had to be suitably accommodated.

By the early 1980s, most diplomatic missions had their own premises and accommodation, often imposing buildings well taken care of. As I am writing this in the early 1990s, we know that before the decade is out all diplomatic missions will have to re-establish themselves in the new capital, Abuja, where plots are earmarked for them. Over one hundred embassies and the representative offices of international organizations like FAO, the World Bank, etc. are now established in Lagos.

To settle in, one had to procure essential services. Diplomatic privileges could be claimed and sometimes had to be insisted upon to overcome bureaucratic obstacles, inertia, or an eye for a quick buck. Local staff had to be recruited, although some embassies preferred to be staffed exclusively by their own nationals. To work for an embassy was very desirable as the pay was much better, there was prestige attached to the job, and one could hope to travel abroad. Men and women were selected by recommendation and the turnover initially was rapid.

I was involved in facilitating the opening of Sweden's embassy. Minor obstacles on a low level notwithstanding, the Ministry of External Affairs did its best to help when difficulties were encountered. Nigeria was anxious to be seen in a good light by the newcomers and it was an opportunity to cut loose from the apron strings of the old colonial masters. The new missions were well aware of this sentiment.

The social scene too changed dramatically. Under the colonial regime, the intellectual and artistic parameters had been set by a core of well-educated civil servants. Some of the commercials contributed, and slowly Nigerians educated abroad also swelled the numbers.

Into this restricted and well circumscribed pattern came a sudden influx of several hundred diplomats and their wives handpicked for the assignment of taking care of their countries' new interests: career diplomats, university graduates of high calibre, and senior members widely travelled and experienced in the ways of the world.

A new glamour descended on Lagos. It began with the Nigerian government's independence celebrations in 1960, which were attended by high-ranking ministers of the various nations soon to be represented in Lagos. Britain sent royalty.

The embassy receptions more than replaced the governor-general's garden parties. There were the receptions to celebrate the National Days of each country, and also those to honour visiting dignitaries or to introduce new ambassadors and say farewell to retiring ones. The scene was always interesting, sometimes fascinating, occasionally repetitive. The Nigerians themselves loved parties and were good at holding them. As they found their feet, embassies organized cultural events, bringing over renowned artists. Each country strove to put its best foot forward. The larger the mission, the more it could offer.

Officers who had earlier been posted to India, Pakistan, Indonesia or Brazil found their feet more quickly than those who had had little or no knowledge of the developing world (it was called 'underdeveloped world' in those days). The interest in the assignment to Lagos varied. Some found it challenging; some had a deep feeling for the underdeveloped world. Some took it as just another job that had to be done as well as possible. Some found the climate, lack of cultural life, and the many petty obstacles unpleasant and were happy to leave. With time some of the problems eased. There are now schools where diplomats can send their children, international telephones work better, the large diplomatic and foreign community has established a cultural life, and of course there is much going on in Nigeria with its many universities, its artistic life and its business community - plenty to keep one occupied.

Sweden had for many years been in the forefront of opposition to colonialism, apartheid and discrimination, and had a high reputation in Nigeria as a sincere friend of the black man striving for emancipation. The embassy staff reflected these sentiments. In no way did Sweden try to make capital out of her pro-African stance in the UN and other international bodies. On the contrary, I would say that advantage was taken of her liberal and positive approach and her help solicited with little thought of reciprocity. It took some years for this to filter through the corridors of the Foreign Office in Stockholm.

By contrast, countries like Brazil made much of reminding her hosts that offspring of Nigerian slaves in Bahia still remembered their language and customs and translated this into profitable business. If the Germans considered the negro the lowest form of humanity but fifteen years before Nigerian Independence, lower even than the Jews whom they accused of Negroid features when they wanted really to insult them, it did not deter the Nigerians from seeking close business contacts and vice versa.

Modern communications may have reduced the functions of embassies, but they can still play an important part in representing their country and advancing its interests. The impact depends on the personality and inclination of the office holder; this is certainly so in a country like Nigeria.

One of the Soviet ambassadors invited his colleagues to hunting trips near Oyo and was famous for his hospitality: caviar and Crimean champagne were the order of the day. I was friendly with one of the Finnish ambassadors, a melancholy figure, divorced and living alone. We spent many a night in his study talking. He would take the balalaika, play a sad melody, and sing. He had been in the army during the war and Lagos was his last post before retiring. He said he could find little to motivate him in Nigeria. He died on his way home in a Madrid Hotel – very sad. The Lebanese rented one of our houses. They had responsibilities for the thousands of their citizens living in Nigeria. The Argentinians also rented one of our houses. There were only a handful of their compatriots to be looked after.

The Commonwealth countries call their ambassadors 'high commissioners', though their rank is that of an ambassador. Of the British high commissioners I met over the fifteen years they were in Kajola House, Sir David Hunt stands out as the most flamboyant character. He had a powerful intellect, later proved when he became the winner of the BBC Mastermind contest.

Sir David had served in Nigeria before in a junior capacity and came back just as the Civil War was raging in full force. He knew I travelled much in the country and would call me down from time to time to hear what I had to say.

Such meetings with senior diplomats had a less attractive side. When it suited them they would quote your opinions mentioning the source, especially when it was an item of news they did not care to come out of their own mouths but wanted to relay.

One of the less happy British high commissioners was Sir Martin Le Quesne, whose recall was insisted upon because the failed coup leader, Dimka, went to the high commission, revolver in hand, asking to be put in touch with General Gowon, the deposed dictator, which triggered off demonstrations against Britain and windows were smashed. Le Quesne's prompt demand for an apology and material compensation before Dimka's victim, General Murtala Mohammed, was cold in his grave was considered to be unfriendly and soured relations between Britain and Nigeria.

One of the Czechoslovak ambassadors stayed in Lagos for over ten years. He became doyen of the Diplomatic Corps for a long time. As such it fell to him to give receptions for all departing ambassadors, at which he made the customary speech and handed over a gift. The speech was always the same and so was the gift from his colleagues to the departing officer – a silver salver appropriately engraved. His long tenure was quite exceptional.

I remember one amusing incident. The chief of protocol organized a farewell dinner party for an ambassador posted out. After some delay the guests were seated at the tables laid out for them yet still dinner was not served. 'What are we waiting for?' asked the ambassador sitting next to the chief of protocol.

'Why, we are waiting for the ambassador.'

'Sir, you have been sitting next to him for the last twenty minutes.' The chief, in his embarrassment, roared with laughter and apologized.

The Italians gave memorable musical evenings in their splendid building, which had a large concert room most elegantly furnished. I was invited to dinner once by the ambassador, whose mother had come to visit him. We got talking to each other and she told me that her father had served as a diplomat in Ethiopia, or Abyssinia as it was then called.

'Madam,' I said, 'you must have known my father-in-law, Plowman, in Ethiopia or Somalia.' Indeed she remembered him. He was then a British diplomat. I had heard of the lady; she was English and as a young girl had fallen in love with the Italian military attaché. Her parents disapproved and sent her home, but the romance persisted and they married. Now one of her sons was Italian ambassador to Nigeria.

A more recent event worth mentioning was the party given by the German embassy to celebrate the reunification of their country. On arrival we lined up in the usual way to shake hands with our host. When it was my turn to congratulate the ambassador on the happy event, he said to me in German, 'Mr. Brandler, I did not think I would live to see the day and neither did you, did you?' I concurred. I had expected the Germans attending to be full of themselves and boastful, but the event was dignified and there was no sign of arrogance or triumph. Rather they seemed thankful it had come to pass and anxious as to how it would work out. At that reception I joined a small group of Nigerians celebrating and saying how wonderful it was to see Germany reunited. It was something they felt they had to say. I allowed myself to mention that my grandfather had also attended a party to celebrate German unification and I wondered if one of my grandsons would do the same. They looked at me in bewilderment and thought I was not all there.

'When was that?' one of them asked.

'In 1871,' I informed him.

'What happened in 1871?' he asked.

'Germany was united,' I replied. He shook his head until one of the party remembered that he had read of it at school when learning about the Franco–Prussian war.

In 1990, at the annual reception given at the embassy of the USSR to celebrate the October Revolution, I became aware of the undertones of unrest in the various republics making up the Soviet Union. This reception was well attended by most of the ambassadors, all probably noting the curious atmosphere. The East Europeans were reticent and seemed unsettled.

Pickering, the one-time Ambassador of the USA, became prominent as American Ambassador to the UN and was much in the news during the conflict with Iraq in 1991.

I met many Nigerian ambassadors, initially seldom career officers as the service was in its infancy. They were a varied collection – retired generals, politicians, businessmen – well selected and quick to learn the ropes, impressive in their native gowns which they wore on most occasions. One of their outstanding men was a career officer who served in Liberia, Sweden, France, and latterly Great Britain, where he was sent to improve relations which, as already mentioned, had turned sour and were yet to be fully repaired – Dove-Edwin.

I knew, of course, all the Swedish ambassadors, who were professionals: no retired generals, admirals or businessmen amongst them. A few took Swedish restraint to extremes, as when I saw one waiting in the crowd to meet his children at the airport. He did not want to abuse his diplomatic status by requesting to be let into the customs hall to ease immigration control and save his children the bother of queueing up. That would not impress any Nigerian.

I spent many a long evening with Lars Stalberg, the First Secretary to the Embassy and at times Chargé d'Affaires. One evening, towards the end of 1965, as we sat talking, I said to Lars, 'Quite off the record and on no account to be reported to Stockholm in your despatches, I think we are going to see an Army coup here very soon.'

'What makes you say that?'

'I can't put my finger on it, Lars; let's say it's a hunch. A whisper here, an odd remark there, students' agitation, rash newspaper articles – it just seems to me it may happen soon. But I have nothing concrete to go on so you must forget it for now and don't make us look foolish in the Stockholm ministry.'

Lars knew where his duty lay: he did report the conversation. It was feather in my cap. 'We knew of it', they could say in the Foreign Office in Stockholm.

What a civilized people the Swedes are. Liberal, disciplined, with a great sense of responsibility, orderly and hard working, proud of their achievements without belittling those of others. Their concern for the underprivileged, their sense of fair play and common decency did on occasion make them fall for deceit and simulation, but they took it in good grace and learnt their lesson. In Sweden, of course, there are also prisons holding pickpockets, thieves and murderers, offenders against the accepted social order – one knows that. On balance, however, the country has built a way of life in the 20th century which if repeated in all other countries would make humanity less vicious, more orderly, perhaps duller, but certainly nearer the ideals of democracy so often protested and so rarely practised. I did not understand much Swedish and spoke less; it did not matter. I did my best and they rewarded me with high honours.

18

The Americans Take Over

The progress of the Cross River operations remained disappointing. Yet there were vast stands of ilomba *(Pycnanthus combo)*, especially in the northern part of the forests, a wood similar to the South American virola which was used extensively in the USA for the production of plywood. As log export it could be sold from time to time to Italy but not in great quantities, and it had the disadvantage that it split very easily (in the Cameroon the villagers cut the tree lengthwise with an axe quite easily and make planks for house-building – they call it 'carraboard').

The Rockefeller Brothers Fund were looking for viable projects in West Africa to promote industry utilizing a country's raw materials. I knew Bob Fleming, who was in charge, and one day late in 1963 mentioned our Cross River problem.

'What do you think we could do?' he asked.

'You could organize and fund a feasibility study to set up a veneer mill near our sawmill installation. We have an established logging operation which could be extended and the product, using the large ilomba stands in the main, could be exported to the USA and other markets.'

'Can you let me have a memorandum on this setting out your ideas?'

'I will, but it may take some time.'

Three months later, I submitted the requested paper. I included in my study the availability of areas not then under our licence, much further north and almost reaching the border of the Cameroon, where extraction would be physically isolated and seasonal; the logs would have to be floated to Obubra on the Cross River. But the stands in the north were rich in ilomba and logging would be inexpensive.

Bob read the report. 'Interesting,' he said, 'something we have been looking for. I'm not a timber man and we would have to get experts out from the USA.'

I invited him to Obubra and we took him round. He met Efiom Okon, now the Chief Conservator of Forests, who was stationed in Enugu. Okon was enthusiastic at the prospect of extending forest operations in his region and Bob took good note of the chief conservator's point. 'You can have 1,000 square miles of forest if you will establish a veneer and plywood mill and increase the sawmilling operation. At an eighty-year rotation that will give you 12.5 square miles per annum, not to mention the free areas which lie between the reserves.'

Back in Lagos, Fleming prepared a memorandum for his HQ which he showed me for comment before sending it off.

After many weeks he asked me to call on him. 'We are going ahead with a feasibility study on your project. New York have commissioned one Zaug to head it, and will be sending out a forest expert, Dr. Bruce Lamb, to evaluate the stands of trees, the terrain, labour conditions, and so on. He will be with us within a month. Dr. Lamb is well experienced in tropical forestry, though his field so far as been Central and South America and the Far East.'

Bruce Lamb arrived in the second quarter of 1964 and walked the forests, talked to government bodies, and looked at roads and rivers.

He then sat down with us. 'My report will be positive, advocating a step-by-step development. You have a going concern which can be enlarged without having to spend millions on a green-field start-up.'

He explained that the large ilomba stands would form the basis of a core veneer operation. A mill would be erected next to our sawmill which could produce 500 M3 core veneer monthly and should generate enough funds within three to five years to be converted into a plywood mill. The snag was the large volume of species unsuitable for veneer and plywood which would have to be sawn and sold mainly on the local market.

'You need not accept the areas which hold little or no ilomba, but get an option on them. I'll report to Zaug, and the Foundation will print a brochure and circulate it to parties in the USA which we think would be interested.' And he went home. 'You should hear something in three or four months,' was his parting shot.

About a fortnight later, we got a long cable from Carl Wheeler, senior vice-president of the New York-based US Plywood Corporation, inviting us to come for discussions.

'That was quick,' Sandy said. 'Indeed,' I echoed, and phoned Bob in his Lagos office.

'Wonderful,' he said, 'Zaug and Lamb must have been impressed. I suppose they talked to some of their friends in the industry.'

I set off to New York alerting our American agent, Randy Valensi. Randy met me at the airport and put me up at the Plaza Hotel, one of the most expensive in town. I protested at the extravagance.

'USP is one of the largest companies in the country,' he retorted. 'You will be talking to senior executives and they like to think they deal with big men.'

'We are big,' I countered, 'but we don't have to impress.'

'You do have to put up a show when dealing with these people. I've made an appointment for tomorrow morning and will come along with you.'

He collected me from the hotel and we went to 777 Third Avenue, the HQ of USP. They occupied many floors of a large skyscraper and we were shown to the executive suite – very plush, but businesslike. We met Carl Wheeler. He had been in charge of their Congo operations which had been very successful.

Wheeler told us that he had been fortunate to see a draft of the Zaug notes and that they were interested in talking to us. 'Where are you staying?' he asked.

Above: The author (front row, second from left) with a platoon of 2421
Company of the Royal West African Frontier Force at Helwan, Egypt,
1945. *Below:* Chief Seriki Fawehinmi, our first important timber
contractor in Ondo, Kajola Village, 1948.

In the 1940s, before the Nigerian timber industry was fully mechanized, logs had to be felled with axes (above left) and hauled through the forest to the river bank by teams of loggers (below left). The logs were then manhandled into the water (above right) and linked together into huge rafts (the one below right is on the Cross River), which were floated downriver to the port.

By the 1960s mechanization was well under way, continuing and gathering pace into the 1970s. Caterpillar tractors, like the one shown above crossing a river in Cameroon in 1961, came into use.

The forests were opened up by logging roads, and with the roads came frontloaders (above) to speed up the movement of logs. Power saws could handle even the largest trees. The cottonwood shown below, felled in 1971, had a diameter of over 100 inches and was too large for the company's sawmills.

Rufus Adesokeji Aderele, Oshemawe of Ondo, in full regalia, 1951.
The Oshemawe was one of the first people with whom Brandler &
Rylke negotiated tree-felling agreements.

Above: A large canoe loaded with petrol drums on Lagos foreshore ready to leave for Ayesan, 1949. Left to right: the author, Twig Branchflower from London, Beachmaster Law Cheke and Sandy Rylke. *Below:* Bridge-building on the River Gi, Liberia, 1962.

Above: Brandler & Rylke's offices, 62 (on the right) in the Brazilian style and 64 Campbell Street, Lagos, 1950. *Right:* By 1956 those offices had been replaced by a dashing new building, Kajola House, 62/64 Campbell Street, *Below:* A function held in Kajola House in 1956 with, left to right, unknown, Lady Bank-Anthony, Pam, Mrs Limoke Balogun and Mrs Oyeronke Lucas.

Above: Calabar Veneer & Plywood Ltd, 1966. Construction nears completion.

Right: The house in Ikoyi, about 1962. Left to right: Dan Daura, the horseboy from the Polo Club, David, Andrew, Penelope, Theresa, our Nanny, and Marcus. Robert came later.

obbett's party at the Savoy Hotel, London, 1954. With the author is
r Nnamdi Azikiwe, who in 1963 became Nigeria's first President.

Above: The directors of Brandler & Rylke Ltd after a board meeting, about 1960. Left to right: Sir Mobolaji Bank-Anthony, the author and Sandy Rylke. *Below:* An Embassy reception, Lagos, about 1962. Left to right: Dr Okpara, the author, Dr Nnamdi Azikiwe, the Israeli Ambassador, Chief Awolowo and Mr Nwachukwu, the Minister of Education.

Above: Colonel Odemegwu Ojukwu, Governor of the Eastern Region, inspecting timber at the Obubra sawmill, 1966. The following year the colonel announced the secession of the Eastern Region and its independence as the Republic of Biafra. *Below:* The author with General Yakubu 'Jack' Gowon, head of Nigeria's military government, at the Lagos Polo Tournament, 1971. General Gowon's forces defeated those of Biafra in the 1967–70 civil war.

The author with two Nigerian heads of state, President Shehu Shagari (above), Lagos, 1981; and President Ibrahim Babangida (below) at Dodan Barracks, 1990.

'Enang', a Calabar beauty, 1972.

The changing face of Lagos Marina business centre: the West African Drug Co Ltd's office, standing proud in 1954 (above) is dwarfed by skyscrapers in 1986 (below); these photographs are reproduced by permission of John and Jill Godwin.

'The Plaza.'

'Fine. I will come and we can have a drink at lunchtime. Perhaps Mr. Valensi will excuse you.' We took our leave.

Randy was put out. 'He wants to get you on your own. He thinks you are some innocent from darkest Africa he can run rings around. Don't be taken in, keep me informed day by day what's going on.'

I was embarrassed. We trusted Randy and counted on his advice, and I thought it was rather rude of Wheeler to try and shut him out *ab initio*. 'We will do nothing without you, Randy.'

Wheeler turned up at the Plaza. He apologized for having asked Randy to keep away. 'We know Mr. Valensi and respect him, but he works for a number of producers in various countries. You can tell him what you wish, of course. I suppose you've heard of us?'

'Indeed I have.'

Over lunch, Wheeler explained that both Zaug and Lamb had been consultants to USP for many years and that USP valued their opinions. Lamb had taken a very positive view on the chances of success from a technical point of view but they knew little about Nigeria. 'We have asked our Lagos embassy to give us a run down on the country,' he added, 'and we wanted to meet you personally.'

'We have not seen the Zaug report yet ourselves,' I pointed out.

'You wouldn't,' he laughed, 'it hasn't been printed yet. We are lucky to have advance information from our friends.'

He outlined the set-up of USP. Their turnover was the third largest in the industry and they had many plywood mills. They owned vast forest resources in the USA, and were operating also in Canada, Peru and the Philippines. He would have to sell the idea of going to Nigeria to his board, which was divided on extending operations overseas. 'They fear the politics of the developing countries. We are having a lot of trouble in the Philippines with civil disorders, armed bands and corruption. You will meet our president, the lawyers, and the financial vice-president.'

209

I gave him a run down of the social, economic and political situation in Nigeria as I saw it. I suggested that either the federal or the regional government should be invited to come in as partners (he did not like that – they preferred private investment); that the country was as stable as could be expected; that independence had come without bloodshed; that there was no discrimination against foreign investment; that we lacked finance and know-how for a veneer/plywood operation, but that if ilomba stayed in demand and we followed Lamb's ideas of gradual growth over a five-year period, the risks should be minimized.

'The veneer mill will have to carry the sawmill operations for some time because there are many heavy trees of relatively unknown species which are difficult to market overseas. The local market is very conservative, buying mainly the species they traditionally use, like iroko. However, we're only at the beginning of development and shall have to educate the market that they cannot build only in iroko.'

It was arranged that I turn up early next morning and we would get down to the nitty-gritty.

I reported back to Randy. 'You know,' he warned me, 'there's a lot of politics in these large corporations. One vice-president has only to suggest something for another to oppose it. But they're big people and wouldn't have asked you to come had they not been interested in principle. You must understand that they have people coming from all over the world with propositions. Your position is stronger – they came to you, they have a report from people they trust; you should be able to make a good deal. But watch out – these large corporations are tigers; they'll eat you if they can. Remember, personalities in these companies change, sometimes rapidly. You're not talking to Wheeler, you're talking to USP.'

I spent four more days in New York. I met the president, an ex-general – a pompous and overbearing man; I met the legal and financial vice-presidents, impressive and quick off the mark; I met some of the marketing people, suave, well dressed and knowledgeable. All talked about Africa and about risks, and how USP could do with extra supplies and could also do without.

I answered many questions and on two evenings was left behind with the legal vice-president's secretary to put into writing what I had told them. She was pleasant and very helpful in giving me tips on the personalities involved. In the end we raided her boss's bar – it must have been almost 10 p.m. – and had a few drinks. 'Send his wife some flowers,' she suggested, 'she'll like that. She took a shine to you when they invited you out to dinner. Would you like me to come to Nigeria?' she asked laughingly.

'You bet.'

I handed the memorandum over to Wheeler. 'A good paper,' he said.

'I have to thank your colleague's secretary.'

He circulated the paper and we had a final meeting. 'We're interested and we'll send out a man to have a look. He's not on our payroll but I've had my eye on him for some time and he would be made the GM were we to proceed. To recruit staff for Africa will be one of our problems.'

He then called for his candidate. His name was Dirk Deboer. He was in his late thirties, a very American-looking chap who had already read not only the Zaug notes and my notes, but had also read up on Nigeria. He had worked for timber companies in South America and the USA. He was very sure of himself.

'Why don't you fellows go out for lunch and make arrangements for Dirk to visit Nigeria as soon as possible?' Wheeler suggested.

We fixed a date a few weeks ahead, which would give me time to alert the Nigerian end and for Deboer to get his inoculations, visa, etc. This visit got off to a bad start when Deboer had difficulties in getting his visa; the consulate prevaricated. 'Worse than South America,' he said. In the end they demanded that he come there in person 'Did they want a tip?' he wondered. 'Not from me,' he said, 'not from me.'

Deboer arrived. We gave him all facilities and introduced him to Okon and others. He spent four weeks looking at everything, walking through the forests, talking to people, visiting the US embassy, and was generally very active. By the

211

time he had finished he felt he knew more about the country than we did.

He turned down Lamb's idea of siting a veneer mill next to the sawmill in Obubra. Encouraged perhaps by Okon, he said that such a project was too small for a company like USP. 'There are 1,000 square miles and we can build a large veneer mill – later to be extended into a plywood mill – in Calabar and add a large sawmill by its side to produce at least 1,000 M3 of veneer and 1,500 M3 of lumber monthly, on a single shift. You can double that if you work another shift,' he exclaimed vigorously. 'In Calabar we have a port and a large local market and labour. I am going to get out some projections to put before the board.' And off he went back to New York.

Volumes of projections followed. Visits to and from the USA were arranged. Lawyers and accountants appeared and disappeared. The project grew to include a turbine power house with a capacity of 3,000 kw. The preliminary expenses must have cost almost as much as Lamb's modest initial scheme.

'Find us a suitable site,' was the next cry.

We scouted around, assisted by one of our staff, Hogan, who was a native of Calabar. Several possible plots were suggested on creeks leading to the Calabar River. I reminded Hogan that we had once travelled by canoe up river and noticed a promontory which might be suitable.

This land was close to the fishing village of Esuk Utan on the Calabar River, an outpost of a larger village, Ikot Ansa, on the road north from Calabar, about six miles outside town. We had to walk three or four miles from Ikot Ansa to Esuk Utan which took us through cassava farms and shrub land. Only a footpath connected the two. On closer inspection it seemed the ideal location.

Our tug, *Nina*, took soundings and traced a wide channel to a depth of thirty feet all the way from the sea to Esuk Utan. It meant that ocean-going vessels could anchor in the river opposite the proposed mill site – the entrance bar to Calabar from the sea was twenty-seven feet.

We talked with the *Ntoe* (chief) of Ikot Ansa and asked if he would let out 300 acres for an industrial complex. He consulted his chiefs and townspeople. Meetings were held; the Americans came over and approved the site. As the financing had not yet been completed, Wheeler asked us to get an option on the place for six months.

Ikot Ansa made conditions. In particular they insisted that we employ a percentage of their men when recruiting; that we pay five years' rent in advance; and that we give their traders an opportunity to buy the products on favourable conditions. They could see their village taking off.

Then a snag appeared. Esuk Utan said that the land was theirs to dispose of, not Ikot Ansa's. We were perplexed; we consulted the local lawyers and chiefs. It transpired that Esuk Utan were 'customary tenants' of Ikot Ansa, with all that this implied.

'You must sort it out between you,' we said. 'If the scheme comes off, we can pay into an escrow account until you have settled. Or we go to another site.' We contacted a Chief Bassey about one of the alternative plots. The news got around quickly and the two communities settled.

Years later the land around these two villages became the industrial centre of Calabar. Our lease was reduced to thirty acres when the land was requisitioned to build the new port of Calabar. We really pioneered this development: Calabar was to have extended south towards Parrot Island, instead it went north to Ikot Ansa and Esuk Utan. Fortunes were made over land deals.

Protracted financial negotiations then began. Such was the reputation of USP that financial institutions queued up to get in on the act, be it as shareholders, debenture holders, or simple lenders. Eventually a complicated packet was agreed on. USP were to hold 51 per cent of the shares, Eastern Region 25 per cent, B & R 9 per cent, Chase Bank, NIDB and a local development agency 5 per cent each. In addition the banks would give out loans against debentures.

This was followed by discussions with many government bodies for approvals, permissions, and so on. If I remember correctly, there were some eighteen different documents to be agreed on: forestry agreements, foreign exchange approvals, immigration permits, business permits, etc. One sensed a sign of unease on the part of USP for having let themselves in for all that. B & R were to be paid for their assets on book values, to stay with the new company for a minimum of five years, and to divest themselves of all other timber interests in Nigeria – preferably in other West African territories as well.

We looked at the volumes of financial projections and compared them with the slim outlines of a technical nature. It was our first excursion into high finance and we did not like it much. It was not our style. However, we had had a rough eighteen months. We too saw good prospects in running an operation holding 1,000 square miles of reserves, and politically we felt a large set-up would be able to face any crisis should it occur.

Deboer's plan was accepted; several million dollars were raised. Papers were finally signed early in November 1965. An impressive ceremony was held and speeches made. Technical plans were approved, consultants were appointed, American staff were recruited, Deboer ordered the machinery. He decided to build with direct labour under his supervision guided by the consultants.

Eighteen Americans arrived, twelve of whom were construction hands. A few were accompanied by their wives. All had to be accommodated; all had extravagant ideas on comfort and facilities. They were quartered in apartments and houses in the town – a minor boom for the local property owners. Rents doubled overnight. They brought their washing machines and other modern household gadgets not then in common use in Calabar. All had to have air conditioning. It was quite an excercise to get them settled in.

They were highly skilled, middle-ranking technicians, typically American. Most came from Oregon, where they had worked for USP; some came from Tennessee. With one or two exceptions they had not worked abroad before.

They took well to working with the Nigerians; such prejudices as they had were against all non-Americans. Their work morale was admirable. They had come to do a job and

214

there was to be no messing about. A timetable had been laid down and as far as they were concerned they would see to it that it was adhered to. If in the end they did not quite make it, the fault lay outside their responsibilities. Any suggestions one made to forward the work were brushed aside. Theirs was the American small town mentality with all its faults and virtues. 'We are going to do it our own way and we know what to do.'

In spite of the heat, the strange conditions and the unskilled help, they got on with the job. They were good at leading their men and training those who showed aptitude and willingness to learn. But they came from God's own country and felt superior to everyone else.

Whatever racial prejudices they may have had at home vanished completely. They fraternized with the locals and nobody took offence. But they were hard taskmasters, and that did not go down too well. 'We come on time and so must you. We don't hang about on the job and neither must you. We have shown you what to do, we shouldn't have to tell you twice. We don't knock off in the evenings half-way through a delicate technical operation and neither must you. If you fail once, you get a severe reprimand. If you fail again, you're fired.'

To the Nigerians a machine was there to be used when needed. If it was not needed today, it would be tomorrow. Our Americans took a very dim view of their attitude. To them an idle machine was an abomination: the machine was something almost holy and its abuse or lack of employment akin to blasphemy. A machine represented money, other peoples labour made available to us at great cost. 'We must make the best possible use of it and not waste it.' This worship of their tools, the care they took over them, the love with which they handled them, could not really be understood by the Nigerians. They did not live for their work; there were other more important aspirations to be taken care of, which should be given preference. If the pay was good, better than anywhere else and often unexpected, it still could not compensate. This applied in particular to the local inhabitants intimately bound up with the customs of Calabar.

215

The Efik and Qua tribes made up the population. They were easy-going people with strong social ties and customs, and proud of their past. Ceremonies and functions were numerous, with both men and women dressed in colourful gowns. These gatherings were taken very seriously, to the detriment of continuity in daily routine.

Life was enjoyable; the tempo was less urgent, and the people hospitable, artistic and culturally active. The women had a charm all of their own, famous for their challenging feminine allure and the skill and subtlety with which they took care of their men. It was said in the Nigerian forces that if a man was posted to Calabar his wife might well lose him. Their work ethic, however, left much to be desired; the very attributes which made the Calabars so attractive mitigated against disciplined hard work. One cannot have it all. What did it matter if completing a shift or getting out production schedules had to wait for a colourful parade through the streets? Well, it mattered to us; the money had to come from somewhere and if you did not work you would not get paid. Priorities did not always coincide. A balance had to be struck between this clash of cultures.

They are a breed all of their own, these Calabars; studious and enterprising, but easily disheartened and fond of cutting corners without knowing what may meet them at the other end. Affectionate and friendly, cliquish even by Nigerian standards, inclined to let their women earn the bread (who counter by marrying out of their tribe more than others), they still dream of the times when Calabar was a premier city on the coast in days gone by, without doing much to recover their lost glory. One day perhaps they will wake up.

The Ibos, who came from further afield, took to the routine more easily. They were strangers who had come to make money and then go home again; they had always been used to hard work. Their fellow Nigerians did not like them much for that; inevitably the Americans soon realized that they could rely on their relative efficiency and attention to the task given them. It led to a split in the labour force which the Americans would not accept. The best man for the job was

216

their philosophy: 'We don't care where they come from.'

The locals resented it. 'This is our town, our forest. We have invited the Company to come here and our men and women must come first.' It was sometimes a delicate situation, which our American friends left to us to sort out.

We did so mainly by seeing to it that Calabar men filled the administrative posts, to which they were well suited. We impressed on all the locals that, however important their social functions might be, they must adapt to the new environment. It worked after a fashion. All were conscious of the opportunities the new venture opened up for themselves and for the community as a whole, though they found it difficult to equate those opportunities with their customs. They also did not want to know that the Americans had come in their own interests, and that looking after these interests was their first priority.

To return to our Americans. One could understand how their country had become big and powerful by their attitude to work, underpinned by the constant stream of new immigrants offering willing and cheap labour. They got on well with each other, they were polite, and in their way considerate as long as one did one's work. We had one elderly man called out of retirement to install the sawmill who was a most pleasant and knowledgeable individual. He was about from morning to night supervising, encouraging, and giving a helping hand. On retirement he had opened a small motel in a little town in Tennessee, run in his absence by his wife, which was to be taken over by his only son on his return from military service in Vietnam. He talked a lot of him and how he had bought a new car for the boy who was to return home within a few weeks. Alas, he was killed in action and it fell to me to acquaint him of this sad fact when the US Embassy in Lagos forwarded the news to us in an official communication. It shattered him: 'What are we doing there? Why should our boys be killed in that faraway land?' The shadow of that cruel war fell even over our Calabar venture. He went back to the States. We exchanged Christmas greetings, but he died soon afterwards.

Despite America's reputation for being the world's most efficient industrial nation, however, this particular enterprise was not too well conceived. Deboer was not a construction engineer; he had never built a veneer mill. The consultants were strangers to Nigeria, yet were supposed to issue contracts for the complicated installations.

The money and time budgets could not quite be met and there was an overrun on costs. But an impressive complex rose where there had been nothing but cassava farms, and a fine road was built from Ikot Ansa to Esuk Utan. The veneer mill and the sawmill were the second largest in Nigeria and the power-house for the mills of a high technical standard. We had hoped to go into production by the end of 1966, but could do so only five months later, by which time disaster had struck on the political front.

The Eastern Region was at loggerheads with the rest of the federation and civil war loomed large. We got away one shipment of core veneer when the federal government decreed a blockade of the ports of Calabar and Port Harcourt in the second quarter of 1967.

19

Civil War: the tragedy unfolds

The German Nazi Minister for Propaganda, Joseph Goebbels, coined the phrase: 'The greater the lie, the more likely that it will be believed'. The theory was not new but it had never been acted upon with the efficiency he brought to the task. He had many pupils.

Then we have the fog of war. Even those at the helm of affairs do not always know what is going on in their country on a given day or week. Communications can be difficult and interrupted, opinions can be divided on facts. This or that national or international faction interprets events as it suits them or their reporters. Rumours abound. In this atmosphere, the unwary will believe what they prefer to believe, out of a sense of loyalty, out of panic, out of self-interest. However neutral and uncommitted an individual, and however experienced, these factors and others of a more personal nature must all intrude on the judgement he or she forms at a given moment.

Sometimes, after months, years, decades, one can look back and re-evaluate a situation. The lies have been unmasked or are no longer relevant. The fog of war has lifted; opinions then held become remote. Neutrality has turned to indifference. Hindsight can be mistaken for fact. In any case, historical appreciations change and change again. There can be no absolute truth embracing all that went before.

In my report to the Swedish Foreign Office upon independence, I wrote that I thought that the federation would hold together. At the same time I drew attention to the differences between North and South which would have to be balanced by give and take from both sides; I thought this was possible. In this, I reflected the approach Sandy and I took to the prevailing situation: positive, with reservations. We also had faith in the leaders' repeated assurances that foreign investment was welcome and would be protected; we propagated these views among our overseas friends.

Our business interests were widely spread between the west and the east of the country and in the southern Cameroon. The north was almost a closed book to us. I had taken one or two trips there in the course of my duties as Swedish Consul and spent a pleasant holiday in the Jos-Bauchi region. There had never been a sustained effort to establish business in the north because there were few forests there. We had met northerners in the corridors of ministries we had dealings with and among our polo-playing friends. We knew the horseboys in the Polo Club, who were all northerners, a decent lot and without any pretensions. This gave us a glimpse of the northern mentality, and we liked what we saw, but it was on a very personal level. We got a whiff of the distrust between these horseboys and the Lagosians, but it was no more than that. In any case, these jealousies and suspicions also existed among Southerners.

We had no hesitation, therefore, in going ahead with negotiations with the huge US Plywood Corporation to join us in an important industrial development in Calabar. In every presentation to the directors in New York, and to their bankers and accountants, I was asked about the political stability of the country. Without ignoring the possibility of conflicts, I always affirmed my belief that nothing would happen to bring the investment in jeopardy and was always more concerned with the practical and technical problems facing the project.

Those favouring the Calabar venture had to lean heavily on me to overcome opposition from those of their colleagues who opposed any move into black Africa as too hazardous no matter what the possible advantages. The vote eventually went in favour because of the availability of large stands of timber assured the company by the government, and, if I may so, our presentation of the case for Nigerian continuity. Had we not believed in it, we pointed out, we would have packed up by the end of 1960. Self-interest played its part. We were anxious for USP to join us; we were prepared to share the inevitable business risks. In any case, we thought these risks acceptable.

It took less than three years for us 'Old Coasters' to be proved wrong and the sceptics right. It might be asked why two men who had witnessed so many wars, revolutions, upheavals and commotions in Europe, Asia and South America should have thought that Nigeria would be immune. Was the wish father to the thought?

At the time, we felt that the economy of the country was fairly well balanced, that there was little to fight over, and that for many years Nigerians would be busy creating wealth over which they might possibly dispute later. It was the development of the oil industry, geographically concentrated, which upset the equilibrium and increased the fear of isolation in the north. We were ill-informed on that point. Once oil was a factor, international considerations followed.

Our interests were traditionally anchored in the west; our eastern operations played a subsidiary role once the Cameroon business had become independent of the Nigerian operations fiscally and politically. Liberia had already been written off.

Our joint venture with the USP and other partners, recently entered into and under construction in 1966, and to be completed within twelve months, was the most important undertaking we were engaged in and the most promising in the medium and long term. It was to set the seal on our timber involvement of the last twenty years and the company was to become an important player on the international hardwood scene. It would offer us personally financial security and standing. All that was threatened. Also, we were seen to be fallible as 'experts' on Nigerian business prospects.

We were not only powerless to guide the cause of events; we could not and would not be seen to interfere. At the same time, we had friends on many levels all over the federation and were deeply concerned on the personal side. We had responsibilities towards our staff. We were alarmed for the investors. We were asked questions and had to give opinions.

221

We had to make decisions.

I did not subscribe to the universal view that the conflict, if it came to a fight, would be no more than a police action to be resolved within a couple of weeks at most. I made this known to the investors and to my friends in Lagos and elsewhere. Holding this view, I urged that efforts by those who might be listened to should be concentrated on a peaceful solution. I believed that such was entirely feasible because I did not think that either side wanted war.

Whatever the rights and wrongs, it was clear to me that the east was unprepared in the military sense and would stand little chance of success unless they had powerful backing and were ready to take heavy punishment. I doubted either fact. At the same time, I took account of the sense of desperation in the east over the killings in the north, said to run into tens of thousands, and the fear, real or imagined, that they would be multiplied were the federals to re-establish control. The psychological impact of the killings cannot be exaggerated. It came as a great surprise to me on visiting Lagos at that time how little these sentiments were understood in the other parts of Nigeria, or, if they were understood, how little people seemed to care about it. The gulf which was opening up between the east and the rest of the country was not appreciated and, when I pointed this out in my discussions with Nigerian friends, I was not understood. Irrational conclusions could be drawn on both sides. A show of force by the federation might trigger open conflict. An attempt by the east to forestall negotiations might do the same.

Many people, mainly Ibos, were killed in the north during the disturbances prior, during, and after the second coup. Several hundred, as claimed by one side, or tens of thousands, as claimed by the other? No figures were ever published giving casualties or names. How many Ibos lived in the north? That, too, was not officially known. It was said to be in revenge for the killings of prominent northerners in the first coup that the violence erupted. Many refugees streamed back into the east, not only from the north, but also from the west. These certainly ran into many thousands. Fear and insecurity pervaded the towns and villages of the eastern region.

222

That much I can say from personal observation.

Were the killings in the north organized or spontaneous? If organized, with what aim? If spontaneous, what caused them? Either way, the important factor was the suspicion of an attempt by the Ibos to dominate, probably accentuated by the growing dissatisfaction of many northerners with their living conditions. The northern establishment felt threatened and must have made up its mind that the threat had to be eliminated.

Did the Ibo in fact try to dominate the federation? The ever increasing monies accruing from the oil revenues could point that way. I doubt, however, if they thought of secession until the second coup deprived them of their position in the federal set-up. Ironsi had abolished the regions, which were now to be re-imposed in the extreme by the creation of many states, cutting the old Eastern Region into several parts, thus undermining the power base of the Eastern establishment. The fact that the other ex-regions were also to be truncated did not alter that reality. The more the old regions were cut up into several states, the stronger the centre needed to be. The north felt it had to control this centre.

If the east would not accept the proposed new divisions it must be forced to do so. This would set the east back for many years, perhaps for good. The north must have seen this as an opportunity to advance its own long-term aims which it considered essential for its security. The massacres of its people in the north shocked the east and at the same time strengthened the hands of those easterners who were determined to run their own show east of the Niger and south of the Benue once their influence in the centre faded.

Thus there were imperatives on both sides to force a showdown.

The struggle was for oil. For access to the sea, because there must have been a legitimate concern that if eastern secession were to succeed, the west might follow a similar path. And for power.

The east must have thought there was a chance to bring about secession, which was opposed by the centre. It must have calculated on receiving support from outside. Was such support ever promised? It was said that the French would sponsor them; they badly wanted sources of oil. A residue of the old Anglo-French rivalry over Africa was still said to linger in the corridors of Whitehall and the Elysée. Some of the other African states had promised support out of fear of a giant Nigeria dominating the continent south of the Sahara. Liberal democracy, enlightened opinion in the west supportive of national aspirations, Christian sentiments, humanitarian consideration, all were mustered in the minds of the secessionists. The leaders were educated in England and the USA. They were steeped in European thought, forgetting that much of this had been ineffectual and discarded during two world wars. Katanga should have been a warning – the attempt by that province of the Belgian Congo, later Zaire, to break away had received no support from the developed world. On the contrary, the UN was mobilized to squash Katanga by force of arms.

One may well ask why no major players tried to gain from secession in this game of power politics? Surely here was a classic situation where their self-interest could be promoted, where they could profit by supporting a rich territory and obtain hegemony over it?

I don't know the answer to that. France and Spain were the obvious candidates but would not act. There were certainly strong rumours, difficult to substantiate, that private French interests had offered financial support in exchange for crude oil concessions, and loose talk of similar Spanish machinations. Both countries understood Africa and were short of oil resources under their control, but they clearly had weighty political reservations to early overt involvement, and if there were ever such plans they fizzled out. The USA and Britain, as well as the Soviet Union, threw their weight behind the federation.

The west had established the principle that the frontiers of the old colonial regimes were inviolate, although exceptions were permitted; Mali's split from Senegal, and part of the Cameroon being re-united with the larger country after over forty years of being administered by Nigeria. There was an obvious concern that once Nigeria was split up other countries might follow suit, and an unmanageable multitude of small nation-states would straddle the African continent, leading to permanent squabbles and unrest, a fertile ground for communist agitation. The West's policy toward the civil war must have been dominated by its overriding and implacable opposition to communism.

Why, then, did the USSR also support the federation? It is a good question. Did nationalist rather than communist doctrine govern its policies? Was the USSR nervous of reactions in a federation made up of several 'tribes'? Or did they consider that the secessionists were capitalist in their outlook, and that communism would be better served in a weak federation than in a cohesive part of it? Whatever the reasons, two apparently contradictory philosophies found common ground for the time being. One of them must have been mistaken.

There must have been some clandestine support for the Biafrans, as the secessionists called themselves, at least enough to keep them in the field for over two years to the advantage of interests fishing in troubled waters on both sides. Money will always be found for sex and war. Money could also be made in this civil war. For two years it was found, and made.

The interests we represented were on a much lower plane. If war broke out, and an effective blockade of the eastern ports was sustained, we would have to cease operations. We could work only in peaceful and orderly conditions. Most of our production was geared to export and had no home market; and to maintain machinery we had to bring in spare parts and raw materials from Lagos and abroad. We could not expose our workers to risks to life and limb.

Whether any agreement reached to prevent war was on the basis of the old federation, a new concoction like confederation, or a separate recognized Biafra was a minor consideration for us. Either confederation or separatism would surely have posed new problems and delayed expansion, but they could be coped with. War could not.

Armed conflict lasting only a few weeks could possibly also be faced, provided it did not touch the areas in which we

225

worked. This was a point on which there were genuine differences of opinion: I urged to prepare plans for the evacuation
of expatriates – via the Cameroon if necessary – but the
American MD of the company opposed this. It would under-
mine the moral of all the workforce, and he was sure that
enough pressure would be brought on the parties to avoid
serious conflict. Any fighting, he opined, would not last for
more than a couple of weeks. He went to see the American
consul in Enugu, who was non-committal. He had not received
any instructions either way; as soon as he heard something he
would let us know.

The problem was solved by a pronouncement of the federal
government that all expats should leave the east by a given date.
Some interpreted this as putting more pressure on the east by
causing disquiet and denuding them of experts, others as a sign
of the federals' earnest determination to enforce their writ by
mobilizing all available force.

I visited Lagos during this period of uneasy calm several
times; Rylke and I had much more at stake in the capital
than in the east, although those interests in Lagos were well
taken care of and established. Our active commitment was the
Calabar project and we did not want to desert it. A subtle
change had come over the capital. The Ibos we knew had gone.
The papers were full of righteous indignation against the forces
of evil trying to break up the federation. More men and women
could be seen in uniform. There were roadblocks. Patriotic
ladies were gathering to help the charities set up to look
after the welfare of those involved in the conflict. Patriotic
gentlemen joined in appeals for money.

It was an atmosphere one knew well – the brave beating of
the distant drum, the excitement of an unusual situation in
which no danger to oneself could be discerned and in which
one could prove one's willingness to assist the good cause.
There was contempt of the militias of the east such as one often
has for the unknown enemy, and their leader, Ojukwu, was
portrayed as a buffoon or the devil incarnate.

All this was predictable, although hardly conducive to
making a settlement. What worried me was that there was no

understanding at all of the realities as I saw them, namely that this would not be a pushover were it to come to open hostilities. Even my friend Bank-Anthony would not concede the possibility. It was a war psychosis in the confident belief that all would go well in no time at all. It almost seemed as if independence had been gained too easily, without bloodshed, and that this failing had to be corrected. It was depressing, whether one listened to the arrogant talk of the Lagosians or the vain boasts of Enugu, which we also had to visit often since the immediate authorities under whose control our affairs fell were situated there.

Comparisons were drawn then (and more so later) with the American Civil War of the last century – quite out of place. The conflict in the USA had no nationalist undertones. There was no ethnically homogeneous or semi-homogeneous body attempting to break away – it was a clash of interests. If comparisons had to be looked for, they would be nearer the successor states of the Habsburg, Ottoman and Russian empires on their dissolution, the after-effects of which are still with us in the turmoil of eastern Europe in the 1990s.

Calabar was much calmer. Although part of the Eastern Region, it was not populated by Ibo. Its people liked a quiet life and took little obvious part in the unfolding drama. Quite a few of them held senior positions in the government in Enugu. They did not quit, perhaps did not dare to do so. Sitting on the fence by inclination and necessity did not save Calabar and its inhabitants from hardship. Neither side quite knew where they stood and the federal army when taking Calabar treated it as an occupied city.

I understood the people in the east, by which I mean, in the context of what follows, the Ibos. There had been prejudices against them in colonial days. They were not an easy lot to manage: stubborn, suspicious, unimaginative, and organized in small entities. I had come across them in the army where on principle we paid scant attention to a man's tribe.

I met them properly for the first time in our Ondo labour camps. They did all the hard work in the forests; they did it well and had discipline. When we expanded we had several Ibo clerks in the west, and of course more so in the East. Our chief clerk, whom I had taken on in Lagos in 1948, was from Awka. We knew them as reliable, studious, careful, with an aptitude for mechanical skill, and very willing if financially motivated. They were great savers. Socially they were more reserved, they did not smile much nor share the sense of humour which made other Nigerians so agreeable. They were penny-pinchers and quick to take advantage of any weakness or opportunity. They could also be most violent, especially as a body of men or women. And they were poor; their land could not give them a living – it was limited and hard to work. They had large families, accentuated by their adherence to Rome (which reduced polygamy); the urge to breed was nevertheless strong and their wives bore many children, more it seemed to me, than the average western or northern Nigerian women. Family planning as understood in the west was practically unknown and little appreciated. This added to the problem of over-population in relation to the resources on hand. Until oil was found these were limited. They settled in all parts of the federation and prospered as craftsmen, petty traders, clerks and such like, mainly keeping themselves to themselves.

I appreciated their qualities even if I found the men and women socially less attractive than most other Nigerians with whom I had contact. They rarely even made a pretence of friendliness. I am talking here of those we came across in their towns and villages in the days before the Civil War, and not the more cosmopolitan upper crust, but this is much the same wherever one goes.

These Ibos now found themselves under siege. There had been the massacres in the north widely reported in the local papers and believed. The word genocide began to circulate. Was all this really true? The atrocities of thirty-five years ago were too fresh in my mind to ignore what might happen. I did not believe that the north wanted to kill as many Ibos as they could get hold of, but the idea seemed feasible. Had not the Germans tried to exterminate as may Jews and Poles as possible?

As the war progressed, there was much publicity in the

Western press pointing to atrocities. Was it propaganda, was it true? Was it deliberate, was it a by-product of fighting with soldiers getting out of hand? Does a blockade withholding food supplies constitute genocide? It is after all one of the oldest weapons of war to starve one's enemy into submission. When a senior federalist was reported as saying, 'We don't want to kill all the Ibos, we only want to thin them out,' was he being serious? If he was, a Nazi pattern would emerge; deliberate killing of people simply accordingly to the tribe or the race to which they belonged. Any such tendency would have to be vigorously opposed. Looking back, one can say that if it existed it was not prevalent, and that better sense prevailed, underpinned possibly by the staunch and unexpected resistance of the Biafrans.

Bars of one of Sibelius's symphonies became the national anthem of 'Biafra'. There cannot have been many Biafrans who had ever heard of Finland or that country's struggle for independence, let alone of Sibelius. The choice reflected a cultural divergence between a tiny group of leaders steeped in Western thought and the mass of the people as close to the God of Africa as they could be.

This point was countered by an interesting argument: 'This music is no more strange to us than the aeroplane, motorcar, television and radio set, or having to learn Latin to become a lawyer. It is a fine tune and reflects our national aspirations as well as any other we could think of. The Nigerian national anthem is just as foreign, and much more banal into the bargain. You can add Christianity to this register and many other items.' I think all this mirrors the dilemma of black Africa struggling to find an identity, to make its mark in the industrial world, to compete in modern conditions.

The choice of Sibelius illustrates at the same time the rather high intellectual standards of the Biafran elite and their faith in Western civilization and democracy, which served them ill. There was to be no Gladstone thundering against the Armenian massacres of the late 19th century, only the ineffectual voice of well-meaning and often misguided humanitarians who knew little of what went on, but were outraged at what they heard of the sufferings of innocent women and children. This, alas, was the second half of the 20th century when such happenings were commonplace and carried little weight in the chambers of the chancelleries.

This is not to suggest for a moment that the many bodies, organizations and individuals who rose up in protest and who did their best to ameliorate conditions were wrong. Most of them deserve nothing but praise and their work did prevent a great deal of suffering. This applies especially to the missionaries who often stayed at their posts at great personal risk. Politically, however, they were in the main unschooled.

~   ~   ~

Secession was declared on 30 May 1967 with a rousing speech by Colonel Ojukwu who had been Governor of the Eastern Region and was now hailed as head of state of the new Republic of Biafra. The secession was not accepted by the Federal Government who took military measures to oppose it.

The Biafrans cobbled together some sort of defence force based initially on soldiers who had left the federal army to return to their homes, on ex-soldiers retired from the army, and on untrained volunteers who were put through their paces by the NCOs available. The federation had had a fair number of eastern officers, most of whom were available and eager to join. Enugu, the new capital, had been a major garrison and some supplies were in store, although no air or naval complements as far as I was aware.

That this Biafran army in the end offered resistance for over two years against a much larger, better-trained, and better-supplied enemy may be explained perhaps by the fact that they were highly motivated by fear of what would happen to them and their families – remembering or being reminded of the horror stories of the northern massacres.

It was the time of the Israeli victory (1967) over much larger and better-equipped Arab forces, and this was held up as an example of what could be achieved. It was meant as a morale booster, but ignored the fact that the Israelis had material help from countries like the USA and were an internationally recognized entity.

Our evacuation plans were already under way in Calabar when I was called to Enugu to discuss the mill's present position, how we could continue to operate, and in what way we could help to supply urgently needed items for the civil and military establishments. It was a tricky situation. The people I had to talk to were the same civil servants I had dealt with before and their routine was much the same. Even their stationery was the same, though with 'Nigeria' crossed out and 'Biafra' inserted in its place in ink or pencil.

I explained our official policy: I was under instructions to evacuate all expatriates including myself. Whatever sympathy we may have for their cause could not alter that fact. Even if we ignored this order how were we going to pay our men, where were we going to get our spares and chemicals, and how could we justify the risk of getting bogged down in a civil war? 'If we stay,' I added, 'we shall be accused by the federals; if we go, by your people.'

These Biafran civil servants were reasonable men. 'We are not stopping anyone from leaving,' they said (the thought had flashed through my mind that they might). 'Who is going to run your mills?'

'We have appointed a caretaker committee which includes senior staff.'

'Very well,' came the reply, 'we shall deal with them. Can they carry on?'

'They can carry on the sawmill for some time; I doubt if they can run the veneer mill. In any case there is not much you can do with veneers in your situation. The production is geared for export and that is impossible without ships.'

'We will get the ships,' they said, without much conviction, and I took my leave.

I used the opportunity to call on my good friend Sir Louis Mbanefo, now Chief Justice of the new state of Biafra. He knew I was in town and I had made an appointment for which he had called in two of his friends prominent in the new set-up, Professor Kenneth Dike, the historian of rank, and Pius

231

Okigbo, a well-known economist.

We talked freely. I asked them how they thought they could survive without proper communications; without aircraft, civil or military; without ships, civil or naval; and without foreign recognition, whatever clandestine support may have been arranged or might be expected.

'That,' exclaimed Dike, with much emotion and slightly theatrically, 'is how nations are born, in adversity and blood! We shall get recognition and help if we show determination. We cannot submit to northern domination and attempts to enslave us.' He gave no hint of the practical steps designed to fulfil this purpose.

Okigbo shook his head. 'Yes, we must fight but what great tribulations lie ahead of us. I wonder if all my friends are aware of it here. You have touched on some of the difficulties.'

After they left the office, Louis and I continued the discussion. His was a sober temperament. He quite realized what they were up against but felt he had to give his all in the conflict to see that his people won through and were not destroyed. He very much counted on Western support.

These three men were academics of high distinction, Western in upbringing and spirit, as were many of the other leaders of the rebellion. I felt they were politically naive if they thought they would get help because they had been to Oxford and Cambridge, or that there would be understanding for their cause in the chancelleries of London and Washington where many other considerations had to play their part, not least the question of Nigeria's oil reserves.

Would they be ruthless and cunning enough? Was there an international reason for underpinning the tearing up of the old colonial boundaries? How in practical terms would they cope with the enormous problems confronting them? Was the timing carefully thought out? Could they count on sympathizers in the enemy camp?

These questions went through my mind as I left to go back to Calabar, passing many road-blocks manned by Biafran soldiers openly hostile when I produced my British passport. But I was not molested.

232

I can see now that the east was bent on secession or at least on a loose confederation. The slaughter in the north of their countrymen and women had hardened their popular resolve and also, I suspect, their possession of the oil fields gave visions of great riches to the upper echelons of their society.

In the end it was almost miraculous that they lasted as long as they did, put up a great fight, organized their supplies, and kept the country going. I would not have expected it, nor did I foresee the hesitancy of the federals in not quickly mounting an overwhelming attack, which gave the Biafrans time to organize themselves. I suppose they did not have the means to do it nor the cohesion necessary for such a move. And they must surely have misjudged the sense of purpose of their opponents. They talked of a police action, not a war, when the troubles started.

During the Civil War, I met quite a few senior members of the governments of Britain and the USA. I remember in particular being asked by Joseph Palmer, one-time US Ambassador to Lagos, to visit him in Washington where he headed the African desk in the State Department. He had been informed that I was in New York.

'Who is behind this unexpected resistance?' he asked. 'I can't make it out.'

I told him what I knew. All manner of theories were put forward, with the Chinese making the running. They could not blame the USSR, much as they had wanted to, because she was supporting the federals for all she was worth. I thought it most unlikely that Chinese influence was at work and said so to Palmer and some Conservative ex-ministers I met in London (who were then in opposition). I thought the Biafrans bought their arms where they could, since there are always arms dealers ready to supply against good cash. Where the money for this came from is another question, the answer to which I do not know.

~   ~   ~

Hostilities were imminent. We had begun the evacuation of many of our American and other expatriates, but still hung on

233

hoping that a miracle would happen and the crisis be resolved. Unable to ship because of the federal blockade, we had cut down production but had kept a skeleton team working.

Our Danish accountant, Hans Bonde-Henriksen, was one of those who had decided to hang on. 'Let's wait and see,' he said. 'If the worst comes to the worst, we can escape via the Cameroon.'

Keeping a stiff upper lip, we had arranged to play bridge at the weekend at the Dunlop Club fifty miles up the road, where some stalwarts had also decided to wait. As I was about to set off in the car, with Hans sitting beside me, an expat about to leave for safer pastures came up and asked us to take some books which he had borrowed from the Dunlop Club and was anxious to return before leaving.

'Throw them in the back,' I said, which he did, and off we went. It must have been about 5 p.m. The game was to start after an early dinner and we gave ourselves plenty of time. Fifteen miles up the road we came across a road-block manned by five or six Biafran soldiers. We were stopped – no respecters of persons, these men.

'Where are you going?' a corporal asked harshly.

'We are going to the Dunlop Plantation.'

'Why are you going there?'

To say that we were going to play cards seemed wrong so I answered, 'We are going there for dinner.'

'I must search your car; open the boot and the bonnet.'

It went against the grain, but I did so. He looked and was satisfied that we carried nothing suspicious and was about to send us on our way when he spotted the books lying on the back seats. 'What is that?' he asked.

'Books, corporal, to return to the library.'

He opened the rear door and took out the books. He glanced at the first one and threw it back into the car. He looked at the second one and asked, 'What kind of book is that?'

'Corporal,' I replied, 'I don't know. I've never seen these books before. They belong to a friend who asked us to return them to Dunlop's.'

He eyed me with mounting distrust. 'So you don't know

234

what this book is?'

'I don't, corporal. Why? What is it?'

He showed it to me. It was entitled *A Spy in Rome* and he opened the pages which had lots of sketches of roads in the text. 'You are a spy,' he shouted, 'a spy, a British spy! This book is full of codes. You are arrested!'

Hans tried to intervene. 'It's just a library book, corporal.'

'You shut up or I will arrest you as well.'

He called one of his men. 'Take these people back to HQ in Calabar. They are under arrest. Report to the orderly officer. Sit in the back, point your rifle at the driver, and if he stops or takes any suspicious action fire. You,' he said, addressing me, 'get in the car and drive back to Calabar. You heard my orders to the soldier; he will kill you if you try anything funny.'

There was no argument with that, so I got back in the driver's seat with Hans by my side and off we went. I felt something cool at the back of my neck – it was the muzzle of our escort's rifle.

I drove fairly slowly in case some child ran across the road and I would either have to knock him over or get a bullet in the head. We reached the barracks without incident, and were told to get out of the car when a crowd of curious soldiers gathered around us and the soldier. 'They are under arrest,' he said in a loud voice. 'Call the orderly officer.' The orderly officer was not around but a sergeant took charge of the situation and locked us up in cells close by.

'I want to see the commanding officer,' I told the sergeant, 'and promptly.' I was furious and made no secret of my feelings.

The sergeant shrugged his shoulders. 'All in good time.'

After about an hour, an officer came to our cell. 'The CO will see you presently. I think I have seen you before, sir,' he added.

'I bet you have. I'm the MD of Calvenply and we are doing our best to keep things going and this is our reward. Please call your CO.'

'He will be with you soon,' he said, and the door was locked again.

Half an hour later, a tall military chap appeared in native dress. 'I am the CO here,' he said, 'and you are Mr. Brandler. I am sorry, Mr. Brandler, there has been a mistake, but please understand we are almost at war and my men are raw and they are doing the best they can. You British are not very popular at the moment.'

'May I have your name, sir?'

'It doesn't matter, Mr. Brandler. I am the colonel in charge here.' He spoke excellent English and Sandhurst was written all over him. 'I have looked at the book,' he said. 'It could be a code, couldn't it?'

'Well, I suppose it could,' I replied, 'but that is very far-fetched. I assure you I'd never seen it before.'

'You would have to say that, Mr. Brandler, but I have made enquiries. You're no spy and free to go.'

'You realize, colonel, that we are hours late for our dinner party.'

He smiled. 'I am sorry about that. Do you still want to go to Dunlop's?'

'Of course we do, people are waiting for us. But I must ask you, colonel, to give us an escort or we may be arrested again.'

He detailed the soldier who had taken us to his HQ to escort us back to Dunlop's.

'Thank you, colonel. May I make an observation?'

'You may,' he answered politely.

'Well, colonel, when we were arrested nobody searched us. Had we been spies, we could have carried revolvers and your soldier would have been a dead man within a mile of our setting off with him.'

'I told you my men are raw. Good point. Thank you. Goodbye.'

Off we set back to Dunlop's where we arrived hours late; we had to forgo our dinner and settled down to a good game of bridge, having dropped the escort off at his post. We were told there were no further road-blocks.

On our return journey, after midnight, we passed the road-block without being stopped, although they cannot possibly have known who was in the car. I never discovered officially the name of the colonel but believe it was Eze. I hope he survived the war.

I related the story to Sir David Hunt, then British High Commissioner in Lagos. 'I know the book,' was all he would say, 'and I know the author. Jolly good yarn. Poor old Joe, having been done out of your dinner. Have you read the book?'

'I am afraid not.' And I have not to this day.

~ ~ ~

The blockade of the east by the federals had stopped communications except with the Cameroon. A car could still travel to Lagos but once there it could not return. We were evacuating expatriates now via the Cameroon by road and by sea.

We had an efficient organization in Tiko where our motor company was functioning normally. We used this to look after the evacuees and to send them off home. They left in twos and threes; the last to depart handed responsibilities over to a local caretaker committee selected by agreement and supported with funds.

It was a melancholy experience. All our great hopes dashed, all our efforts in vain, the grand design of an integrated timber complex – almost completed – to be left in abeyance. For how long we could not tell. Weeks said the optimists; years said the pessimists. Millions of dollars, hundreds of jobs hanging fire.

Our imminent task, however, was to ensure the safety of all the staff. We had already laid off half the labour force and those not at home in Calabar had left. The others volunteered to stay as long as the company could pay them and would have them.

All was quiet in Calabar and, remarkably, there was still a supply of food and beer. One listened to the radio from Enugu and Lagos, as well as foreign stations like the BBC and the Voice of America – not that the latter gave much information on Nigeria, or that the former could be relied on. Hoping against hope, one still attended the office and the mills, checking files and equipment. The routine continued.

Early in July, I set off by road for Tiko and Douala to check on our people already evacuated. New York urged that their employees be despatched with all possible speed. Some had already been posted to other stations.

On the Nigerian/Biafran side the frontier posts had been abandoned. One could come and go as one pleased. Not so on the Cameroon side, where papers and vehicles were searched with much ado. Nobody had a visa, but they did not make a fuss over that.

Mamfe was the nearest place to the Nigerian border, and it had the air of a little boom town. Official and unofficial trade doubled and trebled, lodging places were full, and near the border one saw many lorries loaded with food and merchandise held up by the Cameroon authorities for checking. The *gendarmes* must have had a field-day. I never found out if they got through.

The Cameroonians had an ambivalent approach to the conflict. They would not mind Nigeria being reduced in territory and population – she was too big for comfort. At the same time secession in a neighbouring country might encourage similar sentiments at home; they also feared that if Biafra won, she might become arrogant and aggressive. So Cameroon sat on the fence waiting to see who would come out on top, and meanwhile made money from the war.

When I got back to Calabar, we sent off more men. One tough female insisted on remaining until her husband was ready to join her. Nothing much had changed in the few days I had been away.

I left for the Cameroon towards the end of July; several expats stayed on under Sandy for a few more days to ensure an orderly hand-over. The fighting was by then well under way, but not near Calabar.

Left behind were not only the mills, cars, trucks, Caterpillar vehicles, office equipment, files and so on, but also all the household goods and chattels: knives, plates, dishwashers, linen, curtains, bedding, furniture, some clothing, the odd bottle of booze, all in the charge of stewards who were locals and had been kept on to guard everything. They enjoyed themselves.

It was too much to hope for. When I visited Calabar four months later only some of the heavy equipment remained – the units we had immobilized and which the army could not re-activate in spite of all the threats they made to the domestic staff (who had no idea how to work them). We recovered several typewriters and cars looted by the locals. Much equipment had been officially requisitioned and if still in working order could be reclaimed. The financial loss was enormous and in fact crippled the company which never recovered.

As soon as it was occupied by the federals, Calabar came under military administration and order was slowly restored. All economic activity, however, was severely curtailed – there was little work for the inhabitants with the enemy not too far away until the very end of the war. The general who took Calabar, Adekunle, was an energetic man, who was worried lest the unemployed gave him trouble. He got hold of cash from the banks and forced the money on the companies with a request, which amounted to an order, to start up again.

Our chief engineer, Dodgson, who had taken up residence again, received boxes of cash for which he had to sign. Money is not enough to work an industrial complex and little happened. There was no infrastructure, no market, no ships, no technicians; men were taken on and paid and the money soon ran out.

The money the general had passed on to us was in notes which had lost their validity in the federation and were legal tender only in the occupied zones. In his imprest account he was to be credited in the new currency; this made him as good a financier as a general. When the Central Bank in Lagos heard of the transaction I was called by the governor to explain why we had accepted this 'loan' without authority.

'There could have been no better authority, governor, than the general in charge of the town. Would you have us argue with him?'

'You're right,' he replied. 'My writ doesn't go very far in

these conditions. Have a coffee.'

They managed the fiscal side very well and there was not the wild inflation which so often accompanies wars. The money held by the easterners was lost, which helped to sustain the currency. The easterners had to start afresh.

We offered the government the use of our facilities to store the foodstuffs donated by the Western charities to ameliorate the starvation widely publicized in the press. Friction arose: the Red Cross, for instance, wanted to distribute its gifts directly to the people, but the Nigerian authorities insisted that they be in charge of it. Not all went smoothly because allocating these gifts generated patronage and influence and it could also be manipulated to enrich a few of those responsible for handing out the food. Some of the items shipped over were of little use. For example, many tons of egg powder had been discharged and stored but found no favour with the people, however hungry they might be.

There were some nasty incidents. Those Ibos found in the town after it was lost by the Biafrans were often shot out of hand. The army feared they might have been Biafran soldiers or spies who could not get away and had taken off their uniforms to look like civilians. Several bodies were found in our well.

On one occasion all males in the town were ordered to report to the stadium where they were held for many hours. Troops then searched the houses and, it is said, took what they liked, including women. The official reason for this action was that they were searching for rebels. The man who told me this story was a banker who said that his daughter had been violated. One knows that wars bring forth atrocities and terrible happenings, and one also knows that it is very difficult to know what to believe.

20

Civil War: The Ruins of Calabar

I returned to the east again in the third week of March 1968. It was a strange Calabar I landed in. Gone were the masses of soldiers, to fight elsewhere. No more were vehicles careering madly through the streets. No more were soldiers tramping up and down with rifles and automatic weapons. Many houses were abandoned, and only here and there did one come across soldiers doing guard duty. The hustle and bustle of an occupied town serving as HQ had turned into an almost empty silence. Civilians were walking about, seemingly without purpose. A few bicycles could be seen passing. The odd car made its way through the streets.

'What has happened?' I asked.

'They have nearly all gone to fight on the other side of the river,' I was informed.

Here was Calabar in all its ugly nakedness. The ruined houses looked even more ruined. The empty spaces even more empty. The civilians even more dowdy and aimless.

Calabar – with its trade and industry destroyed, its many buildings burned, shelled, or otherwise demolished, its citizens without work and without income, the town itself apparently without anyone in authority. After the exodus of the army its last support had gone, and Calabar was left to face an uncertain future. For in this war-torn place the army had been some sort of stability. Now the contractors who had worked for them wondered what would happen to them. The women, forcibly or willingly made into camp-followers, saw their protectors go. The traders would lose the source of their goods as well as most of their customers. Supplies would stop and prices for food soar even higher. The looted goods would be on sale again at low prices to sustain their owners.

A gigantic task faced the civil authorities. Much help would be needed. Would it be forthcoming? Would the new authorities have enough pull in Lagos to get it? Would they know how to go about reconstruction even if the means were at hand? Was the mettle of the population such as to face the task? The transitory period would be painful and the road back to normality long, to be reckoned in months and years rather than weeks. Soon, one hoped, the port would be opened. What would the ships bring? Who had money to import and then, who had money to buy imported goods? What would they take away? Some produce left over, and by and by new harvests; it would take time.

How would the government recruit efficient staff from other parts of the country? What could they offer such people other than sweat and discomfort? Would they find willing helpers or would they have to rely on third-rate officials eager to line their own pockets? Would self-seekers turn informers and *agents provocateurs* to bring yet more sorrow, fear and hatred to this battered town? Such were my thoughts as I drove about and talked to some of the men and women.

Whatever our sympathies, our job was to look after the interests of the company and to do so honourably. We were still dealing with the army authorities, much occupied with their present campaign. Our employees were doing well waiting on this lieutenant, that captain or major, to obtain one concession or another, like petrol, for instance, or beer, or a signature or receipt. It was terribly time-absorbing, and although little was accomplished any degree of success was a morale booster.

Those of us who were older and had served in armies in wars during our lifetime had been through this before. To the younger expatriate, life in these circumstances was something new and not without an air of excitement. To witness shooting, to hear naval guns firing in earnest, to see bombers taking off on missions, to see prisoners walking through the street under heavy guard, to live in unstable times and in relatively primitive conditions, to wonder whether or not one could leave the town, and if so how. All this was very different from working in a settled environment and added a new flavour to life.

Before we could think of going ahead with our work, law and order and a more regular state of affairs would have to be established. We could not have four or five chaps waiting on the pleasure or availability of some junior officer, however co-operative he may wish to be – and we had had few complaints on that score. There had to be better medical facilities, reliable transport between Lagos and Calabar, and petrol and food should be in the town or should be transported into it by us with the knowledge that they would reach us when expected.

It depended on how much of the country's effort was spent on fighting the war, which still had priority. One knew that life had its own logic which made things go round. One lived in hope.

Some of my experiences during my visit were extraordinary. Quite by accident I found myself being a witness to some of the air operations. Calling on a senior officer with a request, I found that this gentleman had left his HQ and I was asked to wait. A sergeant, who felt that so venerable-looking a person as myself could not possibly be left standing, put me on a chair in the divisional operations room where urgent wireless messages were passing between the front and the base. It was an impressive performance, the details of which I have forgotten. At last a second lieutenant – wondering whether I was one of the foreign journalists – asked what I was doing there. I was glad when this ordeal was over.

At the airport a bored Egyptian pilot, in between missions, eventually drew me into conversation. He was not a mercenary, he said, but had been seconded. I was surprised at his derogatory remarks: he would not let a Nigerian touch his plane, and as for being familiar with one – he would rather jump into the river. Cairo was the place for him.

There was considerable air activity. Ilyushin bombers and smaller jets, either MiGs or Dolphins, took off again and again to bomb the Biafrans. A British Procter jet also appeared in

243

between. DC3s came and went, piloted by expatriates. On the naval side one saw some British faces who were hardly on holiday.

A great weight of metal spearheaded the attacks and one wondered how long the Biafran rebels could possibly stand up to it. The principal sufferers in all this were the civilians. To the Nigerian establishment, new and insecure, the Biafrans were heretics who must be rooted out with fire and sword. They were the modern Albigensians in an African setting, out of keeping with the general development of the continent, or perhaps way ahead of their times. Lacking in imagination, however, and taking at face value all they had been taught about liberalism and democracy, their leaders took it for granted that their erstwhile mentors would not, in the end, fail them and see them destroyed. It was a costly illusion.

~   ~   ~

Many journalists were sent out to report on the Biafran conflict. We had three newspaper reporters as tenants in Kajola House and they had many callers; however fierce the competition between them, they helped each other and anyone new to the place could call on his colleagues to get what guidance he could.

I met several in Lagos, where they collected official handouts and on occasion would be conducted up-country by the government to see the troops and other items considered to be of interest. They were shown what officialdom wanted them to see and for the rest relied on rumours, gossip and impressions. Those experienced in these matters imbibed the atmosphere and gave rein to their imagination. Some knew a little about Africa, others did not. It would be Vietnam yesterday, Biafra today, and Afghanistan tomorrow. If they became nosey and their printed reports were too unfavourable, they would be expelled; this happened to Lloyd Garrison of the *New York Herald* and to Angus McDermott of the BBC.

A few adventurous souls made their way into Biafra. To get there they had to travel to Tiko in the Cameroon from where they would go by hired transport up the Mamfe road and into Biafra before that part of the country was sealed off by the federal army. Others flew into Biafra. Two called on us in Tiko. They probably got hold of our name by the journalistic grapevine through our Lagos tenants.

The first to turn up was a young BBC reporter with his camera crew. His name was Frederick Forsyth, later to become well-known as a writer of thrillers which headed many a best-sellers list. We put them up for a couple of nights, and wished them luck. Listening to the BBC World Service we waited eagerly for Forsyth's reports but never heard anything. We thought we must have missed his stories.

Some time later he turned up again. He told us that the BBC considered his reports too favourable to the Biafran cause and had never put them out. He had resigned and was going back into Biafra as a freelance reporter.

Whilst there, he must have got friendly with the secessionist leader, Colonel Ojukwu. When Ojukwu's regime collapsed and he fled to the Ivory Coast, Forsyth visited him there. He also wrote a book on the conflict. Years later, when Ojukwu was allowed to return from exile, Forsyth was on the aeroplane which brought him back to Lagos. I happened to be in Lagos at the time but we did not meet again.

Another interesting type who called on us in Tiko was J. F. Chauvel, a Frenchman, working for *Le Figaro*. He was a hard-bitten war reporter whose despatches were regularly printed in his paper. They were very pro-Biafran, but the French had a soft spot for the secessionists at that time. It did not last as de Gaulle had his hands full with internal problems.

The Biafrans' propaganda was skilful. They received no official assistance but the support given to them by various bodies helped them to sustain their effort to resist re-integration into the federation.

Amongst their sympathizers was a Swede of liberal tendencies, Count von Rosen, who had been active in the civil strife in Ethiopia and transferred his martial spirit to the cause of Biafra. Von Rosen and people like him reminded one of the Spanish Civil War of the 1930s. They must have believed that

Biafra represented popular progress and social democracy, whereas the federals were bloody-minded, corrupt and reactionary cliques ruining Africa's development.

Be that as it may, von Rosen was a man of deeds, a soldier by instinct if not profession, who set to work to organize a small Biafran air force – civil commuter planes of limited size which he collected from various sources. This force he trained and one day it took off, three or four Pipers or similar, to attack Port Harcourt. Their armament consisted of a few homemade bombs and a machine-gun in each plane, hardly very formidable by any standard. The objective of the raid was the airport, a military base from which the federal Migs and bombers took off to harass the Biafran population and military.

They swooped low over the field and obtained a complete surprise. There was panic amongst the defenders who scattered. They were not prepared for action because at no time had such an attack been expected. Some damage was done to buildings and one or two planes on the ground and the whole affair was over within a few minutes.

It hurt the pride of the federals badly and a great howl went up against these foreign mercenaries and warmongers, with von Rosen coming in as the major target. The press was full of it. Sweden as a country got its share of the vituperation. The Swedish Embassy insisted that von Rosen was a private individual and in no way represented official policy in the Civil War, but protests continued and Sweden was considered to be an active friend of the rebels.

One day it was announced that a demonstration would be mounted outside the embassy in Lagos which was in the same building as my consulate. At five o'clock in the afternoon two buses drew up about 100 metres from the office block: twenty to twenty-five students poured out of one on to the street; out of the other came a similar number of women in native dress, later described as market women.

The embassy was on the third floor and by this time had long since closed and the staff gone home. I lived on the premises in a flat on the fifth floor and was present to observe.

The men and women so gathered marched in serried ranks to the building well covered by photographers and joined by a few passers-by. There was no way they could get into the building, which probably was not their objective anyway. Shouting threats and abuse, the small mob became frustrated when there was no response and tried to throw stones; they soon gave this up as they could not reach the third floor. They unfurled a Swedish flag and after summoning the cameramen to take pictures, burned it amongst shouts of derision and triumph. After twenty minutes they all went back to their buses and drove off.

A couple of days later, there were photos in the press and a description of the spontaneous mass meetings outside the Swedish Embassy to protest against the interference by Sweden in the internal affairs of Nigeria. The photos were skilfully taken to give the impression that a great crowd had assembled, not the fifty or so who actually turned up in the two vehicles.

It was a laughable affair, organized by a semi-official body which hired the buses and roped in a few footloose men and women to have some fun. I do not think the embassy even complained, but presumably made it clear to the government that it took no part in the Civil War and that its ban on delivering arms was long-standing. Sweden's refusal to deliver ammunition for the Bofors guns Nigeria had bought in peace-time greatly annoyed the federals; one can understand that. What is the use of selling guns and refusing to sell ammunition when the guns are being used in earnest? Sweden, once adored for its anti-colonialist role in the UN, was now considered to be an unfriendly country as far as the federals were concerned. No arms were sold to the Biafrans either, but there was much sympathy for its people, which, once again, did not reflect official Swedish policy.

This pattern is a common one. Governments may pay lip-service to popular sentiment, may even arouse it, but in the end they follow their own counsel and policies. The masses let off steam. Today it is Ethiopia, tomorrow Biafra, the next day Chile. Not that this popular support is all in vain, but ultimately it rarely forces a change of policy. Unless, that is, the protests boil over, but this does not seem to happen in matters pertaining to distant countries.

Starvation was the federation's major weapon. To still the hunger of their families, women had to accommodate the soldiers. On our mill site, occupied at the time by a guard post, we could see them come and go, young girls mostly, cooking and fetching water for the soldiers and clearly spending the night with them. They could have run away; they stayed for food. The headmistress of a girls' secondary school in Calabar told me that quite a few of her pupils in the upper forms had returned with babies conceived for the military. 'I wouldn't turn them away; they had suffered enough.'

My English secretary in Lagos mentioned that she had taken a cook discharged from the army. He had a wife and child in her compound and they all seemed happy. The wife had been acquired by the ex-serviceman when in the army. In the occupied part of Biafra he had come across a fine-looking girl he took a fancy to. He confronted the father, drew his gun and said, 'I want your daughter and give you five pounds dowry – or else.' He got the woman, and she had not run away. Nature compensates herself in war; people are killed and people are begotten.

Not all stories had a happy ending. A prominent Efik moneylender was falsely denounced by his debtors as a notorious collaborator with the Biafrans and shot out of hand – one way of getting rid of one's debts. His nickname was 'Coins' because he used to lend the workers a few shillings if they were hard up, and he could be seen on pay-days collecting his interest or capital. A banker in embryo, one might say.

It was often a war with personal undertones, as civil wars are prone to become. Dropping an atomic bomb is more detached and professionally efficient – looting and abducting women does not come into it. Is it more civilized?

~　　~　　~

At the end of the war the Biafrans re-integrated into the federation fairly quickly, due in part to the wise policies of General Gowon, the head of state, who received them back without rancour.

Sir Louis Mbanefo called on me shortly after the cessation of hostilities. I was about to attend the wake for Dr. Alakija in the Obalende district of Lagos. Louis had known him – both had been members of the Metropolitan Club - and he asked if he could accompany me: 'I will show my face and see what happens – if it is all right with you.'

I did not hesitate. 'Do come along.'

Our discussions had delayed us a little, and as we entered the compound through a narrow gate there were already many people seated in the open space reserved for the purpose. Alakija had been a prominent doctor in Lagos from a well-known family and many of the guests belonged to the upper strata of society.

A hush came over the assembled guests and a gasp of surprise. Louis, looking pale and thin after years of privation and worry, walked forward with dignity – one of the much-decried leaders of the secession – and greeted one of the men he recognized, who stood up and warmly shook his hand. So did many others who knew him; the ice was broken. It was touching: the fight is over; we were friends once, and we shall be again. Nor did I ever hear a word of criticism of my action in bringing Louis along.

Dike went off to Harvard as a Professor of African History; he came back, too, and died some years later. Pius Okigbo is still an accepted economist active in the affairs of Nigeria (1990). Sir Louis died within a few years and I attended his funeral in the new and not yet completed cathedral in Onitsha. His wife, Lady Elizabeth, is still very much alive and their three sons, products of the best English public schools and universities, are senior members of the establishment.

The easterners concentrated on repairing the ravages of war and on rebuilding their lost fortunes; they kept aloof from national politics and, as far as I know, were not involved in any of the military coups of the last twenty years.

Little by little many of the civil servants were re-absorbed in all parts of the federation: their training made them vitally needed. If some of them occasionally complained of prejudice, one can only say that all Nigerians do so if they cannot make the fast progress which they feel is their prerogative.

Shortly after the collapse of the Biafra secession, I was invited to dinner at the high table of King's College, Cambridge, by an old friend. I was seated next to a professor of high repute, a member of the nobility, who was interested to hear that I spent much time in Nigeria. He questioned me on what I thought of the war, the fighting and the suffering of the civilian population in Biafra, especially the children, which had been given so much coverage in the British press.

'My lord,' I said, quoting the cynical opinion of one of the ambassadors then accredited to Lagos, 'it was a civilized war: only the poor died.' The professor was not amused.

Most of the prominent easterners I had known turned up again after hostilities ended (I am talking of civilians of the upper classes, and not of soldiers). This may have been a coincidence, and not necessarily evidence of the relative sufferings of rich and poor during the war, but it seemed indicative.

The poor died of hunger. It was the old story: whilst the fat men got thinner, the thin men died.

~　　~　　~

In spite of Brigadier Adekunle's interest, we could not re-activate the Calabar industrial complex until hostilities came to an end and a firm administration was active. Loose discussions between the parties involved had been taking place throughout the Civil War. The financial institutions had sent regular demands for payment of interest they knew could not be met. The Americans kept a framework going by paying the salaries and expenses of a skeleton crew on an ad hoc basis. All was in limbo.

Hostilities ended in January 1970; it was time to take stock. The Americans sent over an accountant to prepare projections prior to undertaking a review of the future. The company faced enormous problems.

The old Eastern Region, a partner in the enterprise, had been carved up into three separate states. Calabar was now the capital of the South-Eastern State (later renamed Cross River State) which had been allocated the shareholding in the company. We had to deal with a new regime.

The veneer plant, powerhouse and sawmill had suffered only minor damage but had deteriorated while standing idle for almost three years. The logging and transport equipment had been partly requisitioned and on return was found to be in a poor condition and had to be replaced; some was never recovered. Our tug, also requisitioned, had sunk in naval operations.

Expatriate staff and skilled Ibo hands had dispersed, the former to new appointments, the latter now unwanted by the powers that be. The till was empty and debts enormous, as banks and others had accumulated interest over the whole period of the war. The Americans had turned lukewarm towards the project, the more so as they had found alternative sources of supply. The financiers' preoccupation was recovery of their loans. The new projections showed that a vast additional investment was required to lay the foundations for a successful re-opening of production.

Negotiations embracing all interested bodies were initiated. The principal subject was money. Nobody wanted to engage more capital in the business and nobody dared to let it fall. Talks dragged on for over a year; in vain did I call for attention to the 'nuts and bolts' – these came very low on the list of priorities. Sandy Rylke begged to be excused and remained in Lagos to look after our affairs there. Carl Wheeler was booted out by the Americans. He had formed the Calabar venture and now paid for its failure. He was replaced by Mr. Wells who disliked the whole idea of involvement in West Africa and was horrified to see more government participation.

The new government's representatives understandably looked at everything with suspicion. Most were inexperienced; some had left-wing sympathies; some were anti-Ibo chauvinists; others were opportunists ready to make the most of their positions. The representatives appointed by

251

government to treat with the rest of the shareholders were Charles Abia, an able accountant, and Henry Ikwang, an intellectual with strong anti-capitalist leanings. It was an article of faith with him that no foreign-controlled concern could dispose of the state's raw materials and resources at will: that is, the forests. The state must have control of the company.

It was impossible to reconcile these conflicting views, and compromises were reached which satisfied nobody, and did nothing to effect an efficient running of the mills. Within a year of opening up again, Wells flew over and disposed of his company's interests to the state for a nominal sum to get rid of all possible obligations. They wrote off several million dollars. He withdrew his men.

In disarray, the government asked me to take over as acting caretaker managing director until a new management could be put in place. I agreed on the understanding that urgent steps be taken in this direction and I refused to draw a salary to retain my freedom of action. It was, in retrospect, a mistake on my part.

No action was taken to recruit a permanent replacement. There were constant financial crises and interference by officialdom, much as I objected. Unwanted employees were foisted on us. They must have thought me a bit of a fool for driving about in the company's Beetle car instead of demanding a Mercedes like the other heads of state-controlled unprofitable enterprises.

Then one morning late in 1973, a rumour reached me that the government was discussing the establishment of yet another plywood complex with Romanian participation, and that two senior government officers, Ikwang and Abia, had met Romanian Embassy officials in Lagos and travelled to Bucharest. I found it hard to credit the story. The professed shortage of funds alone would mitigate against the venture when our plant was kept so short of money that we were unable to operate efficiently. Besides, why should they want to compete with themselves? It did not make sense to me.

A few days later I was on an internal flight and met the Commissioner for Industries in one of the western states of the federation. He said he knew me; as a boy he had to carry timber dogs to his father who did business with us near Kajola. He went on to tell me that he was off to Bucharest with his colleagues from Calabar to negotiate the building of two plywood complexes in partnership with the Romanian Government, one in Ondo and one in Calabar. I was astonished.

A few weeks later, Mr. Ikwang called me to his office to appraise me of the new turn of events; he asked me what I thought of it and I replied candidly that in my opinion this was a rash undertaking. The mill they already controlled could not function properly for want of funds, so what was the point in setting up a rival undertaking with people who had no knowledge of African conditions? He brushed this aside as fear of competition and added that a number of Romanian experts would have to be attached to our mills for training and he hoped we would co-operated.

'You own the place, Mr. Ikwang, and can do as you please. I am here as a caretaker MD, unpaid as you know, and in these circumstances must reserve my position.'

'You are our friend, Mr. Brandler, and I know you will help us. There is room for three mills with all the forests we command.'

I disputed this strongly. 'There are forests, Commissioner, but there are no road communications with them.'

'We will see to that,' he replied optimistically.

It was a hare-brained scheme all right, but it was the new baby of the present administration, who not only wanted to show that they were active in promoting industry but wished to be involved in new ventures which would be of personal credit to them. Travelling to Bucharest with all its charms alone was worth some effort.

A few months later, five Romanian gentlemen arrived and were attached to our works. They were a pleasant lot, middle-aged, well educated and polite. They spoke reasonable English. The leader of the mission was a commercial forester who was a servant of the Romanian government wood industry. None of them had ever been to Africa. They knew nothing of conditions in tropical timber extraction or marketing. I wondered how these people thought they could build up a green-field operation, buy and install machinery and equipment, and operate without any previous knowledge of what was involved. One had the suspicion that they would eventually try to recruit some of our staff.

I often talked to the leader about this and other matters. He readily conceded that he foresaw great problems but it was not for him to query the fundamentals. He was an officer of the Romanian government and must do his best to carry out instructions.

In his view conditions in Romania had improved in the last twenty years; the war was a disaster but reconstruction was going ahead and progress was being made.

'Why,' I asked the leader, 'do you spend your scarce foreign exchange on such wild schemes when you need all the money you can muster to improve conditions in your own country?'

'Politics is not for me,' was his reply.

I suggested that it would be preferable for the proposed new venture to be incorporated into our own. We agreed, but it was not for him to make such suggestions.

Practically all of the new machinery would have to be bought from Western countries like Italy and France and be paid for in hard currency; it ran into millions of dollars. The working capital would be supplied by the local administration, which would also undertake the construction of buildings and workshops. One knew what that meant. It would involve government patronage for contracts, supplies and jobs for friends, and a general atmosphere of hustle and bustle. These were transient preferments.

One plywood mill next to another, both owned by government, could not flourish unless a hundred miles and more of roads were built and the markets were hungry enough to absorb all the production. It was feasible, but in this case why not extend the existing mill?

I put the argument to the commissioners: 'Let the Romanians run the whole show if you want to get in with them. Double or treble present facilities. It'll save a lot of money and you'll have a really impressive production if run properly.' All to no avail.

'They will have a new set-up, buy their own machinery, construct their own buildings, run their own log extraction. It's all arranged.'

I happened to meet the Romanian Ambassador to Nigeria at a social function in Lagos and we touched on the matter. I could see that he was keen on the proposal and did not favour combining the two enterprises.

'We are expanding our interests in Africa,' he said. 'There are many good opportunities for co-operation between the developing countries and our own society.' I wished him luck, but privately thought, 'You will have a lot to learn, my friend.'

Neither mill made a profit; they kept open, and are still open, although I cannot say if the Romanians remained partners in the venture. Millions of dollars and local currency were spent. The initial inexperience of the Romanians was exploited to the full by local interests. Their Nigerian partners did rather better, although the commissioners did not last very long and were soon replaced, but this was quite normal.

Meanwhile they relied on my unpaid services. My warnings that I would soon depart fell on deaf ears. They began to ignore me; I was not, for instance, invited to attend the opening of the Calabar University to which most heads of departments and such like were asked to come along. It did not worry me greatly but gave me a good reason to leave at short notice. I drafted a brief letter addressed to the governor and chief secretary announcing my long-delayed departure and closing it by writing that 'my presence seemed to be of little consequence anyway'.

I flew to Lagos that same afternoon without waiting for a reaction. It was 27 May 1974. Alighting from the aircraft I was met on the tarmac by my driver, Johnson. He was in tears.

'What's troubling you, Johnson?'

Sobbing, he informed me that a message from England had been received that morning that Sandy Rylke had died totally unexpectedly the previous night of a haemorrhage brought on by a coughing fit. He had to be the first to tell me. The news came as a terrible shock and made my resignation from Calabar that much more poignant.

I flew to London to attend the funeral on 1 June. Several of his old regimental colleagues were present and many other friends. He was sixty-seven years of age. We had been partners and close friends for twenty-six years without any serious disagreement in all that long time.

21

Clubland

S andy Rylke had joined the Lagos Polo Club early in 1950 and persuaded me to follow suit. I had done very little riding but the place had a lovely atmosphere and I became a member late in 1950.

The Lagos Polo Club was part of the colonial establishment. There were polo clubs in many towns, mainly in the north: Kano, Katsina, Kaduna, etc., but also some in the south – in Ibadan and Lagos. Enugu and Calabar, too had organized polo clubs in the old days but they were closed for fear of the tsetse fly.

The Lagos Polo Club had a large field situated between the town and what was then the underdeveloped outlying district of Ikoyi where the whites lived. It had stabling for fifty ponies, and quarters for the staff who lived there, the horseboys; it had a little bar, a rectangle no more than 10 feet by 6 feet, with a store tucked on behind it. This was later extended to a half-circle, which doubled the room for those of us who hung around the bar instead of taking the drinks to the seats which lined one side of the field. Such was the conservatism of the club members that it took two years of deliberation before this bar extension was passed at an AGM. I sat at that bar many an evening with a bachelor, one Barker, who was the accountant-general. We talked and talked and kept the barman hanging about wondering when we would pack it in.

All the Lagos members were white. In the early 1950s the first black face appeared, a Yoruba who worked for the Water Works and who was introduced by Mrs. Maclaren, wife of a government officer with liberal tendencies. He must have felt fairly uncomfortable, nice man that he was, not being much of a horseman into the bargain. The northerners looked at him with astonishment when they saw him ride on their visits to the club, mainly for the annual tournament.

By tradition the president of the club was the general commanding Nigeria District. Only one declined this honour in my time because he did not care for horses; he was replaced by a senior civil servant. The Polo Club was one of the few places where civil servants and commercials met freely and openly, and even then there was an unspoken gulf between these two groups of whites.

The club was well-run and strict accounts were kept for every penny that was spent. The welfare of the horses was paramount, followed by the welfare of the horse boys.

Committees were elected; there were pony welfare members and ground members and bar members, all of whom did their job as best they could. Then there was the secretary, and above all the president. Additionally, there were three trustees, of whom I was one for many years. Membership was by introduction and election, the usual procedure.

Into this hierarchical set-up drifted slowly and almost imperceptibly a new breed of member. As more and more white businessmen and professionals turned up in Lagos, so it was the dear wish of many of them to become members of the club. Some came from other colonies and knew the form and could ride very well. Others came to learn, and others again, who little by little became the majority, came for the atmosphere, the drinks, the company, and, last but not least, the kudos.

The bar became too small and it was decided to build a large club-house with better facilities. A hard rearguard battle was fought by the old gang (of whom, I am ashamed to say, I was one) until plans were approved and a building contract given to the firm of one of the members engaged in that trade. I made up for my early opposition by giving the timbers required to erect the new building, entirely of wood.

The Polo Club, towards the end of the 1960s, became the 'in' club to belong to. Prominent Lagosians joined, mostly non-horsemen. The white exclusivity faded here as elsewhere, and was replaced by an exclusivity of rank and means. After independence, the white civil servants and military soon became a small minority of members. They were replaced by some of the diplomatic corps, by the many commercials, and by Nigerians.

The Nigerian riding members were at first mainly the northern military and police, but gradually the southerners too learnt to ride until years later their sons took up the game and now dominate it, along with the military. The president is still a senior military or administrative officer. *Plus ca change ...* except that there has also been an influx of Lebanese who in colonial times had been discouraged from joining, good horsemen though many of them were.

If one came to the club during the Civil War in the 1960s, one would find, after dark, a large crowd of prominent people sitting around discussing current affairs and business; one had the feeling that more was accomplished here in an hour or two than in days of official meetings and deliberations. The decision makers, or many of them, could be found at the Polo Club, plus their supplicants and other interested parties – the equivalent, one might say, of the Carlton Club. However undemocratic this may sound, Nigeria was governed then by a military regime and in the end much must have begun there that was good and above board.

As the old guard drifted away and the younger elements took over, the scene changed once again. The club became more the abode of the wealthy youngsters whose fathers ruled the land, and it became much more expensive to belong to. One of the factors responsible for that was the introduction of Argentinian polo ponies.

We had always played on the local ponies bred in the north. Fast and sturdy they were, well under fourteen hands, and cheap to buy. Then, one day, an Argentinian ambassador imported three or four ponies from home which he presented to the head of state, General Gowon, who kept them at the club. Very fine animals they were, hand-picked. They were much larger and heavier than the local horses and any attempt to play against them led to uneven collision. Riding off was a very one-sided affair when one came up against Argentinian ponies – one had either to ban them from playing or to get more of them. The latter option prevailed, at great expense, aggravated by the fact that many of them could not stand the climate and died. The northerners would only sell stallions to the south. The Argentinians, on the other hand, would send only mares out of the country and some cross-breeding took place.

The bitter dislike with which the Nigerian intelligentsia of the 1950s and early 1960s looked at the Polo Club is no more. It is less prominent at the moment; but it still has its grounds, now right in the middle of town, well protected by an unseen hand. At one time a Lagos governor wanted to seize the field to build on it; his surveyors were driven off and never came back.

The annual tournaments were, and still are, grand affairs, well attended. Often the head of state would come for an afternoon, the diplomats and their ladies would turn up, and visiting teams from other parts of Nigeria and occasionally from other countries would be invited to play.

I first met my future wife at the club. I had acquired a new pony, Blue Peter, of which I had a high opinion, but felt I could not do it justice in a forthcoming polo scurry. I was too heavy (it was catch weights). My friend Jeff Duncan suggested we ask Pam Plowman to take the ride.

'Who is she?' I asked.

'Surely you know Pam,' he replied.

'I don't ' I said, and he pointed her out to me. 'Oh, that girl, I never knew her name.' She was a single girl working in Lagos for the War Office. Her father had at one time been British Consul in Harrar, Ethiopia, where she was born.

So we asked Pam and she consented to take the ride. Alas, during the race her hat threatened to fall off, she failed to concentrate, and our horse came well down the field. I was furious, but we ended up getting married and having five children. Blue Peter was in fact not all that good; he was a stumbler and we had to get rid of him. Later we had a splendid pony, Nohow, which was as fast as the wind and won a scurry or two.

I had in earlier days ridden in some polo scurries but neither horse nor rider were good enough to win; third was the best I could ever record. One nearly always got beaten by some young, good-looking girl half one's weight, but it was great fun and very exciting. These scurries took place on the racecourse during meetings, often attended by great crowds who would applaud or jeer as the case might be.

The football pools put paid to the crowds – there was only that much money to go round – and eventually the racecourse, also in the middle of town, was transformed into a grand ground for parades, ceremonies and such like. This was designed by Robert Atkinson, who had earlier had a hand in building Ibadan University as a junior partner to architects Fry Drew.

My polo-playing days ended with my bad motor accident in Liberia in 1962, but I kept up with the club for many more years, officiating at the annual tournaments.

General Gowon, head of state from 1965 to 1975, came to power as a young man in his early thirties. He was a good friend to the Polo Club and rode himself, time permitting. His tenure of office saw the club blossom, as already described, and it stayed at this pinnacle until he, too, was replaced by a military coup. It was the time of the first oil boom and money was spent freely by everybody, be they businessmen, professionals, military men or civil servants. Champagne was the drink to order, and young Nigerian ladies made their first appearance, accompanying their men to watch them on their fine ponies, riding hard, sweating profusely, and jumping off their mounts after the last chukka to take a drink.

There is something about horses and riding which arouses primitive instincts in men and women, and to see eight men careering over the field at full gallop chasing a ball, making contact on their horses, shouting and swearing, occasionally falling off and remounting, certainly makes the heart beat faster. One becomes a hero for a moment to oneself and to the spectator. A far cry from the swamps and forests of the south, but not so far for the northerner used to horses in daily life, even if replaced in time by Mercedes and Volvos.

I lost touch with the club in the 1980s, visiting only once or twice during the annual tournament. One has one's fun but age creeps up on all of us. Old interests are replaced by more sedentary preoccupations, especially since so many friends have left the field.

There were several other clubs: the Yacht Club, also an exclusive affair; the Ikoyi Club, a more democratic establishment; the Motorboat Club, a latecomer. There was the exclusive Yoruba Tennis Club, a Nigerian counter-blast to the colonial establishments, and then the Island Club, also founded and run by Nigerians. They all still exist and are going strong in this cosmopolitan town.

There is also the Metropolitan Club, an exclusive men's club run on very English lines, which admits ladies only at certain times or in certain of its rooms. This was founded in 1959 and its first president was Sir Adetokunboh Ademọla, then chief justice of the federation. I joined within a few weeks of its inauguration when it met in rented premises. Soon the club built its own large house on Victoria Island. It had at first a membership of 300, restricted to 50 per cent expatriates and 50 per cent Nigerians. The ratio was later changed in favour of Nigerians because there was not enough movement on the Nigerian side; once elected, members stayed on, whereas the expats came and went. It was designed to be a meeting place of senior representatives of government, industry, commerce, and the professions. There are not now many expats falling into these categories and the quota cannot be filled, although the diplomatic corps is taking it up to some degree. Because of the long waiting list on the Nigerian side there is a lower age limit of forty. Its Tuesday luncheons, attended by over 100 people are famous.

The president of the club has always been a senior Nigerian and is changed every few years. After Sir Adetokunboh Ademola, who officiated for many years, we elected Chief Dr. M. A. Majekodunmi, who rose to prominence as a young man when appointed sole Commissioner of the Western Region during the turmoil of the 1960s; then Mr. Justice Fatayi-

Williams, one-time chief justice of the federation and son of the man who first gave me accommodation; and at the time of writing, Mr. Akintola Williams, who was the first Nigerian chartered accountant to establish his own practice. Few Northerners are members, and even fewer attend.

One of the oldest and most prestigous social clubs is the Lagos Dining Club, founded in 1933. Its rules and regulations state, *inter alia*, that: 'The Object of the Club shall be to afford an opportunity for Members to meet one another socially at dinner or luncheon at least once a month. That the Club is restricted to males. That there shall not at any time be more than fifty ordinary members and the proportion shall be twenty-five Europeans to twenty-five Africans [sic].'

I joined the club in the late 1950s. We meet at dinner once monthly, changing venues from time to time. There are two hon. secretaries, one European and one African, but no other elected officers. Each meeting has a chairman who presides by alphabetical rotation; black tie is worn by members and their guests. There were eighteen founder members: men prominent in Lagos Nigerian society of the time and senior British government officers.

The club is still going and in 1991 was still meeting on the premises of the Metropolitan Club. At the 500th Meeting, it fell upon me, by rotation, to respond to the toast, 'The Lagos Dining Club', proposed by Chief Adebo, one-time Nigerian Ambassador to the United Nations. In the midst of my speech the electricity failed and we were thrown into darkness for several minutes.

The club is not far short of its 700th meeting. It too now has diplomats on the 'European' quota which includes Americans and Asians, and is probably the last where reputation and standing still play a bigger role than money and wealth. It has, to my mind, a more natural atmosphere today than of old, when the Nigerians, no matter how important within their society, had a complex relationship with the colonials of status; they were largely dependent on them for worldly success, and yet knew that they could be gone tomorrow – superior and inferior at the same time.

22

How Many Beans Make Five?

Returning from Ondo to Lagos one day in the early 1950s, the car broke down in Ibadan. A local mechanic assured us that he could repair it but would have to search the town for spare parts, which would take some hours. It was already late in the afternoon and the mechanic's quest for the parts could well take the rest of the day or spill over until the next morning. There was a flight to Lagos within an hour and I left my driver to await repairs, took a taxi to the airport, and was lucky enough to catch it.

They were small aircraft, Heron twelve-seaters, and sitting next to me was an Englishman who in the course of conversation mentioned that he was a produce trader in the UK on his first visit to Nigeria. His company had been in business for many years but had never traded with West Africa.

'I am here just to see what's going on, and one of the surprises of the visit to Ibadan has been the discovery that they grow butter beans in quantity. There's a big market for these beans in the UK. In pre-war days we used to get most of our beans from Madagascar, but the import of Madagascar beans is banned in the UK now.' He said it had been a political decision.

We had no sooner got into this discussion than the plane landed and I invited him to join me for a drink in my house. We continued to talk about butter beans.

'Why don't you go into this business?' he suggested. 'These beans are grown all around Ibadan and probably in other locations.'

'I know the beans, Mr. Coltman. The locals store them up for the rainy season when food can be scarce. I understand they have to be boiled for ages before they're fit to be eaten.'

'Yes', he said, 'they need a lot of cooking time but they are very nutritious. In the UK and the USA they are used mainly for canning. The Americans call them Lima beans. If you get going now, you can still make a few sample shipments. If all goes well you'll be set up for next season. My company, Anderson & Coltman, are prominent in this business and we would give you a good deal. Think it over and contact me in London – I'm off tomorrow.'

'Fine,' I replied, 'I'll discuss it with my partner and one of our Ibadan friends and let you know. Have you made any other arrangements for the supply of these beans?'

'No, I haven't. Call on me in London anyway next time you're there. Thank you for the drink.'

Sandy and I discussed Coltman's proposition. We wondered why we had not heard of this demand before and why apparently nobody had bothered to engage in this trade.

'Let's try it,' Sandy said, after we had been briefed by our Ibadan man that it would not be difficult to get some tonnage together. However, he warned us not to show too much interest or we would alert competition and the price would shoot up. 'You handle it for us,' we retorted. 'You'll be on your home ground.' We told Anderson & Coltman that we would be shipping trial consignments in the near future.

Our Ibadan contact set up a small buying organization collecting a few bags here and there, and we made a first shipment of fifteen tons. This was followed by another thirty tons before the first lot had been discharged. We knew nothing about beans but took a chance on it because very soon we would be unable to get any supplies and would have to wait until the following year.

It turned out well. Anderson & Coltman were pleased with the quality and sold to advantage. They urged us to prepare for next season when they hoped we could load hundreds, maybe thousands of tons. We could see ourselves making a small fortune out of this sideline.

I met Coltman for lunch in London and he re-confirmed that this was a promising start and that he could sell any quantity we managed to collect and ship. We told our man in Ibadan that good times were ahead if he could organize supplies, so he went round his contacts and advised them that he would buy all they had to offer. The news got to the farmers, who increased their plantings. A great spirit of adventure was reflected in this move, by people who were always quick to cotton on and take a chance. It was, after all, something quite new: a firm in Lagos wanting to buy butter beans in great quantities. But they assumed that if there was one buyer there would surely be more.

The new season was upon us. Others could not have known about the bean business and in no time at all we had collected and loaded several hundred tons with the promise of more to come.

Then a bombshell hit us: a cable from Anderson & Coltman not to ship any more beans as there had been an unexpected change in the market. The Madagascar beans had come off prohibition. The price had weakened considerably and, what was more, buyers preferred the Madagascar bean to the Nigerian. Could I come to London to discuss the situation?

We had engaged considerable funds in this business, relying on the judgement of the brokers and encouraged by our first shipments. In alarm I flew to London to meet Anderson & Coltman in their fine offices in the Minories. An impressive Rolls-Royce stood outside the door. The money we had invested in these beans could have bought two of them, and there would still have been some change left over.

Coltman was most apologetic. Nobody could have foreseen such a sudden *volte-face* by the government. 'Are you strong holders,' he asked, 'or do you have to sell in a hurry? If so I am afraid you will lose a lot of money.'

'We are strong holders, Mr. Coltman. We can afford to wait but we are most disappointed. For how long do we have to hold? Will these beans keep? How much will it cost to store them? Why are Madagascar beans preferred to Nigerian?'

Mr. Coltman was a patient man. It was not after all his

money that was at risk and he set out to pacify me. He explained that the trade had been taken completely by surprise; there had been no inkling of the change of policy. The beans could be kept in store for many months provided they were turned over and sprayed regularly. The charges would be moderate in relation to their value and they would make all the arrangements necessary.

The price had tumbled because the Madagascar merchants had accumulated large quantities which they now had to off load to become liquid again. Once that wave of supply was over, there would again be equilibrium in the market. Unfortunately the Nigerian bean, the canners had discovered, had a serious defect. Where the bean was detached from the pod a small black spot could be seen which, when canned in fluid, became larger. This did not detract from its nourishment, but it did detract from its looks in comparison with the Madagascar bean, which was white throughout.

'You must sit on your beans for while. We'll have to find a market for them but it will take time.'

The dinner he gave me that night was poor compensation for this debacle. We were stuck, I calculated, with enough beans for every man, woman and child in London.

So as not to rely solely on Anderson & Coltman, we mobilized our American agent, Valensi. He asked for a few kilos to be sent so that he could get clearance for the import from the Pure Food and Drug Administration. Alas, he was turned down. The beans, he was advised, had too high a content of arsenic. Valensi thought that the Lima bean lobby might have had a hand in it. We never discovered the truth or otherwise of this assumption; but he did manage to sell 100 tons to Japan and most of the stock was bought, after many months, by Woolworth in England. Why the beans had too much arsenic for the USA but not for the UK or Japan remained a riddle. It is precisely this arsenic content which makes the bean so nourishing and allows the eater to subsist on it when other food is scarce or too expensive.

We made a loss on the deal and forgot about the bean business. The farmers, who, like ourselves, had had high hopes, were landed with quantities of beans which they too had to market at reduced prices. It was a chain reaction. Whether Woolworth were happy with their purchase we never found out. That's how it goes.

We did occasionally experiment, dealing in commodities outside the timber trade. We handled red pepper and ginger from the north. That too we shipped to Anderson & Coltman. Two Czech friends of Sandy's in Sapele persuaded us to finance them in shipping sheet rubber. They had originally been sent to Nigeria by the Czech Bata company. Being staunch anti-communists, they managed to make money for themselves at the nationalized Bata's expense. These men knew their business and we traded successfully with them for a couple of years. Once they had found their feet, our Czechs felt they did not need any partners and we had to let them go.

As for the butter beans, dear reader, make sure you buy those from Madagascar; they are whiter than white. Woolworth, alas, do not seem to handle this type of food any longer, but the Nigerian farmer still plants it and his family still eat it. What does not kill me makes me stronger; so much for the arsenic objected to by the Pure Food and Drug Administration.

23

Strange Interlude

Welsh was one of our local timber competitors in Lagos. He had been a civil servant who had turned to the timber trade when the boom took everybody by storm. Welsh had built up a sizeable business and we ran across each other from time to time; in spite of being competitors we became friendly.

Welsh was in his early forties. His father had indeed been a Welshman who had worked for the PWD and had struck up a liaison with an Ibo girl who bore him a son. Mother and child were well looked after by the Welshman, who soon returned home but cared for the family and made sure that the boy went to a good school and that the mother was not wanting. The son in turn married an Ibo girl and they had four children, three girls and a boy.

By the time we met, Welsh was fairly well off with a house in a good locality of Lagos, his own business, and a small house in England left to him by his father. He was a tall man of pale complexion, quite well-known in the Lagos of those colonial days.

'We will come and visit you one day,' he used to say and he turned up one Sunday morning in 1954 with wife and children. It is customary for Nigerians to go visiting over the weekend without a definite arrangement – one calls on X and if not available goes on to Y. A laudable custom. All the same his visit caused a surprise, if only because his four children turned up as well.

Drinks and biscuits were served and we talked. He took me

to one side and said, 'I wanted you and Rylke to meet the family. We will call on the Rylkes when we leave here. I hope they'll be at home.'

'We are happy to meet your family, Mr. Welsh. They are a lovely lot.'

'Thank you,' he replied. 'I am making my will and I wonder if you and Rylke would be good enough to act as executors and whether I can tell my lawyers to write that in the will?'

I was baffled. I must have shown it because he went on, 'You have no axe to grind as far as my family affairs are concerned. I believe you to be honest gentlemen of acumen and experience. I've seen a lot of trouble in such matters, and would like to avoid any hassle for my wife and children. I pray it will never be necessary and that I will live to see my children grow up, but one never knows, does one?'

'Well, Welsh, I must talk to Rylke about it and get some advice too. Neither of us is a legal expert and I doubt if we are really the right people for you to appoint as executors here in Nigeria.'

'I think you are. Please discuss it with Mr. Rylke and give me a positive reply.' They left for their next port of call.

The more Rylke and I thought about it, the more dubious we became. What if our friend were to pass away whilst the children were still small? What of the rest of the family? What would be their reactions to two white men being in charge of their affairs? We voiced these misgivings to Welsh, who said that it was precisely because he was nervous of family complications that he wanted reliable outsiders to handle the estate.

In the end we agreed, feeling fairly sure that Welsh, who led an active life and seemed in robust health, would live as long as, if not longer than, we would. Our wives supported this view.

About a year later he was dead of tuberculosis.

The will was read and probated. It caused much consternation, not only to us, who were saddled with the responsibility of administering the estate, but much more so to Welsh's family, that is, his mother and other close relatives.

They came from the east to meet us and looked on us with

obvious resentment. They needed money: money to repay the funeral expenses, money to cover their transport, money for the children, and so on. We were not to give any money to the wife – they would take care of all that.

The wife also came, of course, in deep mourning dress. She said that we must take care of her and the children and not give any money to her late husband's mother, who hated her and would never do anything to support her.

In the will, Welsh had left his funds for the executors to dispose of at their discretion. We tried to reason with the mother, and more so her brothers, that we ought in the first place to make sure that wife and children were taken care of. That, we said, was how we understood our responsibilities.

'We don't want so-so white man's talk. Under our customs the man's mother is to look after all that. Who are you?'

'Under the law, madam,' we replied, 'we are charged to use our discretion. Surely, as the wife lives in Lagos with the children and you far away, we must in the first place deal with the wife?'

'What law?' they cried out. 'This is white man's law. You are white men, but we are Africans and have our own laws.'

'Madam, your son appointed us and he must have had his reasons. We don't want this responsibility, but having accepted it we must act according to our conscience, and we shall.' We gave her money to cover her expenses and sent her away. She was far from satisfied and it was clear that we would hear from her again and again.

For the next few months we dealt with the widow, and after a while we noticed that she was pregnant. A posthumous child, as we thought. At the same time the relatives appeared and made dark allegations about the woman's condition, which we ignored. No baby was born until ten months after Welsh's death. The family came down on her like a ton of bricks and came to us in a rage. 'You see, all the money you gave her went to that man. You see, we warned you.'

Shaken, we asked, 'What man?'

'Why, her driver. She had sex with her driver.'

In our embarrassment, and to be absolutely sure, we saw a

doctor friend and asked if it were possible for the child to be born ten months after the father's death. 'I have never experienced it, nor do I find it in the textbooks.'

We went to see a much-distressed Mrs. Welsh. At first she insisted that it was her late husband's child.

'It is unusual, madam, for a child to be born ten and a half months after conception. Grave allegations are being made against you by your husband's relatives. Not that we are setting ourselves up as judges of your morals, but we are in an awkward position.'

'I was forced by the driver,' she admitted eventually.

'And you kept him on all this time?'

'What else could I do? Here at least was a man who could help me with my daily problems,' she said, with tears rolling down her cheeks. 'They hate me; they want to take away my children. I am all alone. I am only a woman and this driver took me by force and after that I could not send him away.'

What her husband's relatives did to her we don't know, but within a few days she went stark raving mad, running naked about the street, screaming and shouting, and we had to make arrangements to have her sent to an asylum in Abeokuta. This was run by Dr. Lambo, who had a high reputation and indeed in time became an internationally acknowledged specialist in nervous disorders.

Welsh's mother's family moved in.

Mrs. Welsh came back from the hospital after a few months, still very melancholy and unable to lead a normal life.

The old woman and her brothers kept badgering us for money until we went to the administrator-general and requested we be relieved of our duties and that the government take over. We were asked to make formal application, present accounts, and after some time handed over our duties, but still kept in touch with the wife and children.

They took Mrs. Welsh away to the east to be healed by a native doctor; the cure was cruel in the extreme. To drive away the evil spirits (and to punish her?) she was fettered in a dark room and viciously beaten for months on end. When she eventually returned we could see the marks on her wrists where irons had been fastened; she looked haggard and frightened and never fully recovered. She died within a few years. Before then, however, the last child had died and we never discovered why. The driver had long since been chased away.

For all that, the children grew up well. The boy went to St Gregory's College and the girls to Holy Child, the best Roman Catholic schools in town. The son came to the UK, where he worked for the railways and became a station-master before returning to Nigeria. The girls married; the first-born a colonel in the army who was killed in the Civil War, after which she married again; the second a successful lawyer, while she herself ran a profitable restaurant after studying catering in England; and the third a young man who worked for us briefly before venturing out on his own. I never lost touch with the second girl, who had several children. She died relatively young of cancer in 1990.

We had been wrong, of course, to fall in with Welsh's wishes. Even had there been no political changes, we could not hope to do justice to the intricacies of local prejudices and customs. Welsh himself was mistaken in his ideas, too much inclined to believe in the power and infallibility of white man's laws, being half-white himself. We repaired the damage by going to the administrator-general, at that time fairly reliable if cumbersome and bureaucratic, and the results speak for themselves: the children retained their property and had their education. All we could do was to keep track of their progress, which may have been of influence.

One felt sorry for the widow. Still young, she was suddenly faced with enormous problems and, whether forced or otherwise, submitted to the driver, who was part of the family, so to speak, and probably took advantage of the situation, expecting financial gain as well as physical gratification by taking hold of the widow of his late master. The widow clung to him , realizing the hostility of her relatives and at the same time answering the awful question: is this the end of my being a woman?

24

Sub Judice

S andy and I had easily concluded our discussions about becoming a company early in 1948 and I had made notes 'on
one sheet of paper', as we used to say in the army, setting out the salient points. We wondered how to give the new
partnership official standing and decided to consult a lawyer.

'Lawyers cost money,' I said.

'Yes,' concurred Sandy, 'and they will make pages out of
your one sheet and confuse the whole issue.' We laughed.

We did not know any legal practitioners; we had read of
them in *The Pickwick Papers*. We found there were three or
four lawyers in Lagos but did not know their relative worth. I
called on Bank-Anthony for recommendations. He suggested
good friends of his, Morgan & Morgan, as very able and
reasonable practitioners.

'Fine. Can you give me a letter of introduction, please?'

'Gladly,' he replied, and did so. Their address was in Kakawa
Street, close to the Foresters Hall, in mid-town.

I showed the letter to Sandy.

'Morgan & Morgan?' he echoed. 'Sounds very grand, but
I've never heard of them.'

'Nor have I, but then we haven't heard of a lot of people
here, have we?'

A suspicion came over Sandy. 'They won't be Africans?'
When earlier I said we had found three or four lawyers in
Lagos, I meant three or four English lawyers; it had not occurred to me that we would be sent to Nigerian lawyers. However, we had been given the introduction and I thought we had

274

better go. We did not have to accept them if we did not like them.

We called on Morgan & Morgan. They had a poky little office and as we looked at it from outside, we almost turned round. We went, however, and were greeted with much respect by the two Morgans, Nigerians in their thirties. For them to have two white chaps appear in their office was a red-letter day in 1948! An immediate step up the ladder. For us, if it became known, it would be a come-down. 'Fancy these chaps going to a black lawyer; they must be hard up.' Prejudice was deep.

The Morgans were charming, learned and full of common sense; we established an instant rapport. they expanded my sheet of paper to a legal document of some four pages with seal and red ribbon. They registered the partnership as 'Brandler & Rylke Timber Company', got a serial number for it, had it fully signed by a registrar, and we had it framed. All this took a few weeks and we were then presented with a bill for £10 which we settled promptly. We were in business vis-à-vis that mighty and mysterious machine of government, the law!

The late 1940s saw quite a few new Nigerian lawyers establish practices. Some had been caught in the UK by the war and could or would not return, and others had to postpone their journey to an English university until hostilities were over, so a whole batch of newly qualified men appeared and started out.

We met and had dealings with several of them. There was Magnus Williams, a famous legal eagle because he had won a land case of major proportions for which he had been paid something like £1,500, a fabulous amount of money which was the talk of the town for months. That was, I fear, the highlight of his career. All the others rose to great prominence after independence: S.O. Lambo, who took his first case for us when one of our drivers killed a pedestrian – he got him off; T.O.S. Benson, my neighbour in Docemo Street; Thomas, Williams & Kayode, who had their chambers in Reclamation Road; and so on. Both Morgans rose to high rank.

One of the stormy characters of the Nigerian bar was Gani Fawehinmi, one of the lawyer sons of Chief Seriki Fawehinmi.

A fearless advocate, he took on the defence in many political cases where the accused had come into conflict with government bodies. He was widely reported in the press and on several occasions detained or arrested, but he would not be deterred. Now a chief, he is still very active. Another son became a judge.

Law was the premier discipline for any Nigerian wishing to enter the professions. One could work for government, albeit with difficulty, or one could set out on one's own. All the other professions were dominated by government service and the prospects for promotion very limited. Besides, one could make money as a lawyer, more money than as a doctor or engineer or surveyor working for a not over-friendly administration. True, the big companies would not look at Nigerian lawyers or give them briefs, but their compatriots would turn to them in ever growing numbers. Litigation became a major industry; it must have been the gambling spirit which motivated the Nigerians to have recourse to the law, or threaten to do so. 'I will sue you' was a common cry. Most of the cases were settled out of court, others went on and on, often for years: the machine of the law ground slowly. The lawyers waxed fat, while the litigants lost weight and money.

We once sued a logging contractor for a considerable sum; he had taken an advance but diverted his logs to a third party and made no effort to settle his debt. We gave the case to T.O.S. Benson, and the contractor hired for his defence two young lawyers fresh out from the UK – the latest model, so to speak. They were serious men who had imbibed the best of the English bar and still breathed its spirit. They realized there was no defence and admitted so in court, asking only for easy terms of repayment; we got judgement and costs.

As we left, an old hand who had happened to listen to the proceedings, H.O. Davies, said to me, 'If I had handled the case you would not have succeeded so easily.'

'How so?' I asked.

'I would have dragged the matter to try and tire you out.'

Justice is one thing and the law another. Lawyers were good at dragging cases out endlessly when it suited the occasion; one side or the other might run out of cash. Part of the job, I guess.

There was also the 'Affair Rasmussen'. Rasmussen had been my predecessor as honorary consul for Sweden; he had been principal shareholder of a successful property company which had developed the Yaba suburb before and after World War II. He had retired, leaving the running of his business to his junior partners. On his death, years later, his rather complicated will in Stockholm was contested between his divorced wife and the widow, and took a long time to be settled. When eventually the matter was clarified, the trustees could attend to his Nigerian estate. The Civil War was raging which slowed everything down, and they turned to the Swedish Embassy and the consul for help. We came up against a brick wall: we could not trace the deeds to the properties nor the present occupiers or owners in spite of engaging lawyers and accountants. Only some cash in the bank was proved and paid over. We advised Stockholm that it would be long-drawn-out effort. We then got a letter from a son, the principal inheritor and a student or recent postgraduate, to say he did not wish to pursue the matter; he felt he had no moral right to deprive poor suffering Nigerians of their meagre means. An idealistic young man, a product of the prevailing sentiment in Sweden that all Africans were starving, victims of colonialism or neo-colonialism. The beneficiaries of this noble gesture were happy; they could add another Volvo to their fleet. The estate was said to be worth millions.

Nearly all the judges were white; it was accepted that they would be fair, having no tribal affinities. They were also incorruptible; such prejudices as they had they reserved for lesser breeds of Europeans and Asians. Many ended their days with a knighthood. The first Nigerian judge, Jibowu, was appointed in September 1944, to be followed slowly by others.

Our offices in Campbell Street were near the courts; we could observe the lawyers going in and out of the portals carrying weighty tomes under their arms, or having them carried by their clerks who followed respectfully. All dressed in wig and gown in best English tradition. Those we knew would quite often call in for a coffee as they waited for their cases to come up, or they would come after the cases were over, mopping their brows and complaining. The practitioners had to be jacks of all trades. Today they would sue a debtor for £50, tomorrow they would defend an alleged murderer. It was many years before specialization could be attempted.

It was after independence that the lawyers came into their own; they were prominent and their services were much sought-after by the new administration. Within less than twenty years all white judges had gone, preceded by the white lawyers, only one or two of whom lingered for a little longer. They rose to great heights, to be followed by a new breed of lawyer: the men and women who had gone to university straight out of school, sometimes public school in England, the second and more prosperous generation. Most of their elders had had a rougher time. They had nearly all started off working for government or a large company as clerks and similar; they had to scrape together the money needed to got to university in the UK or to look for support from family and friends. Sometimes a scholarship was granted by government or employer or charitable educational institutions at home or abroad. One had to admire the guts and determination they showed to reach their goal and get admitted to an English university – with the occasional student making it to the USA or one of the English-speaking dominions. When they enrolled they would find that they were rather older than their fellow students; the fact that they had more experience of life never came amiss, and made them that much better and more versatile professionals.

There are now over twenty universities in Nigeria, many with a faculty of law, which remains a very popular target for admission. The standing of lawyers in the community may have declined a little – there are now too many of them to be worshipped - but they are still very much part of the establishment and likely to remain so. The ministers make the laws. The lawyers draw up the laws and administer them; we may applaud their handiwork or not as the case may be. But we dare not ignore them, even with a gun in our hands.

One must remember that the judiciary system in Nigeria is superimposed by an alien culture, and does not grow out of the roots of African tradition. It may be widely used and enforced, but one suspects that subconsciously it is still seen as the white man's legacy. It represents them versus us. Getting around it is considered to be rather clever and in no way dishonourable, as of old. Moreover, the law is much more visibly an instrument of power, often naked power; it lacks the tradition and facade which hides this fact in the West.

There is a parallel system, 'Native Law and Custom' – itself an expression coined by colonialism. It varies from region to region, but comes much closer to the sentiments of the average man. It cannot, however, cope with the complexities and needs of present conditions.

The wig and gown may strike one as incongruous in the context of old Africa, but old Africa is changing under the pressures of modern civilization; perhaps in time the two systems will converge and become one code of laws to be respected by the majority. It will take much patience, wisdom and good-will to achieve this.

A lawyer who came into prominence in the 1960s and 1970s was Fred Egbe. His father had already been a lawyer before him. He was much sought-after for major commercial work, well-known, highly respected and popular – sentiments we subscribed to in full after dealing with him professionally and privately. Egbe at the same time owned a property company of wide ramifications and was alleged to be very wealthy.

One day in 1978, newspaper headlines announced that Egbe, together with the manager of an insurance company, had been arrested, accused of stealing N450,000 from the insurance company. It was sensational and hardly credible for those who knew them that two senior members of society could be so arraigned. To make matters worse, Egbe was carted off like a common criminal to a distant prison where he was treated humiliatingly, stuck in a primitive cell without sanitation or other basic necessities. He was too important and reputable a person to be left there for long, and once the news reached the upper echelons of government he was released on bail. The case went on for a long time, vigorously pursued by the police, and eventually fell to the ground. The accused were acquitted. The whole affair was a mystery to the public.

The experience had a traumatic effect on Egbe. With grim determination and at great expense, he sued a judge and the inspector-general of police to the courts. An apology was not enough for him. The return of his passport to his office (he refused to collect it when asked to do so – you took it out of my desk, you return it to my desk) did not suffice. He wanted to hold up the culprits and the evil they mirrored for all to see. All this was widely reported in the press over the years.

Eyebrows were raised and his cases never came to a satis-factory conclusion; the judiciary procrastinated. Some of his acquaintances began to distance themselves from him. They felt he had made his money within the system which he now attacked; he had not attacked it when he was poor. That, of course, is the dilemma. If you are poor you cannot make your voice heard – nobody will listen to you. If you are rich and rebel against the system which allowed you to make a fortune, however honestly, you are tarred with the same brush. You are expected to accommodate yourself; if an error has occurred throwing prevailing standards out of line it must be discreetly corrected. If you kick up too much of a fuss, the establishment will close ranks against you.

I showed the draft of this sketch to Mr. Egbe, who was born in 1936 and read law at the London School of Economics. He commented as follows and allowed me to print his letter:

Dear Mr Brandler

I would have preferred some more time within which to comment. You are stating facts which could possibly in-fluence the thinking of many and it is imperative to en-courage the correct insinuations.

(a) All the judges were probably white in Lagos in 1946, but the late Justice Jibowu was in Warri as early as 1943. There were many others. The impression must not be given that there were no Nigerian judges in 1946.

(b) The lawyers did not dress in their wigs and gowns

(in those days) except actually in court or court premises. The spectacle of lawyers in wigs and gowns in cars or walking to court is very recent and was relatively unheard of, even in nineteen hundred and sixty (1960).

(c) Most of the universities may have law faculties, but certainly not all. In fact, until recently very few had law faculties.

(d) Getting past the law may be considered clever and in no way dishonourable only in certain circles. The business is frowned upon by many.

I was arrested and charged to court in March 1978 and not in 1976, along with the expatriate general manager of American International Insurance Company of Nigeria, Mr. Lefevre. He was a white American. We were charged with stealing a sum of four hundred and fifty thousand naira (N450,000), the property of the insurance company of which Mr. Lefevre was general manager.

The insurance company protested about the arrest of its general manager and legal adviser (myself), as it had not lost any money. The insurance company went on to contend that the N450,000 was properly lent by it on mortgage on the security of property in Ikoyi, Lagos.

It then transpired that the charges were contrived initially by the then Inspector General of Police, M.D. Yusufu, who was anxious to prevent me from exposing those who had fraudulently transferred abroad about 22 million dollars of public money through the African Continental Bank. It also became clear that the then Chief Judge of Lagos State, the Hon. Justice Adefarasin was happy to join in the conspiracy against Egbe (me) as the Chief Judge had been made to believe that I had stood in the way of his letting one of his houses in Lagos to a particular tenant of the Chief Judge's choice.

Some of my acquaintances only, distanced themselves. Many stood by me - Adamu Ciroma for one. Making one's money within the system implies obtaining contracts from the system. I would contend that I made whatever money I made in spite of the system that prevailed in 1978. I would have fought the fight regardless of my economic circumstances. It has also to be borne in mind that in the 60s and early 70s, judges were not landlords and chiefs of police did not protect those responsible for the large scale theft of public funds.

We were carted off to Ikoyi prison for 4 days and to Badagry prison for 7 days, making eleven days in all. At both places, I was locked up in a fairly large cell with seventeen others in one place and with ten others in the next. Both cells had very basic amenities.

I have a great deal to say about this experience and I shall let you see my analysis some day.

Yours sincerely
Fred Egbe

25

The New Republic

One could not be a minister and ignore one's grass roots. That had been made clear to us when Ekotie Eboh intervened on behalf of his brother as we cut back on contractors' advances. Heaven knows for how many different people he had to plead in the midst of his heavy duties. He was also known as Mr. Five Per Cent, but he was a very good minister and when he was shot dead in the first *coup d'etat* it was a great loss; besides, when all was said and done, 5 per cent was modest by comparison with what was to follow.

Men like him had dozens, even hundreds, of real and not so real dependants hanging on them. They had risen from their midst but they were still very much part of them. There was no unemployment insurance, no public health, no free education - the extended family took their place. It would have been impossible to refuse favours which people did not consider as such but as their right. Our 'brother' is now a big man and he must look after us. And he did.

A minister's salary was hardly large enough to meet all these demands; it barely covered the ever rising expectations of the immediate family, let alone the wider circle of loyalties. Much of the extra money earned had thus to be distributed. This obviously did not apply only to ministers. Anyone who had been educated, sometimes with the help of his clansmen, had these obligations once he had risen above the crowd – and seemed to accept them. Nor did the average citizen begrudge this new elite its sudden importance and wealth. On the contrary: here are our men driving cars, travelling abroad, having fine houses just like the white masters. There was reflected pride and, of course, hope of better things to come.

It worked for a time while the colonial system staggered on and the old native customs were still accepted, but the seeds of havoc had none the less been planted. The perks got bigger and bigger, as did the appetite for yet more. The masses streamed into the towns and the tight fabric of social life became ever looser. One began to hear the cry of corruption.

Taxed with corruption, the new men demurred. It was the colonial masters who were corrupt, they would counter: they gave the big contracts to the British firms; they controlled finance in the interests of the home country; they made import and export laws for the benefit of their compatriots; they kept Nigerians out of all lucrative positions; they made the laws to suit their own pockets.

It was clever sophistry culled from anti-imperialist ideology and as such, and from that point of view, had some validity, except that it should not be called corruption but colonialism. It was certainly no excuse for the new men to abuse their power to their personal advantage. It could be argued, however, that it was part of their colonial heritage.

It was also part of their native culture. The concept of the nation-state and of the citizen's service and loyalty to it, to the exclusion of older loyalties closer to home, was alien to their experience and traditions. When they served under the colonial regime, they never felt any allegiance to it – self-interest forced them to conform, born of necessity and fear.

The old iron discipline was strongly entrenched; the fear of being found out and dismissed in disgrace remained an inhibiting factor, but this was eroded year by year. The rot started at the top and rapidly spread to the lower echelons. Things became chaotic and anarchic. A parallel state and administration grew up; within it were certain rules and conventions which gave it a sense of balance. The more it was realized that by being in power or being attached to those in power one's economic advantage increased, the more people strove for this power.

As the lower ranks perceived what went on, they followed the example. In the end the policeman on the beat, the messenger responsible for tracing an urgent file, the clerk in charge of stamping paper, the officer issuing a passport or a licence rose to the occasion. It soon permeated the private sector as well: the bank manager who authorized a loan, the storeman who ordered materials, and so on. All felt they were personally involved in granting favours.

We must remember that after independence the state became still more pervasive in many economic activities. Large enterprises like oil, insurance, banking, steel, etc. had the state either as majority or strong minority shareholder. Parastatal companies were set up dealing in exports and imports; marketing boards controlled agriculture. The government's patronage extended to all these manifold activities and thus indirectly also controlled the rest of the economy. The resultant inefficiency, waste and mismanagement deprived the generality of much of the country's resources and channelled them into relatively few private hands.

Foreign interests were not slow to take advantage of this situation; measures taken ostensibly to protect Nigerians against outsiders were ineffectual. The influence of Middle Eastern and Asian participants, especially in industry, grew apace, with most of them working under a Nigerian front which indeed also benefited substantially.

It was said – a point difficult to prove or disprove – that this development was an unavoidable interim step and would eventually encourage Nigerian entrepreneurs to band together and provide a capital base for the indigenous middle class to emulate the foreigners' achievements.

For all that, the young officers who staged the coup in January 1966 did not know what they were doing, encouraged by many influences, sober as well as mischievous. The sons of well-to-do parents, who were privileged enough to send their children to good schools, hand-picked by the white establishment, trained at Sandhurst, imbued with all the Western ideas of honour, loyalty, obedience to orders, and last but not least ruthlessness, they saw the Nigerian scene – their own country – with unrealistic, even alien eyes. Vague idealists (ambition also played a part), they had given little or no thought to the problems of running a country, hoping to change habits and ways of life at a blow. 'We must get rid of the corrupt politicians,' was their main slogan. They had visions of Britain, where they had never come across bribes, where everything seemed orderly, where they could see no oppression and misuse of power. A year at the LSE before returning from Sandhurst might have put them right!

It was at the Polo Club that I came face to face with General Ironsi, who had been made head of state after the first coup. I had met him briefly when he was ADC to the last English governor-general, Sir James Robertson, in the 1950s; I believe he was a captain then. Through seniority and merit he, like so many young officers, had made a rapid career and he was put in charge of the country to get it back to an even keel.

One would not say that the Polo Club members were enthusiastic followers of the new order or of the general. He came from the east where horses were abhorred to the point that they used to be singled out for ritualistic killings by being beaten to death – a symbolic gesture in the old days against the northern horsemen who came down and raided.

Some Polo Club function – the visit of an overseas team – had been arranged and the club diplomatically invited the head of state and others of the new elite to attend. I was surprised when he accepted, as this was hardly in keeping with the new Nigeria which those who had put him in power envisaged, but he came all the same and watched the game, well looked after by the president of the club and other prominent members.

Ironsi was a huge man, who moved slowly and with dignity; very jovial and typically army, well-groomed and polite. We chatted for some time – he was interested to hear that I had served with the RWAFF in which he may have started his military service in colonial days. He clearly knew much about military affairs and we did not, of course, touch on politics. One could sense that he was of the old school, brought up in the British tradition of army life, with little knowledge of or affection for politicians or civil servants. It must have been a bewildering task for him to try to run this new country and he would have had to rely greatly on advisers, few, if any, of whom he could have known intimately. He surrounded himself with the people he knew best, mainly civilians from the part of the country he came from, a group anxious for radical reforms and at the same time intent on consolidating their new power and influence.

True enough, for some weeks after the first coup there was more order in the towns, people queued for buses and in post offices, civil servants dealt with their duties by rotation, and so on. But this was not a new spirit – it was the remembered respect for colonialism and the fear of the strong hand having returned which motivated this fleeting reversion to the old order. The army was something nobody knew much about except that they had guns. It consisted of around 25,000 men. The coup was staged by a few dozen middle-ranking officers. To run the country they had to rely on the same civil servants who had served the politicians and it did not take them long to find that out. The coup showed perhaps what could be done if one had cadres of devoted, well trained and motivated reformers who could be placed in key positions in every part of the country and every major administrative centre of those parts. Those cadres would need to be indoctrinated and to accept a philosophy and social pattern understood and approved by a large part of the population. Otherwise the coup would be a mere palace revolution, a chance for the next team to do what their predecessors had done.

I think Ironsi's base was too narrow, his friends too inexperienced and rash, and the loyalty of the civil service and his fellow army officers, with a few exceptions, dubious. He was gunned down in the counter-coup of August 1966 and his regime collapsed. It was a shame he had to die thus, as the figurehead of an unconsolidated revolt; perhaps he had been too sure of himself and failed to realize the hostility he faced.

At the Polo Club he was all smiles, took his drinks, chatted, and followed the game, asking questions about the rules. He was a good soldier but a bad politician, who should never have allowed himself to be made head of state. Perhaps it was his sense of duty mixed with a sudden vision of glory which made him accept the job, or perhaps he was imposed upon. He paid for it dearly. He cannot have been much over forty years of age when he died.

The second coup of 1966 was also dramatic from a personal point of view. My family – wife and five little children – were on a BOAC flight to Lagos on 19 July when their plane was diverted to Accra, Ghana. We were so informed by the airline in the evening, and next morning I got visas for Benin, Togo and Ghana within three hours (helped by my diplomatic status, which I pulled for once) and set off for Accra. As we passed Ikeja on the Agege road – I had selected that route because I wanted to avoid the barracks on the other – there was still some shooting going on above us on the bridge over our road. The streets were empty, but nobody stopped or interfered with us and we got to Accra in the evening. My appearance caused a minor sensation! The stranded passengers had been well taken care of, and Mr. and Mrs. Morel – he was GM of Barclays Bank in Accra, having previously been stationed in Lagos – were particularly helpful. One of the stranded travellers was Sir Louis Mbanefo, then chief justice of the Eastern Region, returning from a visit to London.

'Louis, here is your counter-coup.'

'What do you mean by that?'

'I mean that the north will not accept Ironsi and his politics of a unitary state.'

'Will it succeed?'

'I think it has succeeded. You will have problems.'

The family went back to England, where I joined them to spend the holidays in Bournemouth instead of Lagos and Calabar. The episode had been an adventure for the three boys; less so for our little girl and baby, not to mention her mother.

The next regime, under General Gowon, lasted ten years. He was well served by his 'Super Permanent Secretaries', Ayida, Asiodu and Atta, who ran the country almost single-handedly during and after the Civil War, a remarkable group of highly intelligent, UK-educated men in their thirties. General Gowon himself was well under forty.

Then coup followed coup, regime followed regime. The more it became obvious that one's tenure of power could be short and limited, the more it seemed necessary to make the most of that power in the shortest possible time. Those governments which remained in office for longer periods, and whose senior officers had had time to take full advantage or, as the saying went, 'had their bellies full', would endeavour to reverse the process, realizing how adverse the system was to the people and ultimately to themselves. That task, however, was and is as yet beyond them. If they tried too hard they would be removed by force by the next hungry candidates waiting for their turn. Some of the wise ones retired of their own accord.

As long as the state remains the major economic power and influence under the guise of private enterprise, so long will malpractices and misuse of office continue, with its overriding temptation to become one of those controlling the government. It is an international malaise.

26

Pennies to Pounds

In money terms there were no excessively rich Nigerians in the 1940s and early 1950s. There were wealthy traders, farmers, timber dealers, cattle owners, licensed produce buyers. Middle- and upper-class men and women owned property; there were transporters and shopkeepers. There were the Emirs and Obas who commanded wealth. But there were no millionaires in the accepted Western sense. The division between rich and poor was measurable.

All 'big business' was in the hands of European/American companies: there was no indigenous industry or farming of size. The customary land laws made inheritance difficult. Polygamy and the great number of children waiting to share their fathers' inheritance – often fighting over it – mitigated against the accumulation of riches from generation to generation, mitigated against a man becoming very rich in the European tradition. Yet within thirty years of independence, hundreds of Nigerian dollar millionaires could be counted, and a good few dozen or more worth tens of millions of dollars. A moneyed middle class had also arisen. How did all this come about?

Independence in October 1960 brought many opportunities. There was a great influx of new interests from countries who before had little chance to do big business in the colony. The riches of the country were therefore tapped more widely after it became independent and , with the political power in few hands, those riches found their way more easily into Nigerian channels.

The Civil War made money for those Nigerians connected with its organization. The discovery and development of large crude oil resources brought untold wealth into the coffers of the state, which filtered through into individual hands. The oil wealth translated itself into a land and building boom in the cities. The enforced Nigerianization of foreign assets found its way into private accounts. And, finally, inflation wiped out many heavy debts and consolidated all that went before.

Some pertinent questions may be asked:

- If there was limited ready cash how were the riches tapped?
- Who made money in the Civil War and how did they do it?
- How could individuals benefit to the tune of millions of dollars from crude oil production?
- Who now owned the land, and how was money found to build houses?
- How did Nigerianization benefit groups of individuals?
- How did inflation consolidate wealth?
- Were not taxation and exchange control inhibiting factors?

There are no simple answers to these questions; mine are views derived only from personal observation.

The colonial British civil servants had been financially secure and incorruptible. They laid the foundations of the Nigerian civil service. The latter, however, was politicized, financially insecure, and open to family and tribal pressure; faced with undreamt of opportunities, it could and did not live up to its tutors' ideals.

Here were young men of good education and talent suddenly given the power to make decisions which would enrich the parties involved to an unheard of degree. Yet their salaries were small and their future uncertain. How long would the job last? (It was much the same with their ministers, but that is a different story – they went into politics for power and all that

291

implied.)

The colonial regime, always strict in its budgeting, had left a sound economy to their way of thinking. There were taxes, import, export and excise duties, and the marketing boards which had accumulated substantial reserves – in theory to balance farmers' incomes through subsidies, in reality a form of taxation on the farmers. Ready cash was in the Bank, to be spent by civil servants under the direction of their ministers. A new world opened up to those in charge of the departments. It did not take them long to appreciate the strength of their position and great temptations were thrown in their way. These were too attractive to be ignored.

How were civil servants to choose between three or four contractors of about even standing, quoting more or less the same price (or encouraged to adjust their price)? Did they take a consideration offered, or even ask for one? These people had struggled all their lives for a few pounds, and were suddenly expected to dispose of millions.

The new foreign companies trying to enter the market soon realized that they could do better by engaging local 'sponsors' to make progress. These 'sponsors' close to the power-base were ready for a fee to act as 'fixers', or were appointed directors of the new concerns. They had to rely on patronage – 'corruption' in this context may be too strong a word. Here was a radically new administration anxious to show that it could distance itself from the old, but it had too little knowledge of industrial and financial forces and readily relied on the middlemen who had, or were thought to have, the necessary know-how and connections. All this happened with remarkable speed, a tribute to the sense of enterprise and adventure of the Nigerians.

It got quickly out of hand, however. Bank accounts swelled by negotiating deals for and with the government, and in this the politicians played a major role. It paid to be in politics! The money so made was at first used sensibly. The politician would build a fine house in his home town; he would support his many hangers-on to cement his position; he would give out bursaries for education. However sensible this spending, it began to open up a gulf, to show a contrast with the past which in the end was noticed and criticized, not least by disappointed rivals. The man who was 'in' had to make more to spend more to keep his seat. It was a vicious circle. It led within five years to the first coup and the Civil War.

The federals and the secessionists had to go on a war footing. They had to build up their armed forces. Equipment was required for that - arms, ammunitions, transport, communications, uniforms - the sinews of war had to be procured in a hurry. In war, price is a minor consideration. In almost three years of hostilities, many Nigerians made large sums as arms dealers or as agents for foreign suppliers.

Oil was first produced by Shell; most was found after World War II, and increasingly so in the 1950s and 1960s, by which time other oil companies also came into the picture and the royalties accruing to government began to mount up. Moreover, government insisted on receiving a percentage of all oil lifted through its own newly formed oil company (NNPC as it is now known). The NNPC disposed of its quota by either selling it back to the companies or disposing of it on the open market. Came the oil crisis of 1972 and the rise in price coupled to the shortage of crude on offer. Prices shot through the roof within months and Lagos was full of oil traders from all over the world anxious to secure contracts with NNPC. Their problem was how to get in with the NNPC and they scouted round for friends. Once again patronage played its part. Government owed favours to individuals and soon discovered an easy way to discharge them: 'Find an acceptable oil company abroad and bring them here; they will sign a contract with us and must pay you a commission.' The oil turnover ran into billions of dollars yearly and the commissions were handsome – to be shared by various parties. They spewed out many millionaires (described in the later chapter, 'Black Gold').

There was a growing shortage of housing in Lagos and other big towns, as people streamed into the cities. When independence came, embassies, consulates and foreign companies were all looking for suitable accommodation. Thousands of houses were required within a short time. Foreigners, however, could not own land except in the colony of Lagos and even there the areas reclaimed from the sea (like Victoria Island, which became a rival to Ikoyi suburb), which represented most of the available land for building, belonged to Lagos State (that is to say, was government-owned).

To provide the housing required, especially for the upper echelon, schemes were devised whereby anyone who had a parcel of land suitable for an adequate house would go to one of the building contractors (foreign companies, mainly Italian) and say, 'If you build this house for me, I will let it to a company who will pay me five years rent in advance, and with that money I will settle the house you have built.' This became common procedure. For the building contractors it was very good business.

To obtain a plot became a licence to print money, which those in charge of the allocations well knew; they used their power as a means of patronage and probably as a means of making money for themselves. Allocations were widely spread and were important in founding the new moneyed middle class. The rents paid for these houses were phenomenal compared to the cost. In later years, the need for more office space became so acute that Victoria Island is today occupied by many businesses like banks and airlines. Reclamation is still continuing.

A sizeable crude oil producer and a member of OPEC, courted and fawned upon by the West in its pretended or real panic during the oil crisis of the mid-1970s, the military regime seized the opportunity to have its nationals take over as many foreign holdings as possible. The junta felt strong enough and were not warned off.

In quick succession the government promulgated two 'Indigenization Decrees' designed to effect a re-alignment of the economic forces in the country. It was to be a sale on a varying scale from 40 per cent to 100 per cent of the companies' businesses. They had to hive off their Nigerian holdings to be floated, if large and sound enough, on the Nigerian stock exchange. Only Nigerians and certain members of the Organization of African Unity (OAU) were allowed to purchase these shares. Strict rules were laid down how to proceed and the regulations demanded that the price at which these shares were offered to the public be approved by a board, as was the number of shares any one party could hold. In harsh bargaining the shares were priced at a low value and their purchase promised a real bonanza.

Within the framework of Nigeria's capital structure of the day the amounts at stake were considerable, and not enough money was in circulation for such substantial investments to be taken up, no matter how favourable the quotation. In consequence, the banks were given guidelines to lend prospective buyers of shares the necessary funds against the security of the certificates. The banks were overrun by applicants and it was left in the end to the managers' discretion to decide who got what; they found themselves in a very privileged position, as did all involved in this exercise. Moreover, the newly indigenized companies had to appoint chairmen and directors with all the perks and advantages attached to such positions, not to mention business openings. The able ones made the most of this opportunity. Lawyers and accountants worked day and night to keep up with the demand for their services. A whole new segment of moneyed Nigerians arose out of this policy.

Companies unsuitable for flotation had to sell their interests by private treaty subjected to the same restrictive provisions. It gave rise to much manoeuvering and occasionally to circumvention by finding Nigerian strawmen willing to act for a consideration, which practice spread later with the influx of new investors from Asia and the Middle East.

It was an economic revolution, a transfer of wealth at a stroke, a take-over by force. It underpinned the emerging capitalist class. It was in line with the sentiment that money could be made without hard work. Serious foreign investment was reduced to a trickle for many years; that was only to be expected and a price the junta seemed willing to pay. Fifteen years later, these laws were drastically revised under General Babangida's regime.

Under the old order much of all these gains would have been

295

syphoned off in taxes, but this was not the case. Also, many Nigerians preferred to invest abroad, which they managed to do in spite of exchange control laws. There must have been many loopholes which allowed them to do this.

Inflation came, and with it the deterioration of the value of the currency, the naira. In the 1970s, one naira was worth $1.80. By 1992, it had fallen to 5 cents. Real estate, share values, the cost of goods and services rose accordingly, while savings were wiped out and pensions suffered – a familiar pattern well known all over the world. Repaying loans to the financial institutions became easy and consolidated many a fortune still in the balance.

Another wealth-creating gimmick under the second republic, which lasted from 1979-83, was the sudden imposition of import licences. Nothing could be brought in effectively without a licence which was issued by a ministry of the federal government. This soon developed into another venue of patronage and licences were traded, often passing through two or three hands, before ending up with the party actually requiring the goods. Again, large fortunes were made.

In common with the international trend, a number of drug barons also surfaced.

A new elite had come into being.

27

Lagos Line is Out of Order

The American GM in Calabar shouted at the telephone operator, 'Why the devil can't you get me Lagos? I have been waiting on this call since yesterday.'

'Sir, Lagos line is out of order.'

'It can't be out of order for two days! Try again.'

She came back after thirty minutes. 'Sir, they say Lagos line is out of order.' She looked at me imploringly as if to say, 'Please tell him it's not my fault.'

'Patricia, is there no way we can help the GM?'

'Sir, if you take him to the telephone exchange maybe they can do something.'

'Dirk, let's jump into the car and go down to the telephone exchange.'

The operator nodded approval and put us wise which entrance to take. The Calabar exchange was small; three or four young women sat on their stools working the switches. I explained our mission to the supervisor.

'Sir, Lagos line is out of order. It is impossible to get connection.'

'Can't you please do something? This call is most urgent. You know us, don't you?'

'We know you, sir, we know Calvenply.' She hesitated. 'Sometimes we can reach Lagos via another station – let me try.'

She fiddled around for minutes calling different towns, talking to her opposite numbers by name, and in the end managed to get through. We thanked her. I said, 'You know my colleague here nearly sacked the operator for failing to get Lagos.'

'Don't do that, sir, she is my friend; I sent her to you. I will try to help you, but we can't do it often; the lines are bad.'

We showed our appreciation and, difficult though it remained, we did speak to Lagos on occasion.

When self-dialling was installed, there was little improvement. For weeks all would be fine, then for months the lines did not work. One was thrown back on the personal contact.

In colonial days, the infrastructure was very limited but what there was worked. There were no power cuts. There was no water shortage. Telephones were hand-operated, and if one made a call one booked it and was connected. One would be advised of any delays. The railways ran on time. The port functioned well. Roads were maintained. The cable service was efficient.

Supply was tailored to demand, and that demand was restricted to a small part of the population, not by design but by prevailing circumstances. Plans for systematic extensions of these services were in hand and slowly executed. In the mid-1950s, for instance, in the area of Lagos where we had our logging beaches 200 additional lines were allocated, which the engineer in charge thought was over-optimistic. His estimate must have been based on past performance.

After independence in October 1960, the economy took off and by the 1970s demand doubled from year to year. The infrastructure deteriorated in proportion to the increased traffic required of it. It could not cope. Nor could it catch up. These installations cannot be provided overnight. For every additional KW installed, three were needed. For every gallon of water provided, three more were required. For every new telephone line made available, many applicants were disappointed. The mail slowed down. The railways, working all-out, could not be maintained and delays became the norm as rolling stock failed. The ports were overloaded. Only the cable service retained reasonable efficiency.

For year after year the electricity supply was cut off almost daily for hours on end. One began to live in darkness and heat.

The power stations simply could not keep up with requirements and a new breed of entrepreneur surfaced: the supplier
of generating sets. Thousands of generating sets were sold to
private houses, factories and government organizations. These
generators, of course, had to be serviced and the lack of skilled
artisans made that difficult.

I cannot give figures, but I know that the English town of
Coventry, for instance, had factories which practically lived on
selling their generators to Nigeria and expanded from year to
year. One can safely assume that the value of these generators
taken as a whole would have built enough modern power stations to ease the problem within a few years, whereas it continued for decades.

There would be no advance warning. Suddenly the light
failed. Those who possessed a generator would switch it on
provided it was in serviceable condition and they had bought
their diesel or petrol in time.

For twenty years and more, civilized life was handicapped
by these difficulties. Surprisingly, perhaps, to the Western
reader, all this was accepted by the majority as a fact of life. In
their youth, after all, they or their parents were unlikely to have
had electricity, so the lack of it was nothing strange to them.
The next generation looked at it with different eyes and the
powers that be reacted accordingly. In this respect the military
regimes appeared to be more efficient, a point not lost on the
populace.

Matters changed for the better after the military coup in
1983. It made one wonder whether some of the discomfort
imposed on the people by the lack of services was due to a
deliberate policy of shortage so dear in the old days to the
traders and importers, both Nigerian and foreign – 99 per cent
supply makes a profit, 101 per cent makes a loss – and to the
middle echelon of civil servants in charge of electricity, telephones, water, etc. If an officer disposed of so many telephone
lines, so many electrical connections, so many aircraft seats, so
much shipping space, and so on, he was a little king. He did
certainly have his official guidelines and priorities, but he
would follow these to the minimum and have his parallel

considerations. He would favour his friends, his townspeople, the big chiefs, all for a consideration, and he would also be set upon by powerful men to short-circuit his instructions and accommodate their protegés.

It went further than that: if your telex malfunctioned or your water supply failed and you reported it, you still had to find the actual men detailed to repair it and coax them to come in time. If you arrived at the airport with a confirmed seat, you might still find that you were not on the passenger list because somebody had gazumped you with a suitable dash.

The evil spread; the more it was successful, the more it was reverted to. As the cost of living shot up and wages did not follow suit, it became a way of life. There is an official world and an unofficial one; they have not yet met.

The population has learnt to accommodate itself. Nothing functions very well but nothing fails totally. The majority are left out but they have always been left out, here as elsewhere.

Nigeria is now full of computers, telex and fax machines. One can telephone London, New York and Tokyo. Nobody sends cables any more. The more privileged one's position, the less one's difficulties. One has influence, one knows the ropes, one pays. It all seems chaotic but in the end sorts itself out. If the best is impossible, the worst rarely happens.

I must end this sketch by singing the praises of one of the more unpopular generals of the military regimes, General Idiagbon, who became number two under General Buhari in the coup of 1983. The art of making friends and influencing people was not his forte; he was considered to be too harsh and altogether unreasonable – too dictatorial, and an enemy of the press.

He did, however, accomplish one thing I would have thought to be impossible: he cleaned up the streets of Lagos and other big cities. They were badly in need of it. The dirt that had accumulated over the years was almost indescribable. Rubbish was thrown out, paper and cans discarded, empty boxes and bits of metal littered the pavements, and, worse still, broken down cars and lorries by the hundreds were abandoned on the roads and left to rot.

General Idiagbon issued a decree ordering owners of these vehicles to collect them off the roads under pain of severe penalties; he mobilized units to tow them away if not moved within a given time. Occupiers of houses were held responsible for the cleanliness of their own property and the pavements and roads in their immediate vicinity. Enforcement officers ensured that these commands were obeyed – some of them service personnel armed with vicious whips they were not slow to use. The last Saturday of every month was declared to be Sanitation Day, when nobody was allowed out in the morning and had to be busy tidying up their compounds and the streets in front.

Enforcement was harsh, but within months Lagos took on a new appearance and so did all the towns. The measure was a great success and was ultimately accepted by the population as worthwhile. Its heritage is still with us – the Sanitation Days are kept up, if not with the vigour of old. It is the one effort for which General Idiagbon is remembered.

It can be done!

28

Cement

One of the most extraordinary sights ever seen in Lagos were the 440 ships lying in the roadsteads awaiting to discharge their cargoes of cement in 1971.

The Civil War had severely restricted building activities, which took off with a vengeance after it ended, fuelled by the oil boom. At the same time, at least two of the cement works in the country had been damaged and were out of production; others suffered from a lack of spare parts and raw materials. They could not satisfy demand. A severe shortage resulted.

The government had to do something about it. Slowly at first, and then with increasing speed, the ministry issued import licences and there was a mad scramble for them. They were only rarely given to the traditional cement importers, but instead were used to pay off obligations the ministry felt bound to discharge, in lots of between 3,000 and 8,000 tons, (that is, a shipload). Hundreds of these licences were issued. Parallel to and independently of the Ministry of Commerce, the armed forces did the same; they deemed cement to be part of their procurement programme.

Double patronage widened the net of the cement licencees. These included market women, general traders, doctors, lawyers, surveyors, relatives of soldiers and civil servants or their girlfriends, and others. The wealth was spread: one had to have the right connections and, either as repayment for favours done or on the understanding of favours to be received, one was given a licence. The more important, affluent and well-connected the party involved, the larger the licence.

It was up to the licencee to find a source of supply, a ship to carry it, and to arrange the finance required to complete the deal. Local purchase orders were issued and payment would be honoured after discharge of the cement. These purchase orders had a demurrage clause. If the vessel arrived and could find no berth to discharge, the ministry/armed forces were liable to pay for the time it took the vessel to get rid of its cargo over and above the stipulated lay-days, a common procedure in shipping.

We were never involved in this affair and I cannot describe the intricacies of the transactions, only the general effect. Several of our Nigerian acquaintances obtained licences and came to us for finance, or at least advice, but we declined; we were exporters and not importers. We had imported a shipload of cement once in the 1950s when we built Kajola House. We were persuaded to do so by a smart salesman of a cement company and we gave the cement as part-payment to the builder who constructed the complex for us. There were unexpected hazards like broken bags, sweepings from the vessel which had to be re-bagged, sudden rains threatening to make the bags into solid rock, all of which had to be dealt with and are no doubt common in this trade.

How then was the licencee to benefit from his windfall, having no knowledge of the trade, no knowledge of shipping procedures, and no money? He sold his licence on to third parties able to handle it. He gave a legal document to that effect and either took his money there and then or, if he were more adventurous, was promised part of the profit when it had been cashed in. People generally chose the former. In this way, cement moguls arose, with licences for tens of thousands of tons who now had to find finance, sources of supply, and ships. It ran into big money.

The Nigerian banks could engage themselves only so far; there were not nearly enough funds available for this sudden upsurge in requests for loans and it must be remembered that there was a rush of imports for other industrial and consumer goods as well when the economy revived.

Foreign banks and foreign financiers began to take an interest, alerted by the canvassing of the licence holders and their contacts, which included the manufacturers of cement almost worldwide. The news spread like wildfire amongst the flotsam and jetsam of international middlemen all anxious to use their connections or to make connections to promote the Nigerian cement business. In Britain, for instance, an ex-government minister and a prominent yachtsman became involved. Mr. Fix-it came out of his hole.

To add to the confusion, forged licences, revoked licences and dishonoured licences appeared out of the blue. Nevertheless, most of the licences were genuine and, once the first few ships had discharged and been paid for their cargo, the stampede took off.

The enormous request for cement translated itself on to the international scene. The traditional suppliers like Britain, Spain, Poland and a few others were unable to satisfy demand. Cement had to be bought from the Middle and Far East, from countries like Romania, Bulgaria and the USSR, from Turkey and Portugal, indeed from anywhere which manufactured the product. Prices soared, and the goods changed hands many times before they were loaded to make their way to the west coast of Africa. The factories, the wholesalers, the banks and money brokers all came into the act, not least the shipowners, their agents and charterers.

Ship after ship arrived off Lagos port, which simply could not cope. The huge Tin Can extension was not yet in operation; only eight or ten berths were available and not all could be allocated to cement vessels. Besides, such facilities as were in operation had inefficient equipment awaiting repair or renewal, but even if all had been in good working order there was no way in which these quantities could be handled. At best I think a vessel could get rid of 500 tons a day. They averaged 5,000 tons and thus needed at least ten days. Makeshifts were organized, such as discharging into barges, but there were not too many of those around either. Off-loading in nearby Cotonou meant endless bureaucratic delays and that port, too, was very limited.

So the ships piled up and had to wait their turn. Taking one's turn to discharge should have been strictly by rotation but a smart shipping agent could with luck and money receive preferential treatment.

Hundreds of bottoms were required and mobilized from every nook and corner of the shipping world. Leaky tramps which had been laid up for years got a coat of paint, or not even that, and sailed to load cement. At the height of this show, some 440 ships were riding at anchor outside Lagos in full view of anyone who cared to look. This was particularly spectacular at night. The twinkling lights of these ships looked like a town transferred to the ocean waves.

A whole new market developed. The sailors got shore leave and crowded the bars; they were a motley crew frustrated by their long stay on board and set on letting their hair down. They were easy meat to be cheated and taken advantage of. Ships' chandlers were kept busy supplying the vessels, and boats by the dozen came and went day and night. After a while, shore leave was severely restricted and the sailors had to be amused on board. Hordes of women were recruited to make the rounds. Food and fuel had to be provided. Eventually the crews were packed off home to come back after a few weeks, while the ships were attended by skeleton crews. Water entered the vessels and some of the cement was damaged.

But that is not all. Large bills of demurrage accumulated. They were doctored, it is said, with the connivance of interested parties, and many a shipowner got repaid the value of his old vessel by just hanging around, not even anxious to see his vessel discharge in time. Stories went about that some of the ships had little cement on board. One or two sank. The waiting time extended to many months, perhaps even more than a year.

Some rash financiers, who were not too strict about either the validity or the origin of the licences, or careless about documentation, and unwilling to meet requests to have the authorities overlook these defects, met with disaster; others made fortunes. Eventually, the authorities stopped issuing licences or revoked those which seemed overdue in delivery. This ended up in the law courts, and in some cases the government had to pay damages.

At first, vast profits were made by the traders handling bags of cement, but prices fluctuated and sometimes crashed. Not for long, however, as the slow rate of discharge made it possible for the glut to be absorbed. Eventually supply exceeded demand and the business petered out.

The last of the cement ships sailed for its home port.

Within two years there was again a shortage of cement in the country; such was the speed of development in Nigeria in the 1970s.

29

Black Gold

'**O**il is big business, Brandler,' Trevor Berry said, as he saw me to the door. 'A lot of money is involved – one makes it, but one can also lose it. It's not for the faint-hearted. Hope to hear from you.'

At the urging of a cousin, himself an oilman, to whom I was under an obligation, I had been invited by Parazone Petroleum Ltd, an important London oil trading concern, to meet them and discuss their quest for Nigerian crude oil. Berry had given me an outline of their business, and how they had built up an important enterprise since starting in the 1920s.

'My Chairman, Mr. Elgar, will have told you who we are and what we are doing. I am in charge of crude oil trading. We handle large quantities, about 150,000 barrels daily, which we buy and sell all over the world. Dealing with Nigeria has so far escaped us; our direct approaches to the government oil agency have been rebuffed. We've had many people call here promising to help us enter the market, well-spoken Nigerians, and others. Most of them insisted that money was needed to get into this business and asked for large amounts which they would repay by deductions from commissions once a contract was signed. We don't pay such money up front, Mr. Brandler, I must be clear about that. I understand you know Nigeria well and may be able to assist us.'

He went on to say that they would like to do business with the Nigerian National Petroleum Corporation (NNPC), but that they had become wary of the visitors who called promising to facilitate an approach, all of whom wanted money before they could move, and of whom nothing was ever heard again. He explained that the oil business had become much more volatile and prices weaker since the boom of 1972 (we were talking in 1976) and that Nigeria interested them because of the grade of oil she produced.

'We have a lot to offer; we are large buyers and command considerable resources. So far we have not met the right men. You don't need to know anything about the oil business, we do. Have you met the oil minister?'

'Ali Manguno – no. As it happens I know his permanent secretary from the time he served in another ministry, but I've had no contact with him lately.'

'Well, there you are,' he exclaimed. 'Why not get in touch with him and tell him about us? I will give you our brochures to take back to Lagos and am ready to come out at short notice if an appointment can be made.'

'Let me think about it, Berry. This is quite outside my spheres of interest – it just happens I owe my cousin a favour. I will be back in Lagos shortly and scout around. If I feel I can do something I will let you know soon enough. I don't like hanging about the antechambers of ministries; we rarely had to do it. I just don't know the sort of reaction I might get.'

I took his brochures with their impressive figures and said good-bye.

Back in Lagos, I mentioned the matter to my secretary, Ekaite, a well-connected young woman. I could see her alert brain going into top gear. 'Oil, sir, is where all the money is these days. If you have a good company, surely we must find ways and means to bring them here.'

A few days later, Ekaite turned up in great excitement. 'Sir, I think I have found a man who can get your friends into NNPC.'

'Who is that?'

'A lawyer I met socially. He told me he had every chance to get oil if he brought the right buyers.'

'Very well, let's meet him.'

So we met lawyer Negus who informed us that he had been promised oil from the highest quarters if he could bring the

308

right company to buy it. One had to take his word for it. I showed him the brochures and he was impressed. His lawyer's training went to work. 'If you want me to act for you . . .'

'Them,' I corrected.

'Them. Then I must have a letter from the company appointing me as their exclusive agent for a minimum period to be agreed, along with some indication of what I, and my friends, would receive as fee or commission. We know the going rate,' he added.

'Thank you, Mr. Negus. I'll report to London and get back to you.'

'Don't leave it too long. These things come and go.'

'We will act promptly,' I assured him, and he left.

'How well do you know this man?' I asked Ekaite.

'I know him quite well. He has the connections all right.'

I sent a note to Berry. 'I think we have a contact who could get you into NNPC. Are you still interested?'

'We are interested,' he replied cautiously, 'if we can get the grade of oil we want at an acceptable price. The market is patchy.'

It was agreed that an application be made by the company to the NNPC. A letter was given to Negus appointing him as exclusive agent for three months in the first place, which would be ratified on a contract being signed within that period for as long as the contract ran. Negus went to work.

It was not long before he came back. 'Good news. Your friends will be invited to come to Lagos to discuss an oil contract; tell them to get their visas from the high commission.'

Berry duly arrived. I met him at the airport and introduced him to Negus who came to see him at the hotel.

Next morning we set off to our appointment with the NNPC, who at the time had their offices in Apapa, the port area of Lagos. It was a tedious journey beset by many hold-ups but we got there in time and, after climbing several floors as the lifts were out of order, we were ushered into a waiting room full of people. The receptionist looked in her diary and said, 'We are expecting you. Please sit down.'

There were four of us: Berry, the lawyer, myself and Ekaite, whom I had asked to come along; perhaps too many. We waited for thirty minutes and nothing happened. Berry got restless. The longish journey through the crowded streets, the out-of-order lifts, and now the long wait made an unfavourable impression on him. 'I thought we had an appointment,' he grunted.

Ekaite went up to the receptionist. 'The manager has a visitor. I'm sorry. He won't be long now,' she said with a smile. It pacified three of us but not our visitor from London.

'I have come a long way,' he fumed. 'Is this how they do business here?'

'Hush, Berry, take it easy. You have come a long way and so have others.'

The receptionist went into the manager's office and came back. 'The manager will see you presently. I'm sorry, we're running behind schedule.'

After almost an hour, we were shown into the manager's presence. He was in charge of crude oil sales, a young-looking, slim fellow, elegantly dressed, very polite, who offered his apologies for the delay. With him was a male secretary to take notes and another man whose functions were not made clear to us.

The discussions began. Berry referred to his company's brochure, their standing in the trade, and their ability to buy crude oil from the NNPC. He mentioned the grades preferred. The manager regretted that these grades were not available, but that he could offer another grade at such and such a price.

'At that price,' cried Berry, 'we would lose a dollar a barrel.'

'I am sorry but that is all we have available. Perhaps, Mr. Berry, you can consult your head office and come back tomorrow morning?'

'All right,' said Berry, 'I will do that but I am due to leave for the USA by midday, so can we meet early please?'

'Nine o'clock,' said the Manager, and we left.

Berry was glum on the way back. 'We don't want the oil he is offering us and the price asked is ridiculous. This is a wild-goosechase. That man has no intention of offering us a deal.'

In the afternoon I took him to see the sights of Lagos and next morning we went back to NNPC. Berry's bags were packed in the back of the car, ready for his flight.

He repeated his views to the manager. 'We are anxious to come into business with you; we are large buyers and can take what you are offering.' He mentioned a figure well below the quoted prices.

'I am sorry, sir,' said the manager, 'we have fixed prices. The grades you request are not available now, perhaps in the future. Why not take what we have now?'

'We would lose our shirt,' replied Berry, and that was that. We took our leave, much disappointed. We drove straight to the airport. There was an awful jam and Berry was frantic. 'I must get on that plane. I have a meeting in New York tomorrow which is much more important than this affair.'

I took the wheel from the driver, crossed the division to the opposite lane, turned on my headlights and with a hand on the horn drove forward and managed to get to within a mile of the airport where we got stuck. I gave the wheel to the driver, told Berry to get out, found a young man willing to carry the luggage, and off we went on foot to check him in with minutes to spare to catch his flight.

'Never again,' he murmured as he said good-bye and left. I returned to my office after a dreary trip.

Ekaite was waiting for me. 'What went wrong?' I asked her. 'I look a fool and so does Negus. Why did they invite the company?'

'I don't know,' she replied.

'Where is Negus?'

'He has gone to his chambers.'

Negus called later in the day. He could not understand why we had failed. He thought it was all buttoned up. 'But your man might have taken a chance.'

'At a loss of $20,000 a day?'

'They would soon make it up if the market turned.'

'That is clearly not their opinion.' Thus ended our first venture into the oil business.

It was only much later that I discovered the cause of the

debacle. Negus had many friends and many enemies, and the latter prevailed when they found out that he was about to clinch a deal. We had got hold of the wrong man.

'Devil take it', I thought, 'This must not be the end. I will try again.' I went to see the permanent secretary, the minister, Ali Manguno, and his successor, Colonel Buhari. All received me politely, but to no avail.

When next in London, I called on Berry. He had by then become managing director of the company as Elgar had retired. He received me cordially, gave me lunch, and recalled with some amusement his Nigerian adventure.

'We can do without that hassle. They are still coming here, your Nigerian friends, offering us oil if we will finance their "expenses" up front. Fat chance,' he chuckled, 'after what I have seen.'

'You must meet the man we have appointed to succeed me,' he went on. 'His name is Mack.'

Mack was an old Nigerian hand who had worked for one of the oil majors as marketing manager in the east of the country: an astute trader who felt that the whole business was more trouble than it was worth. 'I know the country; we will never get anywhere, Brandler. For every barrel of oil produced, there are ten parties who pretend to want it and nine who will fork out money for nothing. It's become a racket.'

'Quite so,' I thought, 'but what if you are the tenth who gets that barrel?' I returned to Lagos and left the oil trade to simmer in the background. We had troubles enough to keep us busy.

Over a year later, my Swedish colleague Lars asked if I knew of any good oil company who might like to do business with Nigeria. 'I met some men who say they can obtain a contract if the buyer is of the right calibre.'

'Lars, I am travelling to the UK next week. Let's leave it until I return. There are so many characters running all over the place who say they can procure oil. I know a good company all right, but I will not easily stick my neck out. Once bitten, twice shy.' I related my experience with lawyer Negus.

'I thought I would just mention it, Joe – I met these people casually.'

'Thanks, Lars. I'm off and you know where to find me.' I left for London as scheduled. Within days of my arrival I had a phone call from a Nigerian who said he had been recommended by Lars and must see me urgently. His name was Mr. Lisan.

'I am in the UK, Mr. Lisan.'

'I am in the UK, too,' came the reply.

'What do you want to see me about?'

'I thought Mr. Lars had told you.'

The penny dropped. 'Lars didn't say you were coming over. Is it that urgent? If you want to see me, you'll have to come out to Cambridgeshire where I'm staying.'

'I will come today. Please tell me how to get there.'

I met him off the train at Huntingdon. He was a quiet Lagosian, in early middle age, who launched at once into the reason for his mission and was very articulate in doing so. 'I have the oil, sir, if you have the buyers.' His story was that friends in high quarters had offered him an allocation. He was looking for a company to lift.

I wondered if this was just the same old tale. One had heard it so often. 'There would be no money in advance, Mr. Lisan.'

'I am not asking for any money in advance. If I find a company we will be in business. I have come over especially to meet you and your friends in the oil business. I have this promise and you know how it is – my man may be moved suddenly and the opportunity missed.'

I was in an awkward situation. If this fellow were bluffing for whatever reason, my credit with Para would go down still further. Yet if he had come over especially to see me, that must be a positive point. He struck me as serious but then most of them did. I excused myself and went to the phone to ring Para. If I talked to Mack he would probably turn it down flat. So I spoke to Berry and told him what was going on.

'Joe, we get them every day here, more than ever.'

'Trevor, I feel this may be different, there may be a chance.'

'Has he brought a current NNPC specimen contract?'

'Hang on, I'll ask him.' I went to the study where Lisan was sitting sipping a coffee my wife had brought in. No, he had no specimen contract, but could get one in forty-eight hours. I went back to the phone and relayed the information.

'All right, Joe, if your friend will bring us a specimen contract, and on the clear understanding that there will be no money up front, you can bring him along when he has the papers.'

I told Lisan, who immediately rose and asked to be taken back to the station. 'I will fly to Lagos tonight and be back the day after tomorrow. Do we meet in London or do I come back here?'

'You will please come back here and, if I am satisfied, we will get together in London the following day. Please ring me on your return.'

I took him to the station. Would he come back? Could he really get those papers in one day? Could he get them at all?

Two days later, early in the morning, he phoned. 'Where are you?' I asked.

'At Heathrow airport.'

I met him for the second time at Huntingdon station. I was impressed at the speed and obvious determination of the man. He pulled out a weighty document from his briefcase and handed it to me. 'This is a current specimen contract, please look at it.'

'Thank you, Mr. Lisan.' I looked at it but it did not mean much to me. It could be genuine, it must be genuine, I thought. Why should he spend all this time and money otherwise? Even then a small voice said: how do you know he went back to Lagos? It can't be that difficult to get such a document from a clerk at the high commission in London. I stilled that voice quickly. I asked myself if I had really become that suspicious.

I phoned Berry. 'My man is back with what you asked for,' I said, and we agreed to meet at 4 p.m.

'May I keep the papers?' I asked, as I drove him to the station.

'Please do.' We duly met in the afternoon as planned and walked over to keep our appointment.

One could not help noticing the quiet atmosphere of Berry's sumptuous, large office: a solid mahogany desk, an oriental carpet, a board table of walnut with chairs to match, flowers in large vases, effective lighting. Lisan took it in with a quick glance. Mack was called down. I made the introductions, then gave Trevor the requested specimen contract.

He opened the proceedings. He briefly repeated the company's history and its present objectives. 'We have been in the business for over fifty years and are one of the largest oil traders in the country. We have had poor experiences, however, over our Nigerian efforts and would not have seen you but for Mr. Brandler's intervention. Please tell us what we can do for you.'

Lisan, quite self-possessed, said that he was a British-trained insurance broker who had done much important work for the government, as well as for individual government officers, and that to show their appreciation they had offered him an allocation of crude, provided that the buyer he brought to the corporation was acceptable. 'I have studied your brochures and listened to Mr. Brandler and I think you would be very acceptable, gentlemen.'

Mack frowned. 'I should think so,' he growled. 'What exactly do you want us to do?' he asked.

'Please let me have your application to NNPC to purchase crude, state the grade you prefer, and the quantity – it must be at least 20,000 barrels per day – financial statements for the last three years, and your latest brochures. I will take this to Lagos by hand over the weekend and submit it to the management. I would also ask for a letter from the company to me confirming that I act for you exclusively against an agreed fee or commission.'

'As for that, Mr. Lisan,' boomed Berry, 'there can be no letter until we have an invitation and the commission will depend on the deal. You must trust us to recompense you and, if we go ahead, not to ask a third party to get between us.'

'The letter, sir, I need for my friends; they like to see things on paper.'

'We will discuss it between ourselves, Mr. Lisan. Can you

please come back tomorrow morning at 10 a.m.? We must study the contract.'

Berry asked me to stay behind and I suggested to Lisan that we meet for a drink an hour later at a nearby hotel. He took his leave.

'I don't know about your friend, Lisan,' said Berry. 'They all come with the same spiel: money and the letter. This chap did not ask for money, that's a great plus. But these letters lead to endless complications later if the deal falls through and another comes up in the end.'

'He can't go back empty-handed, Trevor, if you give him the authority to proceed. I think this man is as good as any you have come across and better than most. You must draft some sort of document which will prove he acts for you.' I left to join Lisan at the hotel.

We talked over a drink. He had spent a few years in England as a student and he was confident that he could swing business with NNPC. 'I did a lot for these people. I know about you, sir, I know you have had rough treatment recently from Lagos State. Don't let that put you off. Without your support I may not succeed. It would be a pity all round.'

'Well, Lisan, there are other oil companies.'

'You have to get to know them first, Mr. Brandler.'

'And if we go ahead, Lisan, when do you think this matter would come to a head? They will ask you that tomorrow. And don't be greedy about commissions. These men are experienced. Get going and everything will fall into place.'

He listened carefully. 'I can't say how soon we would hear if an application were made. We're now in late August and I would hope that by the end of September the contract would be settled for lifting in the last quarter of the year.'

'Fine, we'll meet tomorrow. You'd better come direct to the office.'

In the train home I made some rapid calculations. 20,000 barrels at $16 per barrel came to $320,000 daily. The contract stipulated a letter of credit to cover the quarter, so almost $30 million would have to be found. There was a clause demanding $250,000 (or it may have been $500,000) deposit as earnest

316

money to be deducted from the first lifting. We were talking in large figures. When Para talked of handling 150,000 barrels daily, they probably meant in and out so the real figure was half of that. They were traders used to a quick turnover, not a three months' commitment, that much I knew, so there was more to think about than Mr. Lisan's credibility. And the market was wobbly.

We met next morning. 'We have agreed in principle to go ahead,' said Berry. 'There are some points in the contract which need clarification, but we can handle that when the time comes. I have drafted a letter which should satisfy you, Mr. Lisan,' and he handed him a sheet of paper. 'Please read it.' He gave me a copy. The letter simply stated that the company would be pleased to come to an agreement with Lisan and his associates if through their efforts a contract with the NNPC could be effected, and that commissions would be paid at a rate to be agreed as and when each lifting was complete and the vessel on the high seas. Lisan accepted the draft with good grace. He was to call back later in the day to collect the application and the final letter.

Lisan rang in the evening to thank me for the interest shown in his project and said he would see me in Lagos. He was to fly back the next day.

Berry phoned the following Monday to ask if Lisan had left and I said he must have gone. 'If we do get a contract who will meet your expenses, where do you come in?' he asked.

'Since you are asking,' I responded, 'I come in at your end.'

'OK, as long as we know.'

I was in Lagos by the middle of September, saw Lisan, and enquired if he was making headway. He was optimistic. 'It's coming, we're working on it. They have to go through the application, check the company's financial statements, and so on. All that is done on a lower tier, and if they're satisfied it will go to marketing, who know what's available. I shall be informed of the progress of the application, and when it comes back to the top I will see my friends and press for action.'

Early in October, Lisan came to the office. 'We are nearly

there. An invitation should go out in the next few days and I am
assured that your friends will get what they asked for.'

The appointment was duly scheduled for a Monday in late
October. This was accepted by Para, and I was informed that
Mack and his manager of operations, Tim West, would be
coming out. The latter had never been to Nigeria before.

'Let them bring out our letter of appointment as their sole
agents,' warned Lisan, 'let them not forget the deposit and they
must further have a letter of authority from the company that
they are empowered to negotiate and conclude business.'

I met them at the airport on a Sunday afternoon. In those
days it used to take a considerable time to get through immigration and customs. This was no exception. Long forms
had to be filled in, the most important of which were the decla-
rations showing what foreign currency one brought in, so that
one could take out again any that was not spent.

Well over an hour after the plane had touched down they
appeared, hot and bothered, carrying their luggage.

'Welcome to Nigeria.'

Mack was used to it and had taken it in his stride, but West
was agitated and sweating profusely in the heat. I took them to
the hotel and, after changing to more appropriate clothes, we
sat down to talk.

'Lisan and his partner will be here soon; have you got all the
documents requested? Are you going to go ahead?' I asked.

'Yes, we are going to go ahead if we get what we have asked
for, and all the paperwork is in order. Look, here are the
travellers' cheques, value $250,000, which I declared on the
form presented to me by customs.'

'By Jove, I should have warned you about that. What if
there's no deal? You might have trouble getting that out again!
Let me have a look at this form.' Sure enough, there it was in
black and white: travellers' cheques, value $250,000.

Lisan and his partner, Kolomare, arrived, were called up to
the room, and we started to talk. They looked at their letter,
they looked at the letter of authority. 'Have you got the earnest
money?' Lisan asked.

'Yes, we have.' It was arranged that my driver would pick

them up in the morning, convey them to my offices where Lisan and Kolomare would meet them to keep their appointment with NNPC whose offices had been moved to Ikoyi, closer to my own. Lisan's partner struck me as a very shrewd person. He was a company secretary by profession. Next morning everyone assembled at my place and off they went for the appointment. I asked to be excused. They came back two hours later. 'So far so good,' I was told. 'We are getting down to the nitty gritty and have been asked to come again this afternoon.' Our Nigerian friends did not join them for the second meeting. They too felt they had best keep out of the way of detailed technical negotiations.

Mack and West returned in a cheerful mood. 'We should settle tomorrow morning. A contract may be signed to lift 25,000 barrels daily, effective this very quarter.'

We all dined together that night in great expectations. Lisan and Kolomare opened the subject of commissions. 'We will handle that tomorrow,' Mack said. 'You must realize,' he added, 'that on the present market this is a marginal business which can go a few cents either way. We believe prices will improve and are going ahead on that speculation. The commissions will have to be in line.'

Lisan and Kolomare looked glum but refrained from further comment. The following morning our two Para representatives set off to NNPC. When they turned up again after a rather long time, they said they were kept waiting. All was in order except for one hitch: travellers' cheques were not acceptable as an earnest deposit. They were to bring a banker's draft.

Mack spoke up. 'We have signed a contract and it is kept with the corporation until we bring the draft. We shall be leaving for London tonight. West will come back with the draft.'

'How many barrels?' asked Lisan.

'25,000,' replied Mack. They went into a huddle to talk about commissions. I calculated the figures in my head and thought to myself, 'Not bad for these guys if they receive it.' Mack was going to see old friends in the afternoon and West suggested I showed him something of Lagos. After lunch we set off. We took rather more time than intended and urged the driver to hurry back. He took a short cut, but came against a barrier of a couple of planks which he shifted. We were near the Central Bank. We had hardly moved before a posse of enraged soldiers stopped us. A violent scene ensued. The soldiers tried to drag the driver out of the car and smashed the windscreen with the butts of their rifles. My intervention was ignored; they shouted and eventually made the driver reverse. We must have been in too sensitive a spot.

West was visibly shaken. 'If my wife hears of this, she will never let me come back to Lagos, ' he said. 'I don't really know that I want to, Joe.'

'Forget it,' I shrugged it off. 'The driver was wrong moving the barricade. I've never had this happen before.'

As we got back to his hotel he piped up, 'There's still another problem. Will I get my travellers' cheques out again?'

'Nobody will ever dream you brought in $250,000. They'll think it was $250.00. Keep your cool and casually present your form as you pass out. As likely as not, nobody will inspect the form in detail. Just hand it in.' And so it happened.

West returned with his draft within a week and was handed a contract. 'They tell me,' he said, 'that even if you have a contract you may still be fouled up by shipping difficulties. What do you know about that, Joe?'

'Nothing,' I replied. 'That sounds to me like bazaar gossip. Our friends will surely see to it that you get your crude.'

'It seems to me that I shall have to come out here every time we load to make sure there's no delay. Can we use your office as a channel of communication? You've done a lot of shipping in your time, do you think you could assist us?' I thought we could, provided he alerted the NNPC.

'I shall come out for the first loading for sure, but very roughly this is how it works,' he said, and he explained the process to me.

I listened carefully. 'In the end, West, it's all the same – attention to detail, good communications, and having the right man on the spot.'

'Agreed,' he nodded, deep in thought, impressed by his own

explanations. 'Some of these tankers,' he said, 'cruise like taxis outside the loading points on the high seas. I know the game, don't worry. Let's see how it goes. First we have to open the letter of credit and I feel pretty sure that Berry will want to lay off most of the contract to one of the majors. The three months' termination clause is very long; if the price goes against us we can lose our pants or we would have to default, which we have never done.' Then he remembered that time was passing. 'It's time to go to the airport. Will you give me your driver?'

'Of course, and a clerk to help you with the formalities. My man knows the ropes; please look after him when he's done, a tip for the overtime. "Dash", we call it here.'

He went off, cock-a-hoop, with the contract in his pocket, to catch the flight late in the evening, travelling in style, first class, as did all of these oil negotiators. Before he had left he informed me with a smile that the marketing manager of NNPC with whom he had negotiated was the same man who had sent off Berry a couple of years before empty-handed. As if to say, 'Aren't I smart?'

I had to disillusion him on that. 'West, the marketing manager is most competent but in the end he does as he is told by his superiors. Now when it comes to the shipping manager, that's a different matter altogether.'

On West's return to London, Berry had the courtesy to send me a cable thanking me for my efforts, adding cryptically, 'I think we understand each other.'

I was pleased with myself. I had discharged an obligation and at the same time had caught a glimpse of something new. The operational side would interest us as a new challenge and was much more to our taste and past performance than endless negotiations. If they needed local expertise we could offer it.

Lisan and Kolomare had called on Tim West to say *au revoir* and saw me the next day. 'How long,' they asked, 'do you think it will take the company to open their letter of credit?'

'I've no idea, gentlemen. If their credit is as good as I understand it to be, they should be through in a fortnight. We're not talking about peanuts.'

321

'We hear such stories about these oil traders and people like us being cheated.'

'No fear of that,' I reassured them. 'The man has only arrived back this morning. You, however, must make sure that as soon as the letter of credit is received by the finance sector of the corporation, that fact is passed on to the relevant bodies making the allocations. Sheer bureaucracy and internal politics may come into play.'

'We will take care of that,' they replied confidently.

The letter of credit came in under three weeks, our friends put on pressure, and the first loading was scheduled for the third week of November: 400,000 barrels to be followed in a week by another 700,000 barrels. West announced his arrival to coincide with the first loading and, after some panic cable exchanges over his visa, turned up a few days before the first ship was due. These loadings, of course, took place hundreds of miles from Lagos, mainly off-shore, and it soon transpired that to be physically present was almost impossible and would serve little purpose.

He suggested that I accompany him on his various calls. First we went to the inspection agents who had already been alerted and with whom the company had connections in other parts of the world. They sent representatives to the ship, checked the quantities loaded, and took samples of the oil which they analysed. They then gave their certificates to the buyer.

We called on the marketing manager, who recognized me from my earlier visit with Berry. He took us to the shipping supervisor, a young man with great powers, who in turn introduced us to some of his staff. They all seemed to know their job well, although they worked in poky little offices with people coming and going all the time, papers all over the place, and telephones ringing incessantly.

'Don't worry, Mr. West,' said the shipping supervisor, 'everything will be all right. We handle these matters every hour of every day. I like your shirt,' he added almost absent-mindedly.

'You do?' replied West, naively. 'Thank you.'

Within a day, West had done all he could do; what next? He

scratched his head. 'There's not really anything more for me to handle here.'

Next day we went once more to the inspectors and were told that they had received news that the vessel had reported its arrival and was due to load within the next 48 hours. West used our cable, transport and telephone, all of which facilitated his work greatly, and went back to London that night. I had taken him for lunch to the Metropolitan Club where he met many of the leading lights of Lagos and he enjoyed himself.

'About that shirt,' I explained, 'Maybe next time you come you can bring out a couple as a sign of appreciation for what is being done.'

He was startled, thinking perhaps I was in need of shirts and then he remembered. 'Ah, but I must know his size. Can you find that out?'

The next loadings were scheduled for the end of December. Before leaving for Christmas, I called on the shipping supervisor to make sure all was going smoothly, told him I would be away for two weeks, but that if he had any problems over communications with Para he could make use of our offices. Before leaving, I casually asked him his collar size, which he gave me without batting an eyelid.

Indeed, he did use our office to contact Para. Communications out of NNPC were very cumbersome and his official messages to Para usually reached them two or three days later, so he felt it wise to duplicate them and save time - an important factor when it came to handling shipping.

After Christmas, I called on Para and was received with loud hellos. The first transactions had gone well and although, as they said, there was not much profit, the future looked promising.

'You must let us know your expenses,' said Mack, 'and as for the deal itself, if you feel we owe you anything you must talk to Trevor.'

I went up to greet West, who was beaming all over his round face – the third and fourth loadings had been completed without trouble. The business was under way. 'So far so good. Your office has been a great help. You must let us know your expenses.'

I said I had already discussed that with Mack. 'By the way it's 15½.'

'What's 15½?'

'The collar size of the shipping bloke.'

Back in Lagos, Lisan and Kolomore were also happy and let us know that they expected the allocation to be raised to 30,000 barrels daily. Could Para absorb the extra quantity? London confirmed that they would accept the larger allocation if offered.

Then fate took a hand. The Shah of Iran was overthrown, throwing the oil market into turmoil; prices rocketed. Para's contract turned into a little goldmine. We had built up a good rapport with NNPC's shipping offices and they would often turn to us if a ship had room to spare and they were anxious to load an extra few barrels to clear their tanks. These were very small quantities, but it showed that the two parties could rely on each other. Sitting a mile apart proved to be a great advantage. It brought in a few extra pennies - small beer compared to our Nigerian partners who had been able to jack up their commissions many times and were literally making a fortune without obvious risks to themselves. One is reminded of Mr. Gulbenkian and his 5 per cent (Gulbenkian was the agent who originally introduced British oil companies to Iran and became a multi-millionaire).

In this shifting scene, at both ends there were adventurers ready to take a chance or to exploit greed and gullibility. Not knowing or ignoring the ropes, innumerable applications to buy crude were made direct to NNPC, and were filed away, often without reply. Some of them were submitted by gamblers who reckoned that if they could get a contract they would sell it on and make a quick legitimate buck; others by small refineries prepared to dabble in the market; others again by established concerns who were anxious to see their name registered as applicant.

On the other hand, there were the patronagees, total strangers to the oil business, who were looking for acceptable buyers. And in between a lot of men who smelled money. They had not been promised any oil but set off to find buyers, sometimes getting names from the junior staff of the Corporation who rummaged through the filed applications and passed on those they thought might be worthwhile approaching.

Thus it came about that all over Europe and the USA well-dressed and plausible Nigerians would call on the managing directors of oil traders, refineries or general merchants to offer their services for the procurement of an oil contract with Nigeria. They asked for money as they discussed the prospects, partly to cover their personal expenses and mainly, as they explained, to buy the patronage essential to get the oil.

One could not say that these men were swindlers. They reckoned that if they had enough cash they could bring it off, because they knew this or that official, general or civil servant to help them. But they took a big chance. And so did the men paying out.

There were, of course, also dishonest characters who set out to get money by deceit, and who were unable and had no intention to procure an oil contract. Sometimes it came off; a chap would pocket a few thousand dollars or more and disappear. The more devious the story the more likely it was to succeed. The listener would listen to the complicated yarn being spun for his benefit and pay for his greed.

By and large, though, the Corporation had no need to trade with dubious buyers, since there were enough good ones knocking at the door.

Nigeria's foreign trade was now dominated by her crude oil production. Well over 90 per cent of all foreign exchange earning originated from her sale of crude, which was controlled directly or indirectly by government. The majors had their agreements with government, which disposed of a percentage of the crude available at its discretion, and used it as a major source of patronage. Money flowed. The government spent and the individual spent. Many fortunes were made and often wisely consolidated.

Much of the money found its way into trade and industry, but as time went on and outcries were raised against these enormous fortunes being syphoned off the country's wealth, those who accumulated these riches preferred to keep quiet and to invest their gains overseas.

The oil companies abroad also made vast profits, but many, less wise than their Nigerian counterparts, rushed ahead mindless of the consequences and were caught by the slump in oil prices in the early 1980s and found themselves broke. The pattern repeated itself as slump followed boom but in lesser proportions and in somewhat more orderly fashion. The great days of the 1970s have yet to return and may never be repeated.

Para continued to lift for two years and their allocation was increased to 40,000 barrels daily. This increase they owed partly to the energy of Lisan and Kolomare, who had become rich over this business and wanted to become richer, and partly to the efficient manner in which the business rolled. Ships came on time, payments were made on time, and extra quantities were accepted if they were required to do so. A close rapport had been established between the contracting parties; the sellers, in a business full of operational headaches, appreciated a buyer who knew what he was doing.

When the time came to renew the contract, it was brusquely terminated by the Corporation. Their letter, however, added that if the company so desired, a new contract would be negotiated.

Para were given to understand that Lisan and Kolomare were no longer *personae gratae* as their promoters. A change in government had brought new powers to the fore who had their own patronage to dispense.

This turn of events coincided with a fall in the market and Para were in no hurry to open discussions; they had expanded rapidly and now felt the cold wind of a sharp drop in prices. They were caught in a vicious spiral and lost large amounts of money.

Years later they did find a new sponsor and signed a contract, but the shine had gone off the oil trade and all the parties concerned earned merely a fraction of what had been the norm in the heydays of the 1970s.

But oil still flows and remains by far the most important export of Nigeria. Respectable deals are concluded and executed. The oil trade is so enormous and so important world-wide that it will always offer opportunities until oil is replaced by some other means of propulsion.

30

The Rice Deal

At a lunchtime reception in 1981 given by the Algerian Embassy, I met the Ambassador of Uruguay. We established an easy rapport as one sometimes does on these occasions.

The ambassador mentioned that his was a new mission. Uruguay had to switch some of her crude oil purchases to Nigeria because of the troubles in Iran, and had decided to open an embassy in Lagos in the hope that reciprocal business could be established to balance the payments for the oil. 'We can sell rice, fish and beef, all of which are wanted in this market. Businessmen like you may be interested.'

We met again quite soon. The Uruguayan Embassy sent me an invitation to attend a small cocktail party. The ambassador, Pedro Vidal Salaberry, returned to our earlier conversation. 'Our crude purchases here run into millions of dollars monthly, but they buy nothing in return. It is a drain on our foreign exchange. If you, Consul, are aware of any openings please let us know.'

I had to admit that the commodities mentioned were outside our past experience and that all I knew about Uruguay was the battle of the River Plate when the German pocket battleship, *Graf Spee*, was sunk in 1940. 'But of course one never knows what may turn up. I understand that increasing quantities of American rice are placed in this market and that frozen fish is imported, although I have not heard of beef.'

That evening we talked about Nigeria and Uruguay, and I went home glad to have come across this man again. I doubted, however, whether we could develop common interests in commerce. Trade in fish to me meant stockfish from Norway and Iceland and sardines from Morocco, though I had heard that frozen fish from South America was now in the stores. Rice had been a luxury item bought by Nigerians at Christmas and Easter, mostly 'Uncle Ben' in one-pound packets. It was also planted in limited quantities inside the country. Its popularity had grown; it was easier to prepare than yam and cassava, and was preferred by many women living in towns. Local supplies were augmented by shipments from the USA. As for meat, I knew that the cook would occasionally buy New Zealand lamb at a price out of the reach of the ordinary Nigerian. We had never dealt in these commodities.

Nearly a month later, I had a visitor from Kaduna, *Alhaji* Musa, who at one time had bought great quantities of Swedish hardboard through our associates; we had not met for months. We enquired after each other's health and present circumstances. 'And what brings you here, *Alhaji*?'

He went into a long explanation that the Minister of Transport, Umaru Dikko, was a friend who owed him a favour; that this minister was now in charge of the Task Force for Rice, which had been formed to control the increasing imports; that the minister would listen to him if he brought a reliable and cheap source of supply and would give him a contract. 'The trade is in the hands of a few men who are making a lot of money. The minister will consider me, I am sure, but I don't know where to find the rice, so I came to you.'

'Thank you, *Alhaji*. What made you come to us? I suppose you've tried elsewhere?'

Yes, he had tried and failed, and just took a chance to see if we could help.

I had to weigh it up. I knew Musa as a serious man. He knew the minister – but so did hundreds of others. How well did he know the minister? How far was he deserving of patronage? How many people had he alerted to the possibility?

The ambassador had talked of rice. Would they be able to meet Nigerian conditions? Would they have rice available at the right price when wanted? Should I take these approaches seriously – both from the *alhaji* and from the Embassy? Did we want to get involved?

As I was pondering, the *alhaji* excused himself to pray on the veranda. It happened from time to time that business discussions with northerners were interrupted in this way. I always respected it; it added an extra dimension to the relationship. Think of a London stockbroker in his City office halting a business deal to prostrate himself in a corner in earnest worship of his god. For a few minutes, at least, profit and loss are set aside.

'*Alhaji*, I know nothing about rice and nor do you. You know the minister and I know an ambassador whose country produces rice. Perhaps the two can meet. Let me think about it and I'll come back to you soon. Meantime, if you see the minister mention to him that you may have found a source of supply and note his reaction.'

The *alhaji* shook his head. 'I have already done that; you should know that I would not come here without some assurances. The minister is a countryman of mine, we are old friends. If your ambassador can offer rice there is a good chance, believe me.'

'Very good, *Alhaji*. I take your point; we'll be in touch.'

I went to see Pedro and told him of the *alhaji*'s call. 'The equation as I see it runs like this. The *alhaji* knows the Rice Minister, who owes him a favour. Uruguay produces rice and buys crude oil from Nigeria. Nigeria buys rice from abroad. If we get these strands together it would have the makings of a mutually attractive proposition. Would you be interested?'

'It sounds fine. What would be the obstacles?'

'First, the obvious commercial ones: price, availability, payment terms. Then, politics – how strongly are present suppliers entrenched, who is supporting them, what vested interests may oppose a new source? And last, just how close is the *alhaji* to the minister? This one can never tell, and it can change from week to week. It's a long shot at the best.'

'Formidable. What can I do?'

'Please find out how far your rice producers are interested

and have supplies available. I don't suppose there's a problem there. More delicately – how far can we play the oil card?'

'I will report to Montevideo and let you know what transpires. Thank you for your interest.'

I heard from him within days. Yes, their rice producers' co-operative was keen to enter into business with Nigeria; their rice, under the trade mark of Arrozur, was already being sold there via a Swiss trading company. They would like to come into direct contact with the market. The oil card, however, should be used diplomatically – the crude was essential.

I was not too happy with Pedro's news. To my mind, the oil card was an ace if we could play it for what it was worth. If a Swiss trading company was already selling Uruguayan rice, they must have backers and there was bound to be opposition. Besides, I wondered what the Uruguayans would gain by cutting out their middleman. For a few cents extra per kilo they would expose themselves to all the hazards of dealing with a notoriously fickle government body.

Pedro did not agree. 'We buy oil direct. Why shouldn't we sell rice direct? That's what we're here for. You will be with us and guard our interests, won't you?'

I called on the *alhaji*. '*Alhaji*, about the rice: Uruguay, a country in South America, produces rice as good as, if not better than, the USA's. You may have seen the mark Arrozur on offer in the markets – it is theirs. The embassy in Lagos would help us to promote a sale and the producers would come over to negotiate. Before I initiate this affair, *Alhaji*, I want you to contact the minister again to make certain there is an interest in principle. You know yourself how these things go; we would look very stupid if this turned out to be a wild-goose-chase. Please confirm with the minister that we can expect an invitation. I will then take you to the embassy and introduce you.'

'The minister has travelled overseas. I will call on him as soon as he returns.'

'I will await your news, *Alhaji*.'

In the old days many a senior officer was 'not on seat' when one wanted him; nowadays he 'has travelled overseas'. It came to the same – one had to wait. There were these endless missions, meetings, seminars, conferences, conventions and what have you, all to be attended by a head of delegation and suitable entourage to meet like-minded delegates from other countries, not to mention semi-official and unofficial gatherings and private visits. One could get more done by seeing whoever one was trying to contact abroad, where he could relax and concentrate, than by calling at the office where he was constantly being interrupted by telephones ringing and people barging in, announced and unannounced.

In time the *alhaji* met the minister and then requested an interview with the ambassador, who asked me to be present. The *alhaji* arrived with an assistant, both in traditional white Hausa garb. They were in no way overawed by the company, and the *alhaji* repeated his confidence in the minister's goodwill, describing him as most able and decisive, a man who did not waste time on trivialities. That was indeed his reputation from afar.

The *alhaji* soon came to the point: how much was he going to get paid in this business?

Pedro looked at me in perplexity. I intervened to tell the *alhaji* that this was not part of the ambassador's brief. He would have to wait until the sellers came over.

From time to time a certain commodity catches the imagination of traders and they rush to get in on the act. News of shortage of supply will trigger this off; by the time most people hear of it the cream may already have gone, but enough will still be left for the adventurous to have a go. The tail-enders come into the act when everybody's goods have arrived, the market is flooded, and the price is depressed, more so if the goods are perishable. One time it is cement, another sugar, then again paper, motor spares, baby milk. This time it was rice. The import of the commodity had risen many times, exceeding 500,000 MT per annum and rising. Most of it came from the USA, originally probably part of some aid programme, later translated into commercial ventures.

To get a licence for the import of rice was at first manna from heaven; when the government realized the ramifications it became the principal importer itself. To sell rice, one had to get a contract from the ministry, which fixed the prices at which it would buy.

A web of intrigue ruled the rice business, and although many were involved only a few large shippers and importers really mattered. The patronage of giving out contracts was sometimes a hollow gesture; more likely the fortunate man or woman would sell on his licence/contract. That much our research had brought to light. Uruguay was coming not as a trader, but as a producer of rice, with the added angle of the oil contract. And there was patronage. It looked a strong hand to play.

The *alhaji* obtained an appointment with the minister and the Uruguayans sent over two senior representatives, Ferres and Cardoso; we all met at the embassy before setting off to the ministry and the *alhaji* once more emphasized the importance of the commission to be paid to him. Unless that was satisfactorily settled there would be no transaction. The ambassador thought it premature for himself to be with the party.

We saw the minister, Umaru Dikko, an imposing figure with alert eyes, in his office, with lots of papers on the desk and many pairs of shoes on the floor. He greeted the *alhaji* cordially, who then introduced us. The minister bid us welcome and listened attentively to Cardoso putting the Uruguayans' case.

Their rice was from source; it was of the best quality; they could ship 30-50,000 MT yearly; it was known and liked in the market; and they could meet the prices of the American producers. Last but not least, Uruguay was a small developing country with much sympathy for Africa, and of course there was the mutual interest in crude oil as seller and buyer.

The bit about Africa and the developing world was unrehearsed; had I known of it, I would have advised against it. It had a patronizing air, it meant nothing, and coming from a country with three million inhabitants to one with ninety million it sounded unreal. What was worse, it was impossible for the other party to say anything in response.

The minister thanked the spokesman for coming to Lagos. 'We buy a lot of rice for our people and we have heard of

Arrozur. If we can buy from you, perhaps in our local currency,' he smiled mischievously, 'we shall be happy to do so.' He pointed to a middle-aged lady sitting next to him. 'Mrs Archibong will negotiate with you. But, yes, in principle we can do business. As for the oil, let's not bring that in. You buy a very small quantity and that will not influence us one way or the other. I shall follow progress of the talks with interest. Please, Mrs. Archibong, take these gentlemen to your office.'

He rose to say good-bye. As we left he detained the *alhaji* who rejoined us a few minutes later.

The lady lost little time in deflating expectations. The ministry had covered its requirements and was short of foreign exchange. If, however, sellers were prepared to accept local currency, a trial shipment of 10,000 MT might be bought because they liked the Arrozur brand and direct dealings with the producers were desirable. Cardoso reacted by asking how his company would be able to convert the payment into dollars.

Mrs. Archibong replied that this would be a matter between the sellers and the Central Bank. When I pointed out that the Uruguayans had no base in Nigeria and no bank account, and could not therefore treat with the Central Bank, she proposed that the *alhaji*'s firm act as principals: she would make out the contract to him, and he would buy the rice from Uruguay and arrange payments. Our friends listened in disbelief; were they to give credit to the *alhaji*? Or could he open a letter of credit in dollars when the ministry could not? 'Stranger things than that happen every week,' I thought to myself.

Ferres cut short these thoughts: 'Our Central Bank would not allow us to sell in naira. If the *alhaji* can open the letter of credit that is acceptable. We pay for your oil in dollars and would expect to be paid for our rice in dollars, or are you suggesting a barter deal?'

We were getting nowhere and it was time for the *alhaji* to speak. 'Madam, can you please let us have a specimen contract and an indication of price? We will study this and come back tomorrow morning. I hope you will be free to see us.'

She confirmed the appointment for the next day and we left for the embassy to digest the result of the morning. The specimen contract caused no further comment except for the price offered. Our friends said it was very low. All eyes turned on the *alhaji*.

'When we go again tomorrow, we will tell them that you cannot sell for local currency. The minister assured me of a trial contract for 10,000 MT.'

Next morning, back at the ministry, we met the *alhaji* and saw Mrs. Archibong. She had gone carefully into the position. They were anxious to assist the *alhaji*, who had been so helpful in the past; they were well aware of the high quality of the Uruguayan rice and exceptionally they would squeeze in a 10,000 MT shipment for delivery in six months' time provided a satisfactory contract could be drawn up. She invited the Uruguayans to submit a written offer. Payment would be by a letter of credit in dollars to be opened thirty days before shipment. The minister was too busy to see us.

Back at the embassy, the *alhaji* impressed on our friends that they must accept the price, and must quote the freight in addition to the f.o.b.. Over and above that, an amount which he indicated would have to be added to the offer.

The Uruguayans were no simpletons, but the sudden *volte-face* unsettled them, as did the *alhaji's* demand. Nevertheless, they returned to the ministry within a few hours to hand in their offer. Neither the *alhaji* nor I accompanied them.

That evening at dinner they related their experience to Pedro and myself. Mrs. Archibong had thanked them for their prompt response; the offer would be submitted to the committee and the minister and they would hear in due course. What did we make of it?

'The *alhaji* will have the answer, gentlemen. Let's enjoy our Uruguayan beef.'

To my mind they had come a long way; formalities had to be observed. If the *alhaji* had the minister's goodwill, and in turn indicated that he was satisfied with what he stood to gain, the contract should be confirmed promptly. And indeed the *alhaji* phoned next morning asking them to stay for a couple of days; he expected to bring the contract before they left for home.

He was as good as his word and turned up with a contract

in forty-eight hours, signed by an officer and counter-signed by the minister. Great rejoicings and congratulations all round. Loth as I was to do it, I had to throw cold water on the high spirits.

'Gentlemen, you have done well, you are nearly there. But until you have the letter of credit. . .'

They interrupted me. 'Surely a contract signed by the minister will not be reneged on?'

'It will not willingly be reneged on. However, the Ministry of Finance now comes into the act; there could be delays. I noted you wisely stipulate for the letter of credit to be opened sixty days before shipment. Make sure you can dispose of your rice to another party should the need arise.'

It put a damper on the proceedings. 'You are a real Jeremiah.'

'I have been here a long time.'

We saw them off at the airport. On our way back the ambassador asked me what I really thought. 'Will it come off? Final success would be a feather in the mission's cap.'

'The contract as I see it, Pedro, is a letter of intent. It should be honoured, but you know how things are. We can't look behind the scenes. The *alhaji* will have to pull his finger out. It would be more than a feather in my cap but we must be realistic. I think the minister's willing but he's a busy man under many pressures and obligations. After all, if he's unable to give the *alhaji* a rice deal, he may compensate him with something else. There may be many influences at work inside the ministry.'

'I understand. But do we budget for this shipment?'

'Arrozur have some weeks left. Whatever happens they mustn't load without the letter of credit.'

'They've invited you to visit them in Montevideo. Are you going?'

'I hope to go soon and take our son David along.'

We went to Montevideo and had a lovely week there: courteous people, a civilized town. We flew to Treinta-y-Tres and looked at the rice parboiling factory; saw the cows and a most modern slaughterhouse, grim in its efficiency and hygiene; ate well, drank well, saw the fishing trawlers' catches destined for Nigeria; were entertained by friends and officials; saw the warehouse with the rice awaiting the letter of credit from Lagos.

There was the rub. 'Will it come in time? Will it ever come?'

I said I did not know.

'But surely we have the minister's signature. And the *alhaji*'s commission is very heavy. And they liked our rice; it's the best. Why do you have doubts?'

'Friends, I warned you from the beginning that you must be wary. You can't ship until you have the letter of credit. Normally the minister's signature should be a guarantee. Unfortunately, the more I've studied it, the more I realize that this rice business is far from normal. I'm hopeful that the letter of credit will come in time, but it hasn't come yet, has it?'

On our return I had an official meeting with Mrs. Archibong at the ministry. Yes, she had been instructed to give the Uruguayans a contract. 'The minister does that from time to time. It upsets our planning. We have many people coming here trying to sell rice they haven't got. All these *alhajis*,' she said in a quiet voice. 'The Ministry of Finance still has to authorize the opening of a letter of credit.'

I felt she sounded distinctly hostile.

'Madam, Uruguay is a major producer of rice and Arrozur is their foremost brand. You're well aware of that, I think. This is no fly-by-night offer. It comes straight from the source. The *alhaji* is assisting them. You will be well served. It's an opportunity. Besides, Uruguay buys crude oil in Nigeria.'

'I am a civil servant, sir. I obey instructions and work on laid down guidelines.'

'Thank you, madam. Please let us know if we can be of any assistance.'

She looked at me, 'How do you come into this?'

'I am a friend of the ambassador and a friend of Arrozur and glad to help them as I live in Lagos.'

'And a friend of the *alhaji*?'

'Yes, and a friend of the *alhaji*.'

'Thank you for calling. You know, in this country every-thing takes a little time. We will do our best.'

It was a most unsatisfactory interview. They were buying 40,000-50,000 MT monthly, so the 10,000 MT could not be a logistical problem nor a financial one. The product was good and known. Was she protecting some of the big operators and their partners at this end who did not want outsiders to muscle in, or was she being awkward for reasons of her own?

Nothing was heard for several weeks. The *alhaji* asked for patience, then suggested he make an appointment for the am-bassador to meet the minister. The minister assured the am-bassador that everything was going ahead; they were happy to deal with Uruguay. As for the crude oil – the ambassador had hinted at it – that was a separate matter.

The time for the letter of credit to be opened had passed; the rice was still awaiting shipment. The ambassador once more saw the minister who promised action, provided the Ministry of Finance would respond. 'Strictly between us,' he said, 'we are having a fight with the Ministry of Finance. Perhaps you can succeed there. Why not call on them?'

We went to the Central Bank and met a senior officer. 'This rice business is giving us nothing but trouble. All foreign ex-change for rice, eh? They are getting so much of it; we don't allocate individually, we cannot deal with every contractor. You must rely on the Rice Task Force.'

Next we had a visit from a big trader, Abdul, whom we knew by name only. He was well-connected politically. On asking what we could do for him, he replied, 'You have a rice con-tract - let me handle it for you. We have a mutual friend who suggested I approach you.'

'We have no contract, sir. We're assisting the Uruguay co-operative, that's all.'

'I understand, Mr. Brandler. I will take you to the minis-ter's house right now and everything will be clear to you.' I hesitated. 'Mr. Brandler, please come with me. I know it's not your contract, but you are with these people and can give them advice.'

'Very well. Let's go and see the minister.'

338

I did not think we would get anywhere near him. There were dozens of supplicants hanging around waiting to see the big man, but my man walked straight into the secretary's office and we were in the presence of the minister within a minute. It shook me.

The minister sat at his desk, again surrounded by many pairs of shoes, and smiled in recognition. He and Abdul talked in Hausa and the minister turned to me.

'This *alhaji* is a large rice dealer, Mr. Brandler. I thought you ought to know him. He can save us all a lot of trouble – the Ministry of Finance is delaying my letter of credit and I don't want to fail the Uruguayans. Maybe you can negotiate with this *alhaji* and find a way out.'

'Thank you, Minister. I will report our conversation.'

We were out again in a few minutes. Abdul had not bluffed – he had access to the minister all right. And the minister intimated that we might have to wait a long time for the letter of credit and suggested we deal instead with Abdul. I wondered on what basis he had done this.

Abdul soon made it clear. 'I will buy their contract for a consideration but I cannot buy their rice. Let them sell that to their Swiss connection. I need a decision promptly. Please contact your friends in Montevideo. I took you to the minister only to reassure you of my credentials.'

'Thank you, *Alhaji*, I will meet with the ambassador at once.'

When I had finished telling Pedro of the morning's adventure, he was taken aback. We summoned our *alhaji* from the north but he regretted that he could not come to Lagos; urgent business held him back. Could we come to Kaduna? We told him what had happened. He said he was sorry, but he had done everything in his power and this matter must now be left with the ministry. 'But if this deal fails, *Alhaji*, you will forgo a lot of money.'

'Allah,' he replied. 'All will be well.'

'We must alert Montevideo, Pedro.'

He was terribly upset. 'The minister's signature to be so dishonoured? In many years of service that has never happened to me before. I think we must insist that the contract be fulfilled.'

It was decided to hold out for the letter of credit. Abdul was informed by me that Montevideo thanked him for his offer and regretted it was not acceptable.

Abdul called again. 'Mr. Brandler, let me tell you in confidence that they are mistaken in turning me down. They will wait a long, long time before they see a letter of credit, if ever. As for your friend in Kaduna – he has been given a building contract in the new capital, Abuja. I thought you should know.'

When I heard this, I knew that Arrozur stood little chance.

Many weeks went by. We saw Mrs. Archibong and, after she was suddenly replaced, her successor. Always the same reply: a letter of credit would be opened as soon as the Ministry of Finance made the funds available.

When a message reached me from Montevideo that the Swiss trader had made an offer to take the rice earmarked for Lagos, I had to recommend that they accept it. The letter of credit might never come. The Uruguayans sold to the Swiss who resold to Lagos at a higher price than that given to Arrozur on their contract.

Abdul was cross: 'I told you to let me deal. I warned you. I took you to the minister. How could you have misread the situation so badly? We would all have been better off.'

'Well, Abdul, it was politics all round. You know politics, don't you?'

'All right, Mr. Brandler. We will wait. In a few months' time I shall come to your friends to buy some rice. They will know better and listen.'

Alas, it was not to be. In a few months there was a *coup d'état* which swept the government out of power and into detention, except for those who got wind of it in time. The minister escaped – on a motor bike, they say, across the border to Benin. He became Public Enemy Number One and they even tried to kidnap him from the streets of London. He was rumoured to be worth hundreds of millions. Abdul went to Paris.

The Rice Task Force was dissolved. The importation of rice

was banned. From then on, it was to be grown inside the country. The American rice lobby was furious. The new government pleaded poverty.

The Uruguay Embassy in Nigeria was closed as uneconomical.

Rice is still popular. The thud of the pestle pounding yam or cassava in the mortar is heard less and less. It was, and still is, music to my ears, its ready rhythm full of promise of the better things of life; a loving woman and good food.

31

Great Minds Think Alike

Chief J. K. Randle is a prominent Lagos socialite, a chartered accountant partner in one of the large international firms, a polished public speaker, and son of the late Chief J. K. Randle, himself a leading light in Lagos in the days after the Second World War. The family has been well known in Lagos for generations.

JK, as he is generally called, is also a writer of renown. Several of his books have been published commenting on the social, economic and political scene of Nigeria, all done with considerable style and wit. He spices his work with anecdotes and little stories which have a moral point.

In his book, *The Natives are Friendly?*, published in 1986 by Hambleside Group Ltd, Randle tells an amusing story of a fake general in the Zimboda army testing the reliability and discretion of a Swiss bank manager by pretending that he is checking on his countrymen's illegal foreign deposits. The bank manager, pleading Swiss secrecy laws, will give no information, even when threatened with a gun. Satisfied, the general brings out several million dollars in crisp banknotes and opens an account.

I was surprised to read a similar story in Jeffrey Archer's book, *A Twist in the Tale*, published in 1988 by Hodder & Stoughton. In Archer's book, however, the general is a Nigerian. Mr (now Lord) Archer is a well-known British author, a busy man of high political standing. It is inconceivable that he would have read Randle's book or that, if he had, he would publish so similar a yarn. Nor does one know where

Randle got hold of the story.

There was a bit of brouhaha over the Randle/Archer duplication and it petered out. It is a funny story and should not be taken too literally. There may be Nigerian generals who were able to make money outside their profession which they prefer to be discreet about; they are, however, an intelligent lot unlikely to expose themselves to clumsy manoeuvres.

One hears many tales, often with a basis of truth. A politician out of favour and reduced to earning his living in business was about to clinch an important government contract. The documents had been signed and he was to collect them on the understanding that he would bring a large amount of money to deposit as a show of goodwill.

Unfortunately he could not raise the cash and went to a friend for a loan, explaining his predicament. 'I need the funds for less than a week.' It sounded plausible and, in a moment of weakness and for old time's sake, the friend made the money available. Our man went off to the provincial capital where the deal was to be consummated and proudly handed over the money. Great rejoicing all round. Instructions were issued to pass on the contract the following day.

That night there was a *coup d'état*. The officers involved in the affair were dismissed on the spot and the contract torn up by their successors. The goodwill money, however, was not returned, nor could our man sue for it because such payments were unofficial. He lost out and had to go to his friend with the sorry news. Much consternation, of course. 'I will pay back as soon as I can, I promise by all that is holy.' What could his friend say? He accepted the promise and in his mind wrote off the loan. He wondered how this chap would ever make enough to repay it and, even if he did, whether he would remember his debt – years might have passed by then.

Six months later, a cheque was received in full settlement!

Such are the twists and turns in the developing world. There is more to come. Our businessman went back into politics and within a couple of years rose to a very important position, lucrative and influential. He was big-minded enough in his days of glory to acknowledge publicly the help he had been given when down on his luck. In time another *coup d'état* sent him into the wilderness once again. He lived to try once more: '*Dum spiro spero*' is the motto – you never give up until you are dead.

In the rough and tumble of politics, you may lose out, or even be shot. But if you survive a crisis, you live to fight another day. Those who follow you may say harsh words and even deprive you of most of your wealth, but they are well aware that the same fate may await them and they normally draw the line at total annihilation. In return they would expect the same treatment. These are the times of Queen Elizabeth I in a different setting. Some of our contemporaries have forgotten or do not want to know of this.

Two incidents come to mind which left a sour taste for me personally. For a period of a few months in the army, one W. W. Hamilton served in the same unit as myself. We knew each other quite well and had the odd drink together. He was a budding politician and stood, when the time came, against the only Communist MP, Willie Gallagher. Hamilton himself was Labour to the left of centre, and he was eventually elected to parliament, where he served for many years. We lost touch when posted to different regiments.

In the late 1950s I heard that Hamilton was to visit Lagos as a member of an official delegation. On his arrival I traced his quarters: he was staying with a government official in Ikoyi. I called at the address but he was out, so I left a note to say where he could find me and expressed the hope that we could meet, however briefly, and talk about old times. I mentioned that I had been in Lagos for some years, and left my address and telephone number. There was no reaction.

I later heard that Hamilton did not want to be seen in the company of a white businessman for fear that it might be misinterpreted. He had come out as a left-wing Labour man to show sympathy with the oppressed colonial masses, and would have no truck with a person he must have considered to be a white exploiter of the poor blacks. Whether that was so I cannot say, but it would have been true to form.

Those were the days when left-wing publications like *The*

344

New Statesman were ranting against colonial exploitation, describing how the whites were living in luxury and idling their days away while the poor natives were suffering untold hardships. The fact that even then class differences between the Nigerians were widening, and that many of them were amassing riches, was ignored. It was a political platform, in the end partly responsible for the ills of the newly independent colonies. The colour question in reverse: the black man could do no wrong – and how quickly he saw that and made the most of it.

At the other end of the scale, I had a visit in the early 1970s from Sir John Colville, at that time working for a London merchant bank. Sir John was the epitome of the establishment. He had spent many years as secretary to Winston Churchill.

He had called at the British High Commission, our tenants in Kajola House, and the high commissioner had suggested he call on me to get another view of the situation. An impressive person, no longer young, walked in, clearly a man of great acumen and experience as we began to talk over a cup of coffee. He described his bank's interests in Nigeria and asked questions in a manner which suggested to me that he was expecting confirmation of the way he interpreted the problems he had come up against.

I felt uneasy. I could neither confirm his views, which seemed mistaken, nor did I want to contradict him when that was the last thing he expected. I could not know where that would end up. I pointed out with as much diplomacy as I could muster that the way business was conducted in Lagos should not be compared with the City of London, that the ethics were different, and that care should be taken in accepting undertakings demanding a long-term view. 'Everything is still very fluid here, Sir John.'

He listened to that with obvious displeasure. 'I know that people talk of irregularities in the conduct of affairs; that may be so on occasion on a lower level. I have just come from a meeting with the head of state, General Gowon, and he surely is a perfect gentleman.'

I was quick to agree. 'Indeed, Sir John, he is a perfect

gentleman, but then he does not control personally every aspect of government or private business.' I left it at that. What was the good of sticking my neck out for nothing? This man had not come for my opinions. He had come to add another name to his report to underpin his preconceived ideas that everything was correct as understood in the City.

It was, to put it indelicately, sheer humbug. A man of his standing and background must have known perfectly well what went on and how results were achieved; that a London banker anxious to do business in the developing world had to make allowances for unavoidable or deliberate lapses of organization calling for remedies not necessarily acceptable or usual within the citadel of modern capitalism. I was not even thinking of bribery and corruption; that I felt they would know how to deal with. I was thinking rather of the lack of training, lack of experience, difficulties of communications, petty obstacles, and the many tribulations which one faced at the best of times.

I have often thought that perhaps one over-estimates the integrity of the City. They may not cheat each other, but they will have dealings with uncertain sources if the money involved is big enough. The scandals of the last few years seem to bear this out.

I do not want to sit in judgement on either Hamilton or Sir John Colville. They must have known that they were visiting a new country stitched together a mere half-century before in the interests of the colonial power, and that it would be quite unrealistic to compare the life-style, mores and traditions of the one with the other. But they had come out on a specific assignment – the one to propagate social democracy as laid down by his party, the other to seek business on the lines acceptable to his directors – and that is what they set out to accomplish and report back.

32

A Son of Modern Nigeria

O ne morning in 1970, or early in 1971, I was sitting at my office desk in the mill at Esuk Utan when the intercom buzzed. It was the receptionist. 'A visitor to see you, sir.'

'Who is it?'

'It's a visitor, sir, a gentleman.'

'What is his name?'

'He says he knows you, sir.'

I gave up and said, 'Please send him in.'

There was a knock at the door and a well-dressed young man entered. 'My name is Victor Akan. Good morning Mr. Brandler. We met at Afi Ekong's party last week.'

'Please sit down, Mr Akan. Yes, I remember we met at Miss Ekong's party. What can I do for you?'

So began a close relationship which lasted until his untimely death at the early age of fifty-one, just before Christmas 1988.

Akan was a son of a senior chief in Oron who later became the paramount chief. He had been trained as a quantity surveyor in England and on his return in the 1960s established his own practice along with a number of equally young partners. They had their head office in Calabar and a branch office in Port Harcourt. When the Civil War came he had to join the Biafran army, in which he was commissioned, and returned to find his practice in ruins. He had to start all over again which he did with great acumen and energy. When I met him he had been going about a year. He called on me to offer his firm's services

347

to our company, should we require them. I took an immediate liking to him.

We met socially quite often and I watched his progress with admiration. We could not offer Akan any work at that time, but as we were impressed with his activities we introduced him to a number of architect friends, including Mr. Borys of whom I talked earlier, and Akan obtained some lucrative commissions arising out of these introductions. He was appreciative of this assistance.

A few months later he called on me and said, 'Mr. Brandler, I have decided to undertake further studies abroad to widen my experience and knowledge.'

I was astonished because his practice was already doing well and growing. But he explained that he felt he needed to widen his horizons and was planning to visit Australia where he hoped to gain admission to one of the universities. It so happened that I was friendly with High Commissioner Hutton in Lagos, and I intervened on his behalf so that in a relatively short time he set off for Sydney in New South Wales, where he had been admitted to the university for postgraduate studies.

He returned to Calabar eighteen months later. His practice had been looked after by his junior partners and he set about extending it with a vengeance. He took off in a big way. The fact that he had been involved on the wrong side during the Civil War proved no handicap, a point worth noting. The family was well connected in Calabar and he soon obtained much work from the local government and the private sector. He was made chairman of the State Housing Committee and came into contact with many decision-makers and important people who were impressed by his intelligence and resourcefulness. In no time he had accumulated influence and goodwill and had made some money, which he used to good advantage.

When the military regime was about to be replaced by what became known later as the Second Republic, he entered politics. At the same time he established industries in Calabar, which was badly in need of such enterprises. One was a metal working company, and another engaged in the manufacture of plastics. Much of his business was involved also with the federal government and, as all the banks and large financial institutions had their head offices in Lagos, he took an apartment in Ikoyi.

Whenever we were in the same place together, be it Lagos or Calabar, we would meet almost weekly to have a chat and exchange views. I was fortunate enough from time to time to give him advice which proved to be advantageous. In particular I urged him that, being a native of Calabar, he should invest locally in property, and indeed he constructed the first multi-storey office block in Calabar which he let out to a government agency. He then built a large housing estate in the town which was a model of its kind. By sheer good luck, I should say, I also tipped him off on one or two currency speculations where he followed my hunch profitably. All that cemented a relationship which was not just a business contact, but grew much closer: a friendship between an older, experienced man and a younger, more active one.

When politics came into their own with the elections for the new civil administration in 1979 he stood for senator at Oron, supporting the NPC party, and was elected with a large majority. In the senate he soon made his mark and became chairman of the very important Finance and Banking Committee, a position which brought him many opportunities inside and outside Nigeria. He became a very important person in the Second Republic, a busy man who travelled widely. He continued to visit me almost weekly and discussed problems which had arisen in his official or business career and, in turn, gave me advice when sought. It says much for his character that this relationship continued in spite of varying fortunes. When, later, two of my sons established their own business, which was heavily involved with Nigeria, he was of great help to them.

Victor Akan was a man of his time: the modern Nigerian, of good family and well-educated; well-dressed; fond of fast cars and beautiful women; not afraid to take a chance; ready for intrigue; suspicious of people's motives when he could not fathom them; adventurous in business; and ambitious in politics. At the same time, he was always ready to help his immediate family and friends and the wider circles of his town and his constituency. Money was spent as freely as it was made.

When, on New Year's Eve 1983, the Second Republic collapsed overnight, toppled by General Buhari, Victor Akan's political life came to an end, at least for the time being, and he was one of the many politicians detained by the military regime. Detaining politicians was popular with the masses, who accused them of having abused their positions as representatives of the people and of having enriched themselves. But are not politics as much for looking after oneself as for looking after other people?

He was soon released from detention, but he and his companies had to pay out vast amounts of money. He was in trouble, but not totally ruined by any means. He vigorously set about repairing his fortunes and was soon on the way up again. His investments did well, difficult commercial circumstances notwithstanding.

We continued to meet in Calabar, in Lagos and in London, where he had taken an apartment in the West End. I recollect visiting him in London one afternoon and we got talking on the situation in the country and the prospects for a new regime once the military had bowed out. He said to me with conviction that he fully expected one day to become president of the republic. He said this in spite of the fact that he had not accepted any of the official positions offered to him by the Supreme Military Council because he wanted to stay out of the political limelight for the time being. But he did keep in touch with many personalities, and was often consulted by state and federal government on issues where it was known that he had wide knowledge, experience and connections.

Victor was taken ill early in 1988, and was in and out of hospital in both Nigeria and London. At the time we did not know what was wrong with him; whether he knew I cannot say. One of his brothers was a doctor; he looked after him and came to London with him early in November 1988 for further consultations with specialists. I called on them on 14 December, which was a Thursday, when Victor told me he had to go back to hospital for further check-ups within the next few days. He mentioned that one of his companies owed us a considerable amount of money which he was anxious to liquidate. I said, 'Victor, you will surely be back in Nigeria early in the New Year. Why not wait until then, and we can attend to this matter?' He smiled and said, 'All right, let's wait.'

A few days later he was dead. It was a great shock to everyone. It was a great shock to me, whom he always called his 'White father'. He left behind many children of a young age, and his old father and mother, both in their eighties. He left behind brothers and sisters and other relatives and friends who had come to look to him for support and sustenance. The communities of Calabar and Oron and many other places inside and outside Nigeria mourned his death. (The outstanding account was settled promptly by the Trustees of the Estate.)

Nigeria had lost one of its great sons at an early age, a loss she could ill afford.

33

Time Marches On

On 26 May 1991, Sir Mobolaji Bank-Anthony died in Lagos. He was buried on Saturday, 1 June, in a specially prepared vault at the Ayinke House Obstetrics and Gynaecology Centre in Ikeja which he had built for the people of Lagos. He was eighty-three years old.

On 13 September 1991, the High Chief Samuel Akinbolaji Oladapo, the Lisa of Ondo, died whilst visiting Lagos and was buried in a specially prepared vault in his family compound in Ondo on Saturday, 16 November. He was eighty-one years old.

I was close to both men and attended their funerals. Two Yoruba notables had passed away in quick succession. Both reached great heights but had followed very different paths.

Sir Mobolaji, the son of a Muslim trader and prominent Lagos undertaker, had been sent to a mission school; he rose on the wave of new opportunities which presented themselves with the change from colonialism to independence. Chief Oladapo, the son and grandson of chiefs, advanced on traditional lines – he engaged in agriculture and related industry and took an active part in the life of his home town.

Sir Mobolaji, or 'Bank' as I had always known and called him, figures early in my story. Then, on the death of our first Nigerian director, E. A. Sanda of Ibadan, we had invited Bank to join our board in the mid-1950s; he remained a director of all of our Nigerian companies for over twenty years. This appointment and its connections became one of the springboards of his rapid progress. I have already mentioned that it was most

352

unusual in colonial times for a Nigerian to join the board of an expatriate company.

He had an alert and quick brain which impressed all who had dealings with him. He realized early on that the foreign companies which streamed into the country just before and after independence would require local knowledge and contacts and soon had astonishing success. He knew how to inspire their confidence and rarely failed his patrons. He cultivated his connections with the British (colonial) administration which recommended him. When independence permeated the economic field he was in his element. He was appointed a director by many new foreign companies and we saw less and less of him but kept in touch. He was knighted in 1963 for his services to the country, which added to his standing and prestige.

How does someone, in early post-colonial times, become a Knight of the British Empire, someone who is not a famous chief, a renowned professional, or a ruler over thousands? What influences, what secret links, were there for this to come to pass? How clever they had been, those colonial administrators. They knew how to listen, to take advice, to pick their men. They recognized Sir Mobolaji as a man they could do business with. A rising star in the world of commerce, a man of standing in the community not overtly engaged in politics, a known anglophile. A man who kept his thoughts to himself, his ears to the ground, and his roots in his people.

Bank was an extraordinary man, his strength being that he was nearly always in the right place at the right time: not so much by luck as by a perspicacious mind, a wonderful memory, some generosity, and some ruthlessness. He was a good social mixer, a bit of a trimmer, a bit of a hypocrite, and a great admirer of the female sex, which he encouraged with education. He was the Nigerian of his time *par excellence*. When we look for comparisons with our own culture, we might say he was a man of the Renaissance or an Elizabethan, but one cannot easily equate one time in history with another.

I sometimes thought that in his later years he modelled himself on the final period of John D. Rockefeller, one of the richest of rich Americans who died in his nineties. Like him, he was wealthy and made money to the last, and like him he gave away much of his money in the end to charity. These charities were well conceived and executed. They brought him much praise and admiration as a benefactor of the sick and needy of his home town of Lagos. He should be remembered in the mythology of the founding fathers of independent Nigeria for his outstanding philanthropy. Unlike the early Rockefeller, though, Bank was not a bogeyman to his compatriots. However, like Rockefeller, the origins of his great wealth were sometimes obscure – but then charity must begin at home.

For all the respect he showed for Western technology and for industrial and political power, he never accepted the Western way of life and, I believe, felt the Yoruba or African to be more humane and realistic. He was a Christian with a Muslim background, but seemed almost like an agnostic, with strong undertones of faith in his local customs. It was that faith which fired his fundamental or philosophical principles.

Unlike his predecessor, Sanda, Bank took no active part in our timber business, attending board meetings as it suited him, and acting when called upon as a guide and liaison man, especially when later we expanded into building interests. Ironically, whilst we knew that his association with us had given him great advantages in the early days, his closer compatriots thought that our success in the wood industry was due to his participation. That was not so at any time.

As his business widened and our affairs ran into difficulties, we drifted apart, accentuated by the complications of indigenization, where we felt that he had failed us and he resented the fact that we would not accept a deal for the properties we were forced to give up. As we grew older and tired of the futility of the feud, we became close again on a personal basis and remained so to the end. He had lost influence under the Second Republic, but was hailed as a grand old man by the Babangida regime which found him useful, appreciated his public spirit, and heaped honours on him.

Chief Oladapo's life and burial took place in a less cosmopolitan setting.

Sixty-four days after he passed away, his body was laid to rest. It is common now for Christian Nigerians of rank to be buried a considerable time after their deaths; refrigerated morgues make this possible for those families who desire and can afford it. It allows time to organize the occasion, to summon family and friends from far away, to plan on an elaborate scale. The mourners use the ceremony to honour the importance of the deceased and, by reflection, to underline their own. The man waiting to be interred will have performed a last great service to his name and to those who follow him. It was my privilege to give the funeral oration. We had known each other since 1948 and often pursued mutual business. His sons are friends of our sons.

The chief grew up a privileged child. He came from an eminent local family of chiefs. These were not hereditary titles; they were bestowed by merit and influence.

As a teenager he had been selected as one of twenty-four young Nigerians to attend the World Scout Jamboree in England in 1929; it made a lasting impression on him and fired his ambition early in life. Ondo Province was rich in forests, cocoa and other agricultural products, and the young man, after a solid grounding working for European concerns, started out on his own as a timber and cocoa producer and trader. His background and connections helped him to get under way. His outlook was modern: any technical innovation he came across would be employed to further his aims. He built up cocoa farms, sawmills and other agricultural enterprises. He teamed up with overseas connections. His status grew, as did his wealth. To his modern outlook was welded the unquestioning acceptance of his traditional society. He submitted to its duties as he expected its privileges. His life revolved around his home town.

If today Nigeria has become the important country she is, much of the credit must go to men and women like Chief Oladapo who formed and must still form the backbone of the state's structure.

At the funeral I met once again men and women I had not seen for years: an ex-employee who had left our service in

1952; one of the widows of Chief Seriki Fawehinmi; Chief
Agunbiade, an ex-timber dealer, now eighty-four, who invited
me to his house and proudly told me that he had thirty graduate
children and had added a new arrival to the collection – his
youngest was just five years old!

Ondo is changing, too, however. Modern communications,
education, radio and TV have brought it much closer to the
mainstream of the country's economic and political life; an-
cient customs and preferences are being eroded. Its people will
have to find answers to the problems these changes are bringing.

That was in part the tenor of the speech I gave at my friend's
coffin. The British Crown had recognized his services and
awarded him the MBE; not equal to the KBE bestowed on his
illustrious compatriot. Under more ascetic regimes the decorations might have been reversed, but they reflect the worth of
their respective activities to the powers that be.

The grandchildren of these men live in a different world.
They are well-educated at home or abroad, and colonial times
are a dim memory passed on in the tales of their elders; already old history to which they listen in wonderment and disbelief. They enter the professions, business or the services.
They travel the world. They have been reared on a thirst for
knowledge and material advancement associated with education. In that attitude one will find no difference between north
and south, east and west, male and female. They lack as yet the
assurance of a class able to consolidate its position and establish
the order necessary to have its wealth and privilege accepted.
The political and social scene is still too fluid to rely on the
protection of an enforceable law offering safeguards, checks
and balances. They need more ruthlessness, cunning and determination than those operating within the genteel Western pattern often held up as an example. These attributes force them
to adopt the very qualities of their seniors which they found
obnoxious as students and protested against. Religious differences in this respect are minimal, whatever the gulf between
Muslim and Christian.

They are an elegant lot, these youngsters: polite, well

dressed and mannered, quick to see an opening and seize it, streaming out of the universities and polytechnics in ever growing numbers and of late finding it hard sometimes to obtain the work and remuneration they were looking forward to. A disgruntled intelligentsia is in the making. Openings for them will have to be found if this is not to lead to more discontent than was met in the first thirty years of independence.

34

Epilogue

'Did you say Lagos, Nigeria?'
'I did.'
'You mean to say you actually live there?'
It was early in 1992. We were propping up the bar of a
men's club in the West End of London, nodding acquaintances
awaiting our respective guests.

'I have lived there most of the time since the war.'

'Since the war? Which war?

'World War II. 1939–45.'

'My God, that's when I was born! A nice old man like you in
that place?!'

'Not so often now – getting on a bit. But what's wrong with
that?'

'What's wrong with that? Why, they say it's rotten to the
core – full of violence, cheating, fraud, drug dealers, the lot.'

'They say so?'

'They do.' He looked at me quizzically. 'Surely you know all
that?'

'I know what everybody else knows. Have you ever been to
Nigeria?'

'As a matter of fact, yes. I was sent there once briefly in
the 1970s by my company. We supplied machinery and lost a
packet. Never got paid; not a penny.'

'I am sorry.'

'So were we. They say you have to bribe your way through
the system – from the minister who approves the contract to
the clerk who types it out. It was awful. The traffic was always

358

jammed; the telephones didn't work, the water in the hotel didn't work, the electricity didn't work, appointments weren't kept. The heat, the dust, the dirt. Everybody after money.'

'You must have been unlucky.'

'Was I? I don't think so. Many tell the same story. Is there an honest man in the whole country, or a virtuous woman? The newspapers are full of tales about Nigerian tricksters. Even the BBC had a programme on it recently. They tell me it's got worse – if that's possible.'

'Yes, I've read some of the reports and I listened to the BBC. Give a dog a bad name. It's all relative.'

'Relative, sir, relative? Are you condoning their way of life? Corrupt from top to bottom?'

'I am neither condoning nor condemning, I am observing. You say they are corrupt from top to bottom. If that were really so, there could be no corruption.'

'What do you mean?'

'I mean what I say. It cancels itself out; if all parties are corrupt it turns into a question of power, doesn't it?'

'You amaze me. Ah, there is my friend. You must excuse me and I hope we can continue our talk some other time. Good-bye.'

'Good-bye.'

The guest I was waiting for came up to me.

'Hello, Joe, I saw you deep in conversation, so I hung back. Did you get a hot tip?'

'Hello, John. No tip; we were talking about Nigeria.'

'Ah, yes. Did you listen to the BBC the other day?'

'Don't you start, John. I have had enough for the moment. Have a drink?'

It has of late become fashionable in the media to highlight alleged Nigerian commercial criminality. It reminds me of the story of the drunk seen at night crawling under a street lamp, who was asked by a policeman what he was doing.

'I'm looking for my keys, officer.'

'Let me help you,' said the kind bobby. They could not find them. 'Are you sure you lost your keys here?'

'Officer, I lost them over the other side.'

'Then why are we looking here?'

'There's more light here, officer.'

Since the Biafran war, Nigeria has figured little in the news. What there was to report rated only small paragraphs. A *coup d'etat* here, a few thousand rioters killed there. Nigeria did not encourage foreign reporters and camera crews to roam about freely. 'Let's keep quiet and get on with business.' The newshounds concentrated their arc lamps on minor fry and made them look important. Big countries like Nigeria and Indonesia figured on the inside pages, if at all.

Suddenly Nigeria had attracted some attention; the journalists found something to get their teeth into. Relatively minor but scandalous – good copy. Their readers knew little of what had gone on before.

The oil boom of the 1970s and early 1980s generated a euphoria, a Klondike atmosphere. The sudden increase of money in circulation accelerated commercial and industrial activities and multiplied the number of men and women seeking work in the towns. Housing and transport problems for the masses became acute and could not keep up with demand. People lived many to a room and moved further and further away from their places of work, throwing ever greater pressures on transport and accommodation. The towns became terribly congested. Still they came, in growing numbers, seeking their fortunes in the big cities like Lagos, Ibadan, Kano. The villages were emptied of the younger generation; agricultural production slumped whilst demand increased; the population exploded.

Migration affected the eating habits of society. Imported rice and wheat became popular in preference to traditional food, which took longer to prepare. The exodus from the land had other consequences. The close family ties were broken as people dispersed: it became more difficult to honour the old obligations of the extended family, and at the same time more expensive and troublesome. Surprisingly, though, they still hold to a wide degree.

Other unpleasant spin-offs inevitably followed the rise in urban population: unemployment, crime, armed violence, prostitution, gang warfare, and all the other accompanying phenomena so familiar to Western society. The police could not cope and became arrogant, oppressive and extortionist. Medical services were limited and expensive. A large flotsam and jetsam of people came into being, and still exists, although the drive to leave the villages slowed down after the mid-1980s.

The upper classes live in attractive small enclaves; the masses in vast conurbations poorly controlled by local governments. Social services like unemployment and health insurance do not exist. Overcrowding, poor sanitation, bad light, limited transport, and low wages are the hallmark of the common people's lives. Whenever the administration succeeds in catching up and improving services, the crowds have increased once more and the game begins all over again. Meantime the rich have accumulated wealth beyond their wildest dreams.

There is an imperative need in present conditions for national and supra-national organizations. This trend in turn generates an instinctive revival of tribalism as people fear a loss of belonging. Tribalism is accused of being reactionary, holding back the consolidation of nation states; yet it cannot be eliminated. It must be harnessed to the support of larger units. Common interests are what matter. They must be understood and be seen to be of benefit.

To suggest that all is well would be a travesty of the facts. Hypocrisy, however, is not the cure. If you deal with the Arab super-rich, you should not denigrate the Nigerian multi-millionaire. If you concede the Duke of Westminster his opulence, you should not decry the Sultan of Sokoto's wealth. If you read of bribery and corruption, remember the history of other nations. After all, the legitimacy of wealth arises out of the social system one inherits or creates, and is flexible.

One must admire the patience, sense of humour and drive that keep most of the inhabitants going, where other peoples would long since have given up or rioted and revolted. That is their strength, and out of this they will in the end build a better Nigeria, time permitting. Such is the verve and potential of Nigeria that she can afford to lose one quarter of her efforts through waste, and another quarter through dishonesty, and still make spectacular advances.

The Nigerian, taxed with an urgent task which little suits him, will answer you: maybe tomorrow, maybe tomorrow. Tomorrow will come one day. No problem.

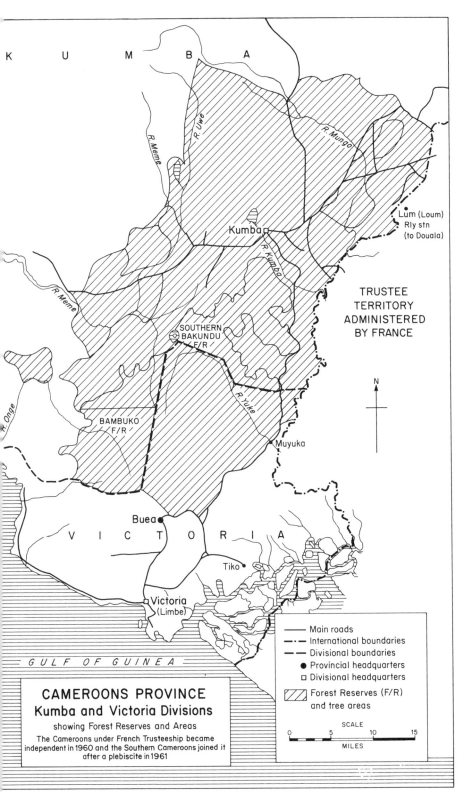

K U M B A

R. Meme

R. Uwe

R. Mungo

Lum (Loum)
Rly stn
(to Douala)

Kumba

R. Kumba

R. Meme

TRUSTEE
TERRITORY
ADMINISTERED
BY FRANCE

SOUTHERN
BAKUNDU
F/R

R. Yuke

N

BAMBUKO
F/R

R. Onge

Muyuka

Buea

V I C T O R I A

Tiko

Victoria
(Limbe)

GULF OF GUINEA

Main roads
International boundaries
Divisional boundaries
Provincial headquarters
Divisional headquarters

Forest Reserves (F/R)
and tree areas

CAMEROONS PROVINCE
Kumba and Victoria Divisions

showing Forest Reserves and Areas

The Cameroons under French Trusteeship became
independent in 1960 and the Southern Cameroons joined it
after a plebiscite in 1961

SCALE
0   5   10   15

MILES

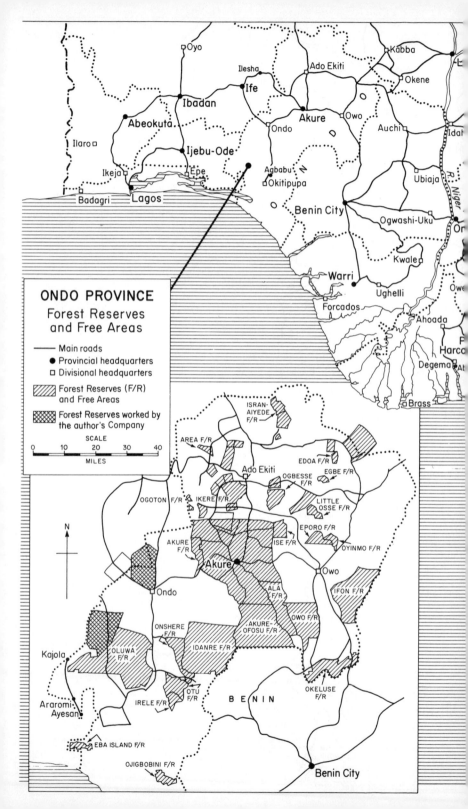

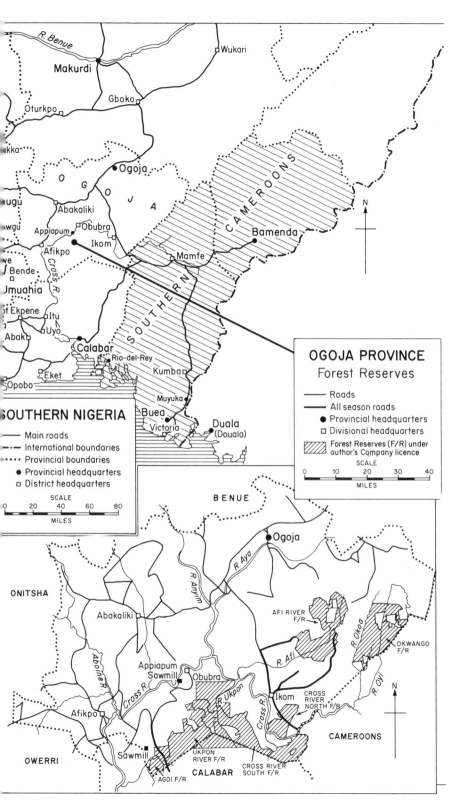

SOUTHERN NIGERIA

— Main roads
—·—·— International boundaries
········· Provincial boundaries
● Provincial headquarters
□ District headquarters

SCALE
0   20   40   60   80
MILES

OGOJA PROVINCE
Forest Reserves

— Roads
━━ All season roads
● Provincial headquarters
□ Divisional headquarters
▨ Forest Reserves (F/R) under author's Company licence

SCALE
0   10   20   30   40
MILES

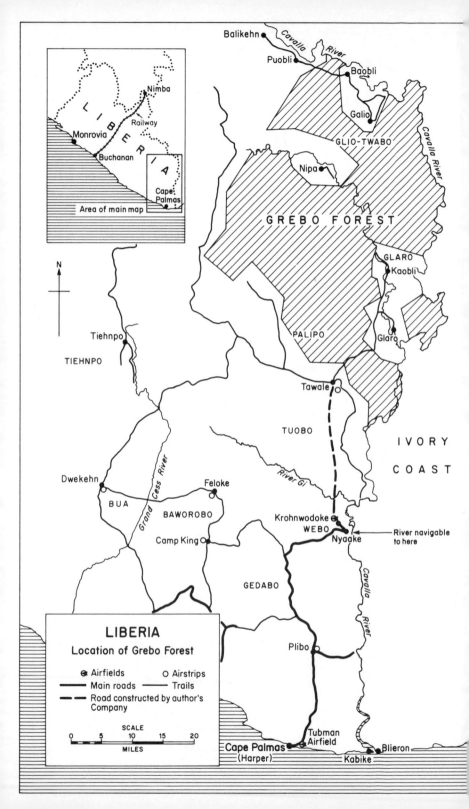

Balikehn

Cavalla River

Puobli

Baobli

Galio

GLIO-TWABO

Nipa

Cavalla River

GREBO FOREST

GLARO
Kaobli

PALIPO

Glaro

Tiehnpo

TIEHNPO

Tawale

TUOBO

IVORY

COAST

River Gi

Dwekehn

Grand Cess River

Feloke

BUA

BAWOROBO

Krohnwodoke

WEBO

River navigable
to here

Camp King

Nyaake

GEDABO

Cavalla River

Plibo

LIBERIA
Location of Grebo Forest

● Airfields   ○ Airstrips
── Main roads   ── Trails
- - - Road constructed by author's
      Company

Tubman
Airfield

Cape Palmas
(Harper)

Blieron

Kabike

SCALE
0   5   10   15   20
MILES

Inset map:

Nimba

LIBERIA

Railway

Monrovia

Buchanan

Cape
Palmas

Area of main map

N

Index

Index

Index